A PHILLIES ODYSSEY

A PHILLIES ODYSSEY

Exploring the Forgotten Players of Fightins Yesteryear

Dave Rueter

Paperback ISBN: 978-1-7356370-2-0

Ebook ISBN: 978-1-7356370-3-7

First paperback edition: October 2021.

Cover art by Ernon Wright

Contact author: PhilliesOdyssey@gmail.com

Table of Contents

Prologue

I wrote another book. We all know the second installment is never as good as the original, so please lower your expectations accordingly. *A Phillies Odyssey* was the logical next step of this series. I've attended way more Sixers and Phillies games than their football and hockey counterparts. In 1989, my dad took my brother and me to an Eagles/Raiders game. The Birds won 10-7, limiting Bo Jackson to just 79 yards rushing on 20 carries. I fell in love – the game, the team, the entire scene. We sat in the 700 Level, and I heard language that a 5-year-old wasn't meant to hear. My dad vowed never again. I didn't go to another Birds game for ten years (The Colts whacked the Eagles, 44-17). Within that span, I sat in the Vet's 700 Level for plenty of Phils games, but it wasn't exactly standing room only for a late summer Bobby Muñoz start. Those same bad words were probably said. I just wasn't in earshot.

For a premise that honors the forgotten Philadelphia athlete, no team better encapsulates the spirit of this series than the Fightins. I didn't witness a playoff berth until I was 9. I wouldn't see another for 14 years. Sandwiched between those seasons were countless memories – some bad, some really bad ('sup, Jeff Conine), and even a few good ones sprinkled in throughout. While *A Phillies Odyssey* covers the former, I tried my best to also capture the latter. A championship or bust mentality is a shitty fan experience. Within even the most disappointing of years, there are small pockets of greatness. Sil Campusano did something extraordinary. So did Jeff Juden, Tomás Pérez, and Wilson Valdez. Let's celebrate that.

Now, writing *A Phillies Odyssey* presented some challenges. For starters, my neighborhood got obliterated by a TORNADO. A Kerry Von Erich or Natural Disasters reference would be too on the nose, so let's just say the storm set me back a bit. Also, these 40-man rosters ran me ragged. There were just SO. MANY. GUYS. I had to either make some really difficult decisions or have a manuscript twice the size of *Atlas Shrugged*. I'd ask myself, "Could I sleep at night knowing Jeff Manship wasn't in this book?" And the answer in this case was 'no.' So please enjoy the chapter on Jeff Manship. But many others were cut. I was comfortable with the final roster of *A Sixers Odyssey*. I left it all out on the floor so to speak. Was there some regret about excluding Dana Barros or Derrick Alston? Sure, but I got over it. With this Phillies rendition, however, I know the angry tweets are coming.

"Where's Garrett Stephenson?"

"Where's So Taguchi?"

"No Steve Lake? No mention of Steve Lake's pet parrot, Ruffles? Is this amateur hour, Dave?"

It's fair criticism. They all should be in here. I have no defense, but we can all agree that Ricky Otero HAD to be included. Now a quick reminder of the rules:

If you're too good in real life, you're too good for this book. Sorry Chase, Jimmy, Ryan, Lenny, Kruk, Dutch, and Schmidt. If you're too well-known around these parts – The Chooches, Lieberthals, Burrells, Brad Lidge and Dave Hollins types – it's nothing personal. You're just not my target demo. If you're still currently playing, your story ain't over. Although, I almost made an exception for Vince Velasquez in the heat of the moment after a 2 inning, 5 ER outing at Pittsburgh. Cooler heads, though, prevailed.

And if you're Curt Schilling, you're not in this book. I don't have time for that shit. Everyone else is on the table: long relief, middle relief, backup catchers, 4th starters, 5th starters, and swing men. Utility infielders? Yep, we got those too. Got a hankering for fourth outfielders? We can seat you now. First door on the right. The reservation is under 'Billy McMillon.'

The nicest compliment I heard about *A Sixers Odyssey* was that they felt the book was written specifically for them. In truth, it was. You and I are exactly alike. We've attached ourselves to these teams and these players for better or worse.

We don't know any better.

"My American League team is the Mariners."

No, it's not. That's not a thing. Loyalty is both our greatest strength and our biggest downfall. Every bullpen implosion just makes us stronger. Every fringe major leaguer pitcher who stifles the Phils' bats fuels us. Make no mistake. We're not stuck with the Fightins. The Fightins are stuck with us.

Grab a bat, Mark Whiten. You're up.

The Altar Server Game

Name: Mark Whiten

Position: Right Field

Career Slash Line: .259/.341/.415

Phillies Tenure: 1995-1996

"It seems like I've been searching for a home for five years," he said.

And why has he been traded so often?

"Everybody wants me. That's the way I see it," he said with a laugh (Hagen 1995).

May 30th, 1996: Altar Server Night at the Stadium. Our parish had recently gone co-ed. It was no longer Altar Boy Night at the Park. Now our exclusive club had girls. The Phillies outing was a big deal. We were 12 – where the hell else were we going? Everyone was piling in Alex's mom's minivan. Who you sat next to – who wanted to sit next to you – this was the table setter. It set the tone for the end-of-the-year roller skating party at The Palace. There were three couple skates planned and you didn't want to be left hanging over by the Loser Wall near the *Cruis'n USA* arcade game. My mom had a lot of misgivings about me going out on a school night, but I explained to her that God wanted me to watch Phils starter, Mike Williams, keep the Dodgers lineup off balance.

I was the only die-hard. The other altar servers were only in it for the pomp and circumstance. They went for the ambience. These fair-weather fans made their laps around the concourse, buying t-shirts and nachos and whatever else. I'd normally never turn down a good nacho, but I had to attend to more pressing matters. Mike Williams was pitching a gem. The offense, though, was stagnant.

Williams and his glorious moustache gave us 7 strong, but he exited the game trailing 2-0. The Phils scratched a run across in the bottom of the 8th off Dodgers starter, Pedro Astacio, but future Phillie Chan Ho Park squelched the rally. Then our chaperone made the horrific decision that still haunts me to this day.

We left.

"I don't want you guys to get home too late."

Come again? It's a 2-1 game in the 9th. What are you scared of, Alex's mom? Zoo traffic? Are you worried about my mom? Did she get to you? Did she give you the whole "It's a school night" song and dance? Mom is all bark and no bite. She's probably just at home watching *J.A.G.* Besides, we can't leave *now*. We still have some power due up. We still have Hard Hittin'. In fact, I told the other kids *exactly* that as we walked through the parking lot.

"Don't worry, guys. Whiten leads off the 9th."

To date, it's still the nerdiest collection of words to ever exit my mouth. My rally cry fell on deaf ears. I was like a parent telling their kids to wait 30 minutes until they jump in the pool after lunch. No one, and let me repeat this again for emphasis, no one gave a shit. Whiten had entered the game as part of a double-switch and hit a two-bagger in the 7th. He was swinging a hot bat, I explained, but Phils apathy reigned supreme. The other kids weren't discussing Whiten's splits, or if Fregosi would burn another bench player if Mark got on. Should we listen to Q102 or Y100 took precedence. I had to act fast. I had to think on my feet. I needed control of the radio, so I volunteered to sit in THE FRONT SEAT with Alex's mom. I may as well have worn a sign on my forehead that said, "I have no interest in ever attending a make-out party."

I have a big forehead.

My fellow servers were bummed, but they let me have this. I had so little. Facing All-Star closer Todd Worrell (not to be confused with former Phillie, Tim Worrell), Whiten hammered a 1-2 pitch over the centerfield wall. I slammed my hands down on the minivan dashboard.

"Hard Hittin', baby! Tie ballgame!"

I think I scared Alex's mom, who later told my mother that, "Dave seems like a really big baseball fan." A few batters later, Pete Incaviglia drove home Mickey Morandini, completing the comeback. Worrell led the league in saves that year. 44 times in 1996 he shut the door, but not on that night. Not on Altar Server Night at the Park. I didn't see it myself, but I heard the collapse was magnificent.

Mark Whiten didn't hit cheapies. He didn't make his living spraying singles to the opposite field. He hit the upper deck at Three Rivers Stadium in Pittsburgh. He mauled an offering at the Metrodome that would've crossed into Ontario if not for that pesky bubble. He mashed homers left-handed. He smashed bombs from the right. Whiten swung from the heels, like your drunk uncle reaching for a wiffleball bat.

"Put it in here, Johnny. Lemme show you why I was all-conference in '87."

The Phils acquired Mark from Boston in July of 1995 for fan-favorite Dave Hollins. Whiten had already played for four different teams in his first five seasons in the league, but his power was intoxicating. He topped out at 25 homers in '93 with St. Louis, but four of those dingers were ripped on the same night. That 4-homer, 12-RBI night in Cincinnati is Whiten's calling card. (His 12 RBIs is tied for the all-time single-game record). That performance was a *moment*. I watched *SportsCenter* every morning, and aside from the clip of the high school kid barking like a dog on the inbounds play, there is no highlight I can recall more than Whiten's monster night. Four home-run games just don't happen. In the NL, Bob Horner accomplished the feat in '86. Before that, it hadn't been done since Schmidt in '76 (In an 18-16 pitchers' duel against the Cubs). The AL hadn't seen a four-HR game since Rocky Colavito in 1959.

Phillies brass hoped Whiten just needed a fresh start. He was hitting a paltry .185 with Boston and spent some time in AAA Pawtucket. But the homers – those majestic homers – always earned him chance after chance. His power from both sides of the plate was like a Spotify playlist. Just when you're over it and about to cut bait, Montell Jordan's "This Is How We Do It" comes on and reels you right back in. Whiten's home run potential kept him employed. 400-foot long balls stand out. When you saw one, you didn't forget it.

He recorded a very useful .846 OPS in 245 plate appearances after joining the club. In an August tilt, he mashed two home runs off Astros starter Greg Swindell (Jeff Juden gave the Phils 7 quality innings, FTW). The Phils re-signed Whiten before the '96 campaign. There was a cautious optimism surrounding the right fielder. Maybe he had finally figured it out – whatever "it" was anyway. Mark struggled, though. His numbers dipped. He didn't anchor the middle part of the lineup as the brass had maybe hoped. He slugged a disappointing .396, a harsh reminder of why so many franchises had passed him from team to team. The power was always there. The consistency was not. He changed his batting stance often, never seemingly finding that comfort level. The coaches mentioned this in a 1996 *Philadelphia Magazine* feature on Jim Fregosi.

"What do you want to do with him?" asks Fregosi.

"Last year, he was all like this," says Menke, demonstrating Whiten's stance, elbows pinched and hands held high.

"That's why he's not a low-ball hitter anymore," says Vukovich. (Feldman 1996).

In June of that same season, the Phils released him. The team tired of waiting for the light bulb to turn on. There was no trade – no player to be named later or cash considerations. The front office had enough. Philadelphia became just another pitstop in Whiten's long-winding career.

"When you see his physical attributes - his arm, speed, power - it is disappointing," Fregosi said. "He has a lot of talent. I don't think he fulfilled anyone's expectations." (Sheridan 1996).

The team brought in a lot of guys of Mark's ilk during this time: Todd Zeile, Danny Tartabull – guys, who in the right scenario and in pristine conditions, may have been able to knock in 100 RBIs. But they weren't Bonds or Sosa. It was discounted power, like finding name brands on a Marshall's clearance rack. The mid-1990s Phils weren't paying top dollar for a premium power bat, so here's, oh, I don't know, J.R. Phillips. Fans didn't judge Whiten as critically as management did, though. We don't label him a bust or a retread, or years later, recount some wild, flailing swing in a key situation. I only remember Hard Hittin's long balls, and, man, were they memorable.

The Doubles Machine

Name: Felipe Crespo

Position: First Base / Outfield

Career Slash Line: .245/.330/.380

Phillies Tenure: 2001

It wouldn't be surprising if relievers Turk Wendell and Dennis Cook, plus utility man Felipe Crespo and catcher Todd Pratt, are the team's only acquisitions. However, Wade said he is in a "listening mode" (Salisbury 2001).

There is an electric counter on the right field wall of Oracle Park in San Francisco. The tracker tallies "splash hits," Giants home runs that hit McCovey Cove on the fly. Barry Bonds owned 23 of the first 25 'splash hits.' The other two? How about that ... Felipe Crespo (MLB 2021). I wasn't surprised that Bonds monopolized the entire list. That was expected. But I was shocked that Crespo was on there to begin with. I don't know Felipe Crespo, Home Run Hitter. I don't recognize that man. I only know and acknowledge Felipe Crespo, Doubles Machine.

All Cris Carter did was catch touchdowns. All Crespo did was hit doubles. That's how it was sold to me at the 2001 trade deadline anyway, when the Phillies moved my favorite reliever ever for the man who *supposedly* never saw a gap he didn't like.

"Dave, I know you literally brought a "Wayne Gomes Fan Club" sign to the Vet but chin up. This Crespo is a doubles machine."

I never signed off on this trade. I didn't agree to it, and I wasn't consulted. The Baltimore Colts moved to Indianapolis in the dark of night. GM Ed Wade traded away one of my favorite players while I was stocking shelves at the Dollar Tree. I was knee-deep in travel toothbrush holders when Wade sold low on the second coming of Goose Gossage. To all my fellow members of the Wayne Gomes Fan Club, I'm sorry. I know the trade went down on my watch, but what was I supposed to do? I needed some scratch. That Incubus CD wasn't going to buy itself. The 'Doubles Machine' label was just some old wives tale. It was whisper down the lane. Someone told Ed Wade, who told Chris Wheeler, who told the viewing audience that the switch-hitting Crespo mashed; that he was a walking extra base hit. By Sunday, a dude from my algebra class was telling me that Felipe hit a double in 18.25% of his at-bats in the Venezuelan Winter League.

"He feasted on fastballs down there, Dave."

I didn't mind the *idea* of Felipe Crespo. I wasn't Anti-Crespo. He had an earned reputation as a pinch-hitting specialist, an exclusive title usually designated for Lenny Harris and John Vander Wal. I could get behind that. And I concede that the '01 Phillies needed some versatility off the bench. As the saying goes, "A bench cannot thrive on Kevin Jordan alone." But the deadline acquisitions for the frisky 57-46 Phillies left fans underwhelmed.

Crespo is a journeyman switch-hitter with more snap and crackle than pop. Felipe is a pedestrian defensive player. Nor is he a John Vander Wal with the stick despite the best numerical stats of any National League pinch hitter last year.

The prized Vander Wal was the other Pirate snared by Sabean in the Jason Schmidt deal - made at the cost of platoon outfielder Armando Rios and Triple A righthander Ryan Vogelsong, the Giants' equivalent of Phillies untouchable Brandon Duckworth (Conlin 2001).

Critics accused Wade of not going for it, and there's nothing Philly talk radio hates more than a coward.

"Let's go to Nick in South Philly."

"King, help me understand. Does Wade not want to win? Who is this Phillip – this Phillip whats his name? I never heard of 'em. Where did we get him from?

San Fran or San Diego or something? And Cook? That bum? He stunk here. We should of sold the farm for Jason Schmidt. Also, I've been reading good things about Na Brown in camp. What are you hearing? Imma hang up and listen."

Eight years had passed since Macho Row. The trade deadline presented a golden opportunity with the Phils sitting just one game behind the NL East lead. Fans wanted rotational help. They wanted a power bat. But while the minor deals frustrated fans, it didn't deter manager Larry Bowa.

"Eddie Wade is showing that this organization is dedicating itself to winning," Bowa said (Carchidi 2001).

But were they? Even "The Big Cat" Andres Gallaraga was available as a cheap rental at the deadline. He also was moved to San Fran, where he recorded an .863 OPS in 174 plate appearances.

The beacon of light, Wayne Gomes, had an 8.41 ERA and a 2-0 record with the Giants, which proved he was a winner. Felipe, to be fair, was also productive post-trade. He hit a very respectable .293 in Philly. Oh, sorry, I misspoke. I meant he *slugged* .293. A .171/.234/.293 line left me scribbling Faith Evans' lyrics from "I'll Be Missing You" into my chemistry textbook. I lost Wayne, and the only thing I got back was three extra base hits in 47 plate appearances.

An ingrown toenail sidelined Crespo for most of spring training in '02. Deciding that the switch-hitter wasn't in their long-term plans, the Phils sold his contract to the Tokyo Yomiuri Giants (Collins 2002). The Marlins and Reds took a gamble on Crespo in later years, but he never was able to climb back to the majors. His final big league hit came in a September 19th game against the Braves, a 5-2 win for the Phils.

It was a ~~double~~ single.

The Bulldog

Name: Geoff Geary

Position: Pitcher

Career Record: 16-10; 3.92 ERA (4.31 FIP)

Phillies Tenure: 2003-2007

Overheard at homeroom

Date: September 16, 2006

Time: Approximately 9:04 AM.

"Bulldog's been lights out this year."

"Well, actually, Ray, if you dig a bit deeper, the advanced numbers say he's been pretty lucky this year."

"Nerd."

I got this weird fascination with Geoff Geary. I don't think I'd go out of my way to attend a Geoff Geary meet-and-greet at Forman Mills, but I'd definitely comment on one of his Instagram photos.

"Looks like a great time, Bulldog! #Its5:00Somewhere"

Even when I wrote a book about the Sixers (available through all online retailers), I couldn't help myself. I'm shoehorning Geoff Geary into a chapter about Andrés Nocioni without the slightest hint of remorse. I could be asked on a first date if I had any pets, then transition into a ten-minute history lesson about the Bulldog's 2.96 ERA in 2006, before asking the lucky lady if she wanted to split the calamari. Toby Borland is my Wayne Gomes who is my Geoff Geary who is my Aaron Fultz who is my Jeanmar Gómez. If I'm building a team of random Phillies relievers, I'm trotting out these five and having them pick up Mike Zagurski full court.

You have a special kinship with the Phils teams that intersected with your college years. Those are some memories, man. Maybe you have a story about the doubleheader against the Padres in '93 – perhaps you were one of the few who filed back into the Vet after last call and witnessed Mitch Williams' R.B.I. single at 4:40 A.M. (Hagen 2013). Or maybe you were an undergrad in the city during the string of NL East titles. You saw Ryan Howard's moonshots at Bonner's, or Drinker's, or wherever you called home. Or perhaps you're a bit younger. Maybe that Grady Sizemore jersey buried in the back of your closet reminds you of some really fun times, and your only regret is that you didn't buy two Grady Sizemore jerseys. We all can relate. The summer nights were the same. The Phils were a comfort food. They were always there for you. I drank a lot of Miller Lites at Whiskey Tango, hoping Ugueth Urbina – sans machete – could see his way out of an 8th inning jam. It built character. It made me who I am today.

Geary may as well have been my college roommate. He and I are going halfsies on a case of bottled water and cutting class to play *Crazy Taxi.* I compare anyone with a goatee to Geoff Geary. I hear "Bulldog" and instantly bypass Davey Boy Smith and the Dynamite Kid, and that's not fair to arguably the greatest wrestling tag team of all time. In 2006, Geary appeared in 81 games, which was good for 7th in baseball that season. Jon Rauch was 2nd in appearances with 85, which is entirely believable because that dude pitched *every* night. 15 years later, I could still describe every wrinkle in Rauch's face to a sketch artist. (1987 Kent Tekulve and his pair of shades holds the Phillies record for single-season appearances with 90).

My love for Geary didn't happen overnight. It was a slow, gradual evolution. I learned to appreciate Geoff. In '04, he rocked a 5.44 ERA, and, yeah, maybe I said some things about the Bulldog that I'd like to have back. No one is perfect. One Ron Blazier comparison in the heat of the moment doesn't make me a bad guy. There was room to grow. For all parties.

"I can honestly say my first year up here I was so nervous I had heartburn," Geary was saying of 2003, when he was first called up (Donnellon 2006).

In '05, Geary turned in a 3.72 ERA in 58 innings of work. My man just needed some Tums and a ginger ale. He became a stalwart the following campaign. He took the pill every night.

"Just need Leiber to get us through six. Bulldog can give us two tonight."

"Just need Scott Mathison to give us 4 1/3. Geoff told Charlie he's available."

"Think Eude Brito is on a pitch count. Gonna need to stretch out Geary tonight."

Geoff coupled his sub-3 ERA in '06 with a tidy 7-1 record. All he did was win games. He inspired. The offense responded; the bats delivered for the Bulldog. Geoff Geary, future closer, was maybe a tangible thing in an alternative reality, but this isn't *Fringe*. Joshua Jackson as FBI consultant, Peter Bishop, isn't walking through that door. He peaked in '06. Geoff regressed the following season, and a strained right elbow kept him off the postseason roster (Hayes 2007). His ERA jumped to 4.41 in 57 games, and I can't help but wonder if this hiccup contributed to the disturbing trend I've seen in later years.

Geary, it seems, is THAT guy. When I search his name on Twitter (standard protocol), people designate him as the de facto shitty Philly bullpen benchmark. If a Fightins reliever gives up a homer, someone is on the internet writing, "I'd rather have Geary" or "Where's Geoff Geary when you need him?" in sarcastic undertones that I can sniff out a mile away. And while I appreciate the 'Gas Can Geary' alliteration, I take exception to its historical accuracy.

I will not sit idly by as you slander G-Squared's good name and passable peripherals. Do Geoff Geary revisionists not know right from wrong? No moral compass to speak of? Show some respect. Of course, you'd rather have the Bulldog than whatever slop Klentak trotted out in 2020. The guy was a competitor. He wanted the ball. And if we're being honest – hot take incoming – Geary deserves a World Series ring.

Now hear me out. He was part of the November '07 trade along with speedster Michael Bourne and Mike Costanzo that brought over Brad Lidge and Eric Bruntlett from Houston. So you're welcome, Delaware Valley. Geoff Geary died, so the Phillies bullpen could live. If Adam Eaton and his 47.09 ERA got a ring, then I'm sure we can pacify us Geary apologists.

So next time the bullpen implodes, and Tom McCarthy says, "Oh no ..." as a ball with an exit velocity of 357 miles per hour leaves the Bank, take a deep breath. Don't type in haste. Choose your reliever comps more carefully before tweeting. Maybe consider Ron Blazier instead.

The Cannon

Name: Glenn Wilson

Position: Right Field

Career Slash Line: .265/.306/.398

Phillies Tenure: 1984-1987

Wilson is a lot smaller, peeping out from behind those aviator glasses, conning runners into screeching into wide turns so he can throw behind them. Or sprinting in for hard hit balls to nail unsuspecting hitters at first base.

"It's something I invented," bragged Wilson, who led the NL in outfield assists the last two seasons. "Oh, I'm sure it was done years ago. But it hasn't been done in this era." (Hochman 1987).

During roster introductions for the 1985 All-Star Game, Glenn Wilson tipped his cap and did a 'smoking gun' hand gesture before placing his imaginary piece back into his imaginary holster (1980s Sports Home 2019). It's the greatest video in the history of the internet. I've watched it so many times that it recently surpassed Baby Shark in total views. Every six months or so, this clip pops up on my Twitter timeline, and I mash the 'Retweet' button like I'm trying to break a tackle with Keith Byars in *Tecmo Super Bowl*.

I dug Wilson's aviators. He looked like someone who was dating your recently divorced aunt. Aunt Jane's boyfriend is probably a dick, but he just pounded eight Bud heavies at a family christening, so you have to appreciate the hustle. You rarely see eyewear on athletes anymore. Every player either wears contacts or has had Lasik surgery. They're all too perfect. I want a team full of Tyler Clippards and Chris Sabos. I want a team who doesn't like driving at night and keeps an extra pair of reading glasses on their nightstand.

But it wasn't *just* the glasses that made Wilson stand out (although his 1986 and 1987 Topps cards are fabulous). Glenn had an absolute rifle in the outfield. Nicknamed 'Glennbo' (an ode to Rambo), Wilson had the biggest arm in the 1980s outside Hulk's 24-inch pythons. The Phillies marketing department capitalized on the moniker. There's this photo of a shirtless Wilson decked out in fatigues with baseballs attached across his chest like ammo. It's fun and weird and very 80s, and his costume looks like his girlfriend is really into cosplay and he's trying his best to fit in with her circle of friends. He led the NL in outfield assists from '85 through '87 (Baseball-Reference 2020). In '87, Wilson hosed down three runners at first after apparent base hits. On June 12th, one such victim was poor Expos pitcher, Bryn Smith.

Because not only were the Expos' 19 hits not cheap last night, but they even got cheated out of one. That came when winning pitcher Bryn Smith lined what looked like a second-inning single to right, but Glenn Wilson gunned him out at first. (Stark 1987).

Stark caught up with Smith the following afternoon.

"It was embarrassing," Smith said. "He was playing me like a rover in a softball game." (Stark 1987).

(On the same day, Sixers center Jeff Ruland announced his retirement. He would return five years later, but his comeback was derailed after being struck by a luggage cart driven by a Boston Celtics ball boy).

The Phils acquired Wilson and C/1B Johnny "Fuss" Wockenfuss in 1984 for Dave Bergman and pitcher Willie Hernandez. Hernandez and his screwball spent just one season in Philly – he was pretty effective here – and he promptly went on to capture the '84 AL MVP and Cy Young in his very first season in Detroit.

Well, shit.

I guess if Steve Nash can win two MVPs, then Willie Hernandez can win one? I'm not gonna defend the Phillies brass, but – BUT – in their defense, awards in the 1980s were basically picked out of a snapback trucker's hat. Hell, Washington kicker Mark Mosely won the NFL MVP in '82, and he missed three extra points and didn't even handle kickoff duties (Barnwell 2015). Hernandez was great, but he wasn't 'AL MVP great.' Wilson, though, struggled with the success of Hernandez and that '84 Detroit team. Seeing his friends and former teammates winning the World Series, and coupled with *his* lackluster first season in Philly, the outfielder briefly considered jumping from a 60th floor balcony while watching the Tigers championship celebration (Macnow 2017).

Offensively, Glenn's numbers were pedestrian, but he had this infectious personality that heightened his perception among fans (Also, more on Mike Sweeney later). In '85, he was voted the Philadelphia athlete fans would most like to have a beer with (Macnow 2017). He also owned a gas station, like Rick Moranis in *Little Giants*. As a member of the Pirates, a reporter asked him how he felt after a hitless night at the dish. He responded, "Pretty good. I went 0 for 4 today, but I sold 16 tires." (Lidz 1989). For the record, that quote would have driven me nuts; although, I blew a gasket every time Rodney Peete smiled after an interception. I'm easily triggered.

His efforts in the field and 102 RBI campaign in 1985 also helped his stature. One of those RBIs came on August 17th when Juan Samuel, Wilson, and Mike Schmidt went back-to-back-to-back at Wrigley Field. Baseball statistics have evolved the last thirty years, but it seemed like everyone back then thought Glennbo was maybe a little bit better than he really was. Mike Schmidt even suggested the Phils had five potential MVP candidates in 1987. "Myself, Lance Parrish, Glenn Wilson, Von Hayes, and Juan Samuel." (Bernstein 1987). "The Hawk" Andre Dawson won NL MVP in '87 for those wondering. Not Lance Parrish. The praise handed down by Schmidt aside, Mike and Wilson had a very strange relationship. Like almost a *frenemies* type deal. *Sports Illustrated* profiled Wilson in a 1989 article and reached out to Michael Jack for his thoughts.

His buddy Mike Schmidt now calls Wilson one of the top three right fielders in the National League. "All right, the top five," Schmidt concedes. "O.K., so maybe the top 10. But write the top three. It sounds better." (Lidz 1989).

Schmidt is kidding there, right? He's joking, just busting Glenn's chops. To me, it's obvious he's messin' around. But in Glenn Wilson's autobiography, *Headed Home*, Glennbo took exception.

In the article that appeared in the 1989 May issue, Mike told Lidz that I was one of the top ten right outfielders in the game, "but say top three because it sounds better" (Lidz, 1989). That disappointed me because I felt that if I had not had those hundred and two RBIs in '85, Mike would not have won his third MVP award in '86, since I was the guy hitting behind him. To this day, Mike never thanked me or acknowledged it." (Wilson and Halk 2012, 40).

Damn. Glenn also said that Schmidt had the personality of a rock, but also became semi-close with him after the '85 season (Wilson and Halk 2012, 40). So I'm sticking with *frenemies*, and tuning into the 1987 Phillies reunion show hosted by Andy Cohen. Glenn registered a Cody Asche-like .689 OPS in his final season here. He was moved to Seattle along with future closer Mike Jackson in a December '87 deal for outfielder Phil Bradley and Tim Fortugno. The Phils replaced Wilson with Chris James who equally struggled. Right field was still a work in progress, but help was on the way.

Eventually. 14-year-old Bobby Abreu was mashing in Venezuela.

The Grand Entrance

Name: Billy McMillon

Position: Left Field

Career Slash Line: .248/.322/.396

Phillies Tenure: 1997

"You don't base a player's career on their first game, but first impressions are also sometimes lasting," manager Terry Francona said. "A lot of things that we heard about him - that he's a professional hitter - looked true." (Associated Press 1997).

I made my first ever sports bet when I was 8. It was a hockey wager and I suppose it was a futures bet if we're being specific. The Flyers had a 19-year-old rookie named Eric Lindros and I was all in. I was a believer. My sister's high school boyfriend came around all the time and I bet him $1 that Eric Lindros would score a goal in every game that season. I didn't leave myself much wiggle room. Wayne Gretzky holds the NHL record for goals in a season with 92, but I didn't need Lindros to be a hero. I only needed 82 tallies from the powerful center. His goal streak ended in Game 3, a 4-2 win over the Capitals. My sister's boyfriend didn't collect though. He was also the biggest benefactor of my brother and I's Sega Genesis Fund (we had a bucket to collect rogue singles and loose change). In turn, I ratted him out to my parents after I saw him smoking a cigarette with his buddies in a Wawa parking lot. It was a shit move on my part. I should've kept quiet. If you're reading this, I'm sorry, Dom. Thanks again for the Sega donations.

When you're young, you latch on to a player's early success. Why not, right? What's wrong with a little optimism? Besides, what the hell did a second grader know about regression to the mean? Lindros was gonna score 150 goals. Chris T. Jones was the perfect complement to Irving Fryar. Ricky Otero (more on him later) was Rickey Henderson and Billy McMillon was the second coming of Hank Aaron. The Fightins acquired McMillon in a July 1997 deal for the beloved Darren Daulton. Dutch was 35 years old and had made the full-time transition from catcher to the outfield. It was weird not seeing Daulton behind the plate. The natural evolution for catchers trying to save their knees is first base. Like, if Rod Barajas went on sudden tear at the dish, I doubt Charlie Manuel's first instinct would be to stick him in left field in the second game of a doubleheader.

"Barajas is playing left tonight. Little worried about his range out there."

"Yeah, but he's crushing lefties, Kevin. Gotta keep his bat in there."

Daulton was having a nice final season with the Phils. While his play in the outfield was a mixed bag, he sported an .860 OPS (.381 OB%). Still, a 35-year-old rental won't fetch you much in the open market. McMillon bounced around between the majors and AAA in '97. He was putting up terrific numbers in the International League (.279/.378/.485), but a 25-year-old minor leaguer is one birthday away from being a dinosaur. It's like being an alum at a frat party. Even though you only graduated five years ago, none of the college kids want you on their flip cup team and they're going to talk shit about you as soon as you leave.

"Who was the old head in the Aeropostale polo?"

I'm between laundry days. Get off my back.

McMillon made his Phillies debut on August 18th in a home game against the Giants. Veteran right-hander Mark Gardner was on the bump for San Fran and ran into trouble in the 3rd. Midre Cummings, as he was known to do, set the table with a lead-off single. MICK-EY MORAN-DINI (that's my Harry Kalas voice) followed with a base knock. Scott Rolen lined out to third, but an errant throw by Bill Mueller advanced the runners. Gardner wanted no parts of Rico Brogna – what pitcher did – and intentionally walked the first baseman. Mike Lieberthal, though, popped out and Gardner could see his way out of the jam. But there are two cardinal rules you never break. You don't wear a band's t-shirt to their concert, and you don't groove a fastball in the zone to Billy McMillon. Billy belted a grand slam into the Phillies bullpen and a legend was born.

Two grand slams.

It was the first time the Phillies had done that in a while.

To be exact, since April 18, 1921, at the Baker Bowl.

Shortstop Ralph Miller and pitcher Spike Meadows, each of whom ended the year with three homers, had no way of knowing after that 11-6 win over the Boston Braves that it would be another 76 years before the Phillies would do that again (Hagen 1997).

(Lieby would later hit the other).

Chase Utley also hit a grand slam in his first Phillies start, but my mind doesn't go to The Man. When I'm asked about a player hitting a grand slam in their Phils debut, and I'm asked that often, my brain instantly recalls that August 18th night. Allow me this metaphor:

McMillon :: Thomas Edison.

Utley :: Ben Franklin.

Franklin was an inventor, sure, but he also was a Founding Father, a statesman, a diplomat, a printer, etc, etc. My first memory about Utley isn't his grand slam. However, as far as I know, the *only* thing Thomas Edison did was invent the light bulb.

"Hey, who was that dude that hit a grand slam in his first start with the Phils?"

"You're thinking of Billy fuckin' McMillon."

I was pumped for the new guy. I then did what every red-blooded 7th grader did in 1997: I traded Darren Daulton for Billy McMillon in my *Triple Play* season. I had plans to use McMillon at short. I expected Virtual Kevin Stocker to be disappointed with my decision, but I was prepared to have that difficult conversation. Billy finished the year with a solid .792 OPS, but he never got back to Philly. After the season, he spent two more campaigns in Scranton/Wilkes-Barre where he again performed admirably, recording an OPS over .800 both years, before signing a free agent deal with the Tigers in the offseason. I wasn't naive. Despite the heroics on that warm August night, I knew Billy McMillon wouldn't homer in *every* game. The math, the odds, just weren't in his favor. But it was fun to dream.

The (Almost) Perfect Season

Name: Mike Grace

Position: Pitcher

Career Record: 16-16; 4.96 ERA (4.44 FIP)

Phillies Tenure: 1995-1999

You may remember Grace from the tail end of the tailspin that was the Phillies' 1995 season. With most of their starting pitchers sporting fresh new surgical scars on their shoulders and elbows, the Phillies called up Grace, who had only been recently promoted to triple A (Sheridan 1996).

My brother and I had this really small box TV in our bedroom. We mostly used it for our *NHL '93* wars on Sega Genesis. It definitely didn't have cable. Hell, I'm not sure it even came with a remote. Once you were in bed, you didn't want to keep getting up. You rolled the dice. You stuck to one channel. You'd settle for a rerun of *The Jeffersons,* but you really hoped for two new episodes of *Roc* and *Herman's Head* on Fox 29. Channels 3, 6, and 10 were useless. The news was either airing or coming up next. Channel 48 showed ECW (shout out to the Blue Meanie) and I once saw a pair of boobs on the New Jersey Network (NJN), which was a nice change of pace from their Seton Hall basketball telecasts. After the great Garden State flashing of '96, I spent the next week trying to convince my parents to move to Cherry Hill. Figured that across the Ben Franklin there was more where that came from.

Phillies road games aired on Channel 17. I saw a lot of west coast games on that TV. Well, I saw the first two innings of a lot of west coast games on that TV. I'm not an old man shouting at a cloud-type guy, but times were different then. If the Phils played the Padres on a Tuesday, I wouldn't find out that Trevor Hoffman pitched a clean 9th until Thursday in the *Inquirer*. I never stayed awake for an entire west coast game on that TV, but I once came close.

Enter Mike Grace. If you're reading this, you probably remember Mike Grace. If you don't, don't sweat it, because Wikipedia doesn't have the slightest idea who he is either.

Michael James Grace (born June 20, 1970), is an American former professional baseball pitcher. He played all or part of five seasons in Major League Baseball (MLB), from 1995 through 1999, all for the Philadelphia Phillies (Wikipedia 2021).

That's the entire entry. I mean, the information is correct. He was a pitcher. He played for the Phillies. I'm not disputing that. But for *years*, the entry was accompanied by a photo of a DIFFERENT MIKE GRACE. It's like looking up heavyweight boxing champion, Jack Johnson, and seeing a picture of the "Bubble Toes" guy. The photo formerly paired with *our* Mike Grace was Mike Grace, a former Reds third baseman. And that is disrespectful. Fake Mike Grace played just five games in the majors in 1978. *Our* Mike Grace threw a complete game shutout against the Yankees in '97 and faced the minimum 27 batters. Store-brand Mike Grace had a .000 OPS in three career at-bats. OUR Mike Grace almost ran the table in 1996. We all remember Summerslam '94. There was only one Undertaker.

12-year-old me was one of the first passengers of the Mike Grace hype train. I knew we had something. Forget his stirrups. Actually, don't forget his stirrups. What a look, what a presentation. Grace was old school. His pants stopped below his knees like they were jean shorts and he was shopping for CDs inside an F.Y.E. There was a lot to like. I bought in early, investing my shares in GraceCoin as soon as my weekly $1 allowance cleared. On April 3rd, he pitched 8 innings in a 3-1 victory over the Rockies. He stumbled in his next start, giving up 5 earned runs over 6 innings, but a potent Phillies offense propelled him to win #2 (Benito Santiago hit a go-ahead, three-run jack in the 6th). By the end of April, he was 4-0.

20-0? 25-0? Everything was on the table. Dream big. And, yeah, the win/loss stat is ultimately meaningless (run support dependency, etc), but not when you're 12. When you're 12, wins are everything. I had this mental checklist.

I needed a quality start from Mike Grace.

If I didn't get that, I needed the bats to come alive.

If I couldn't be assured of A or B, I needed a rainout.

No decisions became my best friend. Mike entered his May 7th start with a 5-0 record and a 2.53 ERA. The Phils lost to the Astros that night, but a no decision kept the streak alive for another week. My joy watching Grace pitch waned, though. Not because of Mike Grace himself – he was a godsend – but because of the pressure. It was too much for me. I watched scared. I no longer was trying to win Mike Grace starts. I was just trying not to lose them. Preserving this perfect record consumed me. I welcomed bad weather to buy myself another day or two. I tried handpicking opposing pitchers, like Jim Boeheim scheduling Colgate and Cornell and other inner-state cupcakes on the non-conference slate. On May 12th, the Phils welcomed the 23-13 Atlanta Braves. Bobby Cox trotted out Greg Maddux against our hero. I countered from my parents' living room floor.

"What about Steve Avery, Bobby? Or how about Neagle? I think Denny needs to get some work in."

Cox wouldn't budge. It was Maddux against Grace with our, well Mike's, undefeated record on the line. FanDuel had Atlanta at -225 on the Money Line. 87% of the public was on the Braves. There was just one problem, though.

No one told Mike Grace he was supposed to roll over.

With Greg Maddux on the mound after Atlanta had pounded Philadelphia pitching two nights running, Grace was supposed to lose. But, like many rookies, he didn't get the message.

"I really don't pay much attention to who I'm pitching against," Grace said after raising his record to 6-0 with a four-hitter as the Phillies ended the Braves' seven-game winning streak with a 6-0 win Sunday at Veterans Stadium (Associated Press

1996).

My confidence was restored. If Mike ain't scared, why should I be? I had been trying to nibble my way to a 5-0 record with 27 no decisions, when I should've been pounding the zone with my fastball. Pitch to contact, Dave. I shouldn't fear the likes of Greg Maddux. Teams should fear Mike Grace. Later that week, the Phils boarded a flight out west. I planned ahead. Catch a quick cat nap after dinner before Mike took the bump at Dodger Stadium. I needed to be fresh. Grace needed 9 innings out of me that night, not my usual 2 ⅓ before I woke up at 7 AM with drool on my pillow. The opposing starter was Hideo Nomo. Nomo was *insanely* popular. The 1995 NL Rookie of the Year and All-Star starter was must-see TV. His funky delivery gave opposing hitters fits. Looking back, I wasn't prepared for Hideo. I had seen Maddux's shit 1000 times. Guy is gonna top out at 88 and try to extend the strike zone. Ho hum. Nomo was a different beast. I had trouble picking up the ball, and it wasn't just because I was squinting at an 10" TV. I sat on the edge of the bed during his first inning warm-ups wondering when the last monsoon hit Los Angeles.

"Is that a cloud over Chavez Ravine? I'd get the tarp out. Can't be too careful."

I needed an exit strategy. What I really needed was a no decision. But the Fightins struck early. Hits by Pete Incaviglia, Todd Zeile, and Kevin Jordan gave the Phils a 2-0 lead in the 2nd inning. Grace was cruising. Throwing strikes, inducing ground balls, etc, etc. My mind drifted in the 3rd, wondering if "Amazing Grace" or "Grace-ful" would be the headline in the newspaper two days from now. Then Mike Piazza homered in the 4th. Raul Mondesi then followed suit. By the bottom half of the 5th, we had an emergency. It was apropos that Brett Butler was in the opposing dugout, because Grace was Under Fire. I was screaming for Johnny Padres to get his ass out to the mound and settle down my guy, and you haven't truly lived until you're screaming for a visit from the pitching coach. By the 6th, it was over. Los Angeles had chased our golden boy to the showers with the Phils down 5-3. The bats turned their back on Mike and me. So did the No Decision gods. I fell asleep in the 7th.

Grace only pitched four more times that year. Injuries disrupted his '96 campaign (described as "a sharp, stabbing pain in his elbow") and dogged him throughout his career (Sheridan 1996). I watched those other four starts, but no longer with that same anxious feeling. I didn't watch those other games through my fingers like a horror film or carry the heavy burden of his pristine record on my 6th grade shoulders. I still loved Mike Grace. I still believed. He just wasn't perfect anymore.

The Phone Call

Name: Rick White

Position: Pitcher

Career Record: 42-54; 4.45 ERA (4.34 FIP)

Phillies Tenure: 2006

With the crowd frenzied, especially after Scott Olsen hit Abraham Nunez, Coste had no idea what White was saying.

"I had to hang up on him," Coste said. "No offense meant." (Hayes 2006).

Relievers and kickers have the longest shelf life in sports. While Gary Anderson and Norm Johnson are probably still humming along in the AFC somewhere, NFL running backs are put out to pasture by 29. Aside from the occasional "The 49ers have signed FA RB Alfred Morris" alert on your phone, the backfield is a young man's game. There is little room for comeback attempts or retreads. Barry Sanders, or even Chris Ivory for that matter, isn't joining the huddle any time soon. But relievers? Bullpen guys? They're just finding their sea legs at 30. These guys are pitching in the bigs for the next decade, maybe even longer if they're a southpaw.

"I'm concerned about Jesse Orosco, Ken. I don't think his body can hold up. He turns 65 next spring, and his two-seamer is topping out at 57."

"Yeah, but lefties are only hitting .223 against him."

And outside of the Trevor Hoffmans and Mariano Riveras who stick with the same franchise, relievers make their rounds. They've done multiple tours across the league. Hard-throwing mercenaries signing one or two-year deals, one after the other, always potential trade bait at the deadline, because if MLBTradeRumors.com has taught me anything, it's that everyone is looking for bullpen help.

It may be easier to list the teams that Rick White *didn't* pitch for, but I'll give this a whirl. The big righty played in eleven cities - Pittsburgh (2x), Tampa, the Mets, Rockies, Cardinals, White Sox, Houston (2x), Cleveland, Cincinnati, Philly, and Seattle. Rick White was Tony Massenburg, if Massenburg was bald with a thick goatee and looked like a member of the WWF's The Disciples of Apocalypse (DOA). Every time I saw White take the bump, I expected an ambush from Savio Vega and Los Boricuas.

"White available tonight?"

"Nah, he twisted an ankle yesterday on *Sunday Night Heat*."

Years before Rick landed in Philadelphia, he was involved in this bizarre incident involving fellow relief pitcher, Jim Mecir. Playing with Tampa in 1999, the bullpen guys were shagging flies during practice. The details are a bit murky, but White collided (?) with Mecir and broke his elbow (Topkin 1999). There were Tampa radio reports that the freak injury was due to roughhousing, a little game of grab ass, and big Rick took things too far. This led to an internal investigation.

Manager Larry Rothschild has determined that Jim Mecir's broken right elbow was the result of an innocent collision with Rick White rather than horseplay, and that no disciplinary measures will be taken. A congenital condition in Mecir's elbow also contributed (Topkin 1999).

"A congenital condition in Mecir's elbow also contributed." The hell? Have we stumbled upon the most underreported cover-up in sports history? Surely, there is a perfectly good explanation here, because right now I'm skeptical.

Mecir, White and several pitchers were in right field when White fielded a ball and threw it towards the infield. He turned around and became entangled with Mecir and the two fell to the ground, with Mecir on top. White then rolled over on to Mecir's arm, causing the break (Topkin 1999).

Oh, that clears everything up. They became entangled. Makes perfect sense. The incident was a weird footnote in White's lengthy, and otherwise unassuming career. The Phils picked-up the 37-year-old pitcher in June of '06 off waivers from the Reds. Rick wore #00, ala Spencer Hawes, becoming only the second Phillie to rock the fake integer. And if you knew that Omar Olivares was the first Fightin to wear #00 back in 1995, then you should be writing this book, not me. White's stint here was only a few months, but he earned a reputation. He stood out. He gained notoriety here for much more endearing reasons.

Rick White was the Telephone Guy.

The bullpen phone rang. Ryan Howard, having returned to the dugout from his home-run trot, was summoned. He picked up the receiver and identified himself.

"Big Sexy Chocolate."

On the other end, Rick White, nonplussed, replied:

"Uh ... White Chocolate."

And so, a tradition was born:

A Phillie hits a home run and White, a middle reliever, gives him the Mr. President phone call - you know, the type presidents deliver to champagne-soaked championship teams (Hayes 2006).

White's bullpen calls became part of the home run pageantry. The telecast cut to Rick and the hitter on the receiving end.

"Rick White giving his customary home run congratulations," Harry Kalas would say with a chuckle.

I popped. I loved it. It was the '06 Phillies' 'thing,' like Brad Miller and his bamboo or the Fightins' Home Run Hat. I don't remember if White was any good that season, but I know that big ol' country boy could use a telephone. It was like a call on your birthday from your grandmother. It wasn't necessary, but it definitely made you feel good inside.

"What I miss?"

"David Dellucci just went deep - second deck. No phone call yet, though."

"Rick will call. Don't worry. He'll call."

White wasn't long for the Fightins. Few relievers were. Locking up your middle relief for the long-term isn't a sound strategy. You don't ink Rudy Seanez to a five-year deal and then focus your attention towards the other 24 roster spots. Teams shuffle these guys in and out, just hoping they keep the ball down during their brief stay. The situation is fungible. A plethora of relievers are always ready, always available, and always on call. And sometimes, they even call you.

The Replacement

Name: Tadahito (Tad) Iguchi

Position: Second Base

Career Slash Line: .268/.338/.401

Phillies Tenure: 2007-2008

"Obviously, you don't replace a Chase Utley," Arbuckle said. "Hopefully he's out for a shorter duration than we originally thought, but we wanted the best possible replacement." (Carchidi 2007).

Since these essays don't cover the Rollins or Howards or Chooches of the world, there isn't one player in here that was universally beloved. No one in this book had a 99.99% approval rating. There's always one naysayer, always one critic, and that goes for any player. Someone is probably out there who's like, "Yeah, Lidge was perfect in '08 and delivered the best moment of my life. Don't get me wrong, the parade was cool and all, BUUUUT ... but, he really regressed the following year." Tadahito (Tad) Iguchi, however, is maybe the exception. He may be the closest thing we have to the Mayor of *A Phillies Odyssey*.

Chase Utley was hitting the cover off the ball in '07, and, at the time, was considered the more likely MVP candidate over eventual winner Jimmy Rollins. On July 26th, Chase was hitting a robust .336/.414/.581 – a NSFW slash line that is more likely to be found on RedTube rather than Baseball-Reference. In that July 26th game with the Nats, horrible human (and future Phillie) John Lannan broke Chase Utley's finger with a fastball. He *claimed* it was unintentional. Right. And Marty Jannetty just fell into the barbershop window. One day after the injury, the organization found – and I can't believe I'm actually writing this – a viable, productive player at the trade deadline. What a breath of fresh air. I didn't think that was possible. (Apologies to all the Turk Wendell fans out there. More on him later).

Welcome, Tadahito Iguchi, the first Asian-born player to wear the red pinstripes. After a successful run in Japan with the Fukuoka Daiei Hawks, the 30-year-old rookie came to the States. He promptly won a ring with the White Sox in '05, proving to be a useful, capable player in the bigs. A year after winning 90 games in '06 (but only finishing 3rd in the AL Central), Chicago bottomed out. They went 72-90 and Iguchi was moved for Michael Dubee, son of pitching coach Rich Dubee.

A week after Tad's arrival, the Fightins mounted an insane 9th inning comeback against the Brewers. Trailing 6-1 in Milwaukee, the Phils rallied for five in their final at-bats. Wes Helms reached on an error, and Werth followed-up with a two-run jack. Chris Coste and Ruiz were then retired. The Phils then scratched across three more runs thanks to two walks, a hit by pitch, an infield single (by Iguchi), and an error by Ryan Braun at third. Helms hit a two-run double in the 11th and old friend Jose Mesa stranded three runners to preserve the win.

It was an absurd finish that is lost in the archives of that incredible '07 season. Those late-inning heroics at Miller Park are just a footnote in Iguchi's Philadelphia story. Tad's defining moment came *after* Utley returned. In the stuff of lore, the Mets held a six-game lead in the NL East when they took the short trip to South Philly for a four-game set.

Game #1: The Phils punked them in the opener, 9-2. J.D. Durbin's stuff was moving. Iguchi homered.

Game #2: Howard hit a walk-off in extras (My brother and I were there. No big deal).

Game #3: Phillie legend Marlon Anderson is called for runner interference in the 9th. The Phils survive.

Game #4: Fuck the '07 Mets. By the time the Business Person Special rolled around, fans at the Bank were ready to take on the '27 Yankees. (We have J.C. Romero warm to face Ruth and Gehrig). This game was an, "I remember where I was" moment. Everyone has a story. I was at work, and you don't have an 11-10 final wrapped up in two hours and twenty minutes. My entire department STAYED at the office. (We did not get paid overtime for this). 5:00 rolled around and no one left. No one wanted the game to end during the walk to their car. There were no live streams in '07. It was 15 people just banging the refresh icon on Yahoo or ESPN or CBS or wherever. The Phils first blew a 5-0 lead and then an 8-5 cushion after the Mets stormed back with five runs in the top of the 8th. Willie Randolph then called on Billy Wagner for the rare two-inning save. With Wags laboring in the 9th and a pitch count over 40, Chase Utley ripped a single to right. Iguchi rounded third, and there was Pat Burrell right behind catcher Paul Lo Duca motioning Tad to get down, get down, get down. The Bank was a madhouse. Kalas' call was (predictably) great. A guy on my team stood up and screamed, "Phillies win!" After a collective cheer, 15 people walked out of the building together. The headline in the *Philadelphia Daily News* the next morning was, "Make Broom for the Phils," which I fully endorsed. (Hayes 2007).

"Gotta hand it to the fans: It was the best it has been since I've been here," said Burrell, the longest tenured Phillie at 8 years. He also homered in the first inning, part of the 5-0 lead the Phils had by the end of the third. "They stuck around."

"I've got to agree," Utley said. "It was crazy." (Hayes 2007).

(Later that night, the Birds lost a closely contested preseason affair to the Jets, 13-11. Backup quarterback, A.J. Feeley, broke his hand in the defeat. John Lannan is not considered a suspect at this time).

With Chase back in the lineup, "Can Tad play third?" became the most uttered phrase in the Delaware Valley. If I had an iPhone in '07, it would have autocorrected every "can't talk" or "call me" text to "Can Tad play third?" Every Wes Helms error or failed at-bat with runners in scoring position added fuel to the fire. I caught myself muttering, "Can Tad play third?" on my commute to work and

I wasn't even carpooling with anyone. Philadelphians love wondering if a guy can play out of position. It's a timeless tradition. Can Okafor play the 4? With Thome at 1B, can Howard play left? On the surface, it wasn't that far-fetched. At least Iguchi played *in* the infield. Hell, I once heard a WIP caller ask if Andy Reid may play Sav Rocca at some fullback because of his rugby background. Iguchi wasn't a third baseman by trade, but he wasn't Wes Helms either.

Manuel never did experiment with Tad at third, though, and Gucci (great nickname) settled into a utility role. He hit a crisp .304 after joining the team and walked in two of his three plate appearances in the NLDS for a gorgeous .667 OB%. See? Told you Charlie should have played Tad at the hot corner.

He then signed with the Padres after the season. Iguchi – and gosh – I completely blanked on this, rejoined the Phils the following September. Tad was back! Why/how did I block this out? I can remap the fifteen minutes that Frank Gore was an Eagle, but I don't recall Iguchi's cup of coffee with the World Series team? I'm getting old. My first question after discovering Tad's reemergence was, "Did Tad get a ring?" Help a brother out, Wikipedia.

Because Iguchi joined the Phillies after September 1, he was ineligible for the team's postseason roster; thus, Iguchi was not with the Phillies when they defeated the Tampa Bay Rays in the World Series (although he did receive a World Series ring) (Wikipedia 2021).

I was able to corroborate Wikipedia's story (Nagatsuka 2010). He did get a ring. 2008 was Iguchi's final season in the big leagues. Tad's fit on the '07 team was perfect, and that *rarely* happens. The list of impeccable midseason deals not involving Cliff Lee is very short. We always concoct these trade scenarios for a contending Philly team, believing that the Fightins/Sixers/Eagles/Flyers are just one missing piece away. It's Chris Webber (oh, come on. You were excited in '05), it's Golden Tate, it's literally any bullpen arm with a pulse. Iguchi was thrusted into an impossible situation, and he performed admirably. He raised the bar. Only problem now is I think there is a Tad Iguchi out there at every trade deadline.

The Picasso

Name: Randy Wolf

Position: Pitcher

Career Record: 133-125; 4.24 ERA (4.38 FIP)

Phillies Tenure: 1999-2006

I watched the '09 postseason from our garden-level apartment. And by 'garden-level,' I mean the basement. Your mind can go to some dark places when you haven't seen sunlight in six months. I paced around the living room, hiding behind the couch for one pitch, then crouching in front of the coffee table for the next. My girlfriend (now wife) caught the Phever. Chooch, Werth, and Victorino were her guys. Game 4 of the NLCS was a nail-biter. I couldn't find a lucky spot. I watched a half inning from the kitchen, another from the bedroom. I was trying to find a rhythm. What's the old expression? Get hot and stay hot? I just couldn't get hot from any spot in our 450 sq. foot apartment. The Phils were trailing 4-3 in the bottom of the 9th. Two outs, two runners on. J-Roll was our last chance. I was spent. I was down on my knees in front of the TV, exasperated, like Todd Pratt catching Paul Abbott in a sweltering August heat.

"If we win this game, I'll take you wherever you want for dinner tomorrow."

The Phils had an off day.

Rollins then ripped a 1-1 offering from Phillies whipping boy, Jonathan Broxton. I caught a second wind and leapt up, waving Chooch home at the crack of the bat.

"Go Chooch! Run Chooch! Run Chooch! Move those little legs!"

I think I tore my rotator cuff. Days later I would be giving my insurance information to the receptionist of Dr. James Andrews. Behind me, my wife was jumping up and down on the couch, waving my '07 NLDS rally towel I used to bite like Jerry Tarkanian.

"P.F. Chang's! P.F. Chang's! P.F. Chang's!"

The lettuce wraps didn't disappoint. Randy Wolf started that game for Los Angeles. It's strange that one of my favorite Phillies memories ever involves an opposing Wolfie, because, man, he was an organization staple. He was a constant: eight seasons, an All-Star berth, 11th on the all-time Phillies strikeout leader list, and the guy who broke in Citizens Bank Park. Randy Wolf deserved to be part of the Phils NL East dominance. He paid his dues. But he departed after the '06 season, and here he was in '09, watching the Bank erupt while donning the Dodger Blue. Randy Wolf wasn't a martyr, but he was in the wrong place at the wrong time.

He made his Phils debut on June 11th, 1999, throwing 5 ⅔ innings of 1 run ball in a win over the Blue Jays. Randy won his first two starts in the bigs, and by game #3 – a home tilt with the Pirates – he had gained a following. In section 739 of the Vet, a handful of fans decked out in wolf masks honored their left-handed hero. The Wolfpack was born. The group consisted of eight brothers, the Wood Brothers, who danced their way through Randy's entire Philly tenure (Nelson 2009).

They had moves, too. As a professional wedding guest for hire, I've been in the center of a lot of banquet hall dance floors. I'm familiar with all the disciplines: modern, interpretive, the Cupid Shuffle, etc. Their strikeout dance was reminiscent of the Lawnmower, a distant cousin to the Shopping Cart, which are the only two dance moves guys have in their toolbox. The Wolfpack could go, and they get bonus points for the synchronized effort. The group gained traction. People wanted to be part of the festivities. While the 700 Level (shout out to Enrico) had the well-earned reputation of being a *bit* rowdy and a *bit* negative, the Wolfpack were outliers. They were upbeat. They were positive. It was easy to see why they themselves became so popular, and later imitated through other fan groups like Sal's Pals, Person's People, and Padilla's Flotillas.

When he formally retired as a Phillie in 2016, Wolf was quick to mention his fanbase during an interview with Gregg Murphy (MLB 2016). The Wolfpack were ahead of their time. This group would've thrived today. Think of the Wolfpack-organized tailgates and merchandise opportunities. An nWo Red and Black t-shirt with Randy Wolf's face on the front? Please take my money. In the mid-2000s, dudes wore a pink polo with its collar popped over ANOTHER pink polo with *its* collar popped. Then a wristband on their *forearm* because (???). It was sad. It was a cry for help. If only they had a Wolfpack or Sal's Pals tee instead.

Wolf stumbled at the end of his rookie year but won 10 plus games the next four seasons. He had a stretch in August of '02, where he tossed 26 consecutive shutout innings across three starts. The final leg was a complete game victory over the Mets, where he outdueled "The Human Rain Delay" Steve Trachsel. The 1-0 final ended in 14 hours and 53 minutes. A 10-4 record at the '03 break with a 3.31 ERA earned him his only All-Star appearance and Wolf finished that campaign with a 16-10 mark. Along with being a dependable middle of the rotation starter, he also developed a reputation as a pretty good hitting pitcher. Broadcasters love that. Pitchers who can handle the bat are like board members of a foundation. Just trying to do all they can to help their cause.

"David Coggin up with two runners on.

"A chance here to help his cause, Harry."

In August '04, Wolfie belted two homers in a win over the Rockies (Thome also homered twice). Randy went 3-3 and left the Bank that night with an eye-popping .907 OPS.

"I could see using him as a pinch-hitter," said manager Larry Bowa, who has no lefty pinch hitters when Utley starts. "He gives you a quality at-bat. The only guy I hit-and-run with more is [No. 2 hitter Placido] Polanco." (Hayes 2004).

I wasn't explicitly asking for Wolf to spell Marlon Byrd in center. I just was curious if Wolfie played any outfield in Little League. It was an innocent question.

His later years were hampered by injuries and he needed Tommy John surgery in '05. Still, the organization hoped the popular pitcher would fill out the rotation in 2007. The California kid spurned the team, however, taking a hometown discount to play with the Dodgers. Along with Wolf, the Phils were also attached to free agent names like Jason Schmidt and Barry Zito, who was linked to the Phillies every offseason and trade deadline for like five years (Zolecki 2006). The team instead settled on Adam Eaton.

Wolf then pitched for everyone. He made Octavio Dotel look like a shut-in. He went from LA to San Diego to Houston, back to LA, then to Milwaukee and then Baltimore (which I think is made up because I have zero recollection of that), then down to Miami and finished in Detroit. He didn't last 16 years by overpowering you. In the latter stages of his career, he cultivated this slow, eephus-style pitch that could bottom out at 49 miles per hour on the radar gun (Made the Cut 2020). It was this evolution that made me appreciate Wolf even more. Its effectiveness was baffling. I threw a mid-40s two-seamer when I was 12, and some kid hit a bomb that broke a window of a nearby Shop-N-Bag. The wind must've been blowing out that day because I hit my spot. All I could do was give the hitter credit in my post-game presser.

Wolf told this story on Gregg Murphy's Podcast, *Glove Stories with Murph*. Shortly after being called up, he saw a can of red paint and a paintbrush inside his locker at Wrigley. As a rite of passage, Curt Schilling told him all rookies had to paint a statue that the team bus passed each day to the park. The statue was of Civil War General, Phillip Henry Sheridan. General Sheridan is riding a horse and the horse's testicles were, as Wolf described them, sculpted above scale (Murphy 2021). Despite some apprehension, he and fellow rookie Cliff Politte moved forward with the prank. They painted the horse's balls and even added a red Phillies "P" onto its leg, while Marlon Anderson and Wayne Gomes filmed the entire excursion. (Lot going on in that sentence).

Wait, isn't it illegal to deface a federal statue or monument, Dave?

Good question. I'm a little rusty with my federal laws, but I believe painting the horse's balls may be illegal according to the Veterans Memorial Preservation and Recognition Act. Though I'm no lawyer and we're no narcs, so to borrow a line from Eazy-E, "don't quote me, boy, 'cause I ain't said shit."

The next morning, the team shares a laugh from the bus as they spot the artwork. Cliff and Randy assume that's the end of it. Mission accomplished. In the clubhouse, however, Terry Francona is pissed.

Francona is accompanied by two Chicago police officers, who call Politte, Wolf, Anderson, and Gomes into the manager's office. Since Wolf and Politte were the ones who *actually* defaced the statue, they're being arrested. Anderson and Gomes were then excused. Randy's fired up and ready to throw Schilling under the bus.

"I'm ready to make him pay my bail money, my legal fees..." (Murphy 2021).

Politte then asked the officers if he could first change out of his uniform before being escorted to the police headquarters.

"No way," they respond. The officers want everyone at the precinct to know who they are, as if anyone in a Chicago jail knew who the hell Phillie long man Cliff Politte was.

"Hey, is that Phillies long man Cliff Politte in cell four?"

"Nah, can't be. No way. Looks more like Billy Brewer."

Before they're escorted out of the stadium, the cops ask the team if they have anything to say to the rookies. The team's prank, their elaborate hazing, got these two arrested after all.

After a long pause, the team yells, "Gotcha!" (Murphy 2021).

Release the footage, Gomesy.

The Comeback

Name: Carmelo Martinez

Position: LF/1B

Career Slash Line: .245/.337/.408

Phillies Tenure: 1990

"What was the final of the Phils/Dodgers game last night, Dad?"

"Not sure, son. I'll put on KYW. It's almost 15 after the hour."

The first card I vividly remember owning, the first one I can picture holding in my hand is a 1990 Topps Carmelo Martinez. I had like fourteen of them. Carmelo and the stale stick of gum were staples in each pack. It was the other fifteen cards that varied. His pose was straight from a grade school yearbook photo and he's wearing a long white t-shirt underneath his Padres jersey, like he just went shopping in Keith Van Horn's closet. (The picture on his Baseball-Reference page is from that same card). I was happy when mom told me the Phils signed Martinez. I knew him well. There was one of his cards in every room, like sage cleansing the home of negative energy.

"We signed *Caramel*?" I asked. Or, to account for my Philly accent, I probably called him, *'car-mole.'*

Before John Kruk became a fixture at first, the Fightins brought in the big righty to spell Ricky Jordan. Ricky was considered a top organizational prospect, ranked #5 in 1988 according to *Baseball America* – just behind Ron Jones. (Pitcher Brad Brink was #1) (The Baseball Cube 2021). The 8-year vet started hot, making the most of his chances when called.

Ricky Jordan came down with a case of Wally Pipp in Atlanta. Carmelo Martinez replaced him at first base. While the Phillies' medical staff hoped that the stomach cramps wracking Jordan were not symptoms of appendicitis, "The Big C" pounded an eighth-inning grand slam Friday night that carried the Phils to a pulse-quickened victory.

The next night, Martinez beat the Braves with a homer in the top of the ninth. (Conlin 1990).

"The Big C?" I LOVE IT.

"If Curt Ford gets on, Zack ..."

"You thinking what I'm thinking?"

"Yessir. It's Big C time."

In early May, Martinez was hitting .318/.400/.591, but the good times didn't roll. Regression reared its ugly head and The Big C's numbers plateaued. He was eventually moved to Pittsburgh as part of a bizarre Wes Chamberlain snafu (more on that later), but in one final parting gift, Carmelo played a vital role in one of the most improbable victories in *all* of sports.

The Phillies were out in Los Angeles for a three-game set. During game one of the series, Lenny Dykstra was called out on strikes in the 5th inning. Nails argued, letting home plate umpire Ron Barnes know that both the call sucked, and he sucked (I'm assuming). Behind the plate was catcher Rick Dempsey. Now, Dempsey was no spring chicken. He was 40 and had made his major league debut way back in 1969! So, Dykstra, up now in the 7th, argued the call from his previous plate appearance once again. He then targeted Dempsey, accusing him of kissing Barnes' ass and buttering up to the ump (Klkatz 2007). The veteran backstop wasn't having it. Getting called an 'ass kisser' is fightin' words. Dempsey popped up and hit Dykstra with a right hand and the benches cleared.

Crew chief Harry Wendelstedt chalked up the fight to "two veteran players trying to intimidate a young umpire." (Bamberger 1990). Rick had this to say about the scuffle:

"Somebody grabbed my face when we rolled on the ground," said Dempsey,

who ended up with a large welt on the side of his face. "After I saw the replay, I saw it was Dykstra. He grabbed me by the side of the face and squeezed every pimple I had."

"What's he mad about?" Dempsey continued. "He made an out. I make four of them a game. If I was hitting .340 I'd be kissing every player on the opposing team." (Klkatz 2007).

(Lenny's averaged dropped to .342 after the 0-3 night).

The next night was the comeback. It was an ESPN telecast and Chris Berman was on the call. The Phils were sloppy, committing three errors that night, so I don't think Berman had the Fightins in mind when he said, "You're with me, leather." The Dodgers led 11-1 going into the top of the 8th thanks to an eight-spot in the fifth. Jason Grimsley didn't have his best stuff. Neither did Bruce Ruffin. Or Darrel Akerfelds for that matter. Tommy Lasorda emptied out his bench with the game in the bag. Von Hayes plated two in the 8th with a meaningless double, but LA clung to an 11-3 lead entering the 9th. Let's pick up the action from there.

Rod Booker walked.

The Big C reached on an error by future Phillie Jose Offerman.

Dickie Thon singled, scoring one.

Dave Hollins singled, plating Carmelo.

Sil Campusano flied out (He would make two outs in the inning).

Tom Nieto walked.

Von Hayes reached on yet another Offerman error. Thon scored.

Dale Murphy doubled, scoring two.

Now it's 11-8, with still only one down. Up next was the Krukker.

"John Kruk was standing out in the field, looking up at the clock, thinking, 'We're not going to make it back to the hotel in time for room service. Room service closes at midnight.' So he started thinking. 'If we're not going to make it back in time for room service, we might as well win.' - Jayson Stark (BaseballDaysofYore 2011).

The Philly favorite roped a drive over the right centerfield wall to knot the game at 11-11. *"I don't believe we're seeing this,"* said Berman, as Krukker rounded the bases (BaseballDaysofYore 2011). The onslaught continued. Rod Booker singled and swiped second. Carmelo's double brought him home, and Don Carman shut the door for his first save of the year. (Sil made the final out in the top half).

Wowsers. The Dodgers ended up finishing one game behind the Reds in the NL West standings. Ok, it was five games, but that would've been a pretty neat footnote.

Mathematically, this was the second-most stunning comeback in MLB history, according to Baseball-Reference.com, surpassed only by a 1952 game in which the Reds had an 8-2 lead with two out and the bases empty in the ninth. But we're splitting graying Tommy Lasorda hairs here. (Weisman 2020).

A week plus later, Martinez was traded. I don't remember the Dodgers game. Those west coast contests aren't conducive to a 6-year-old's sleep schedule. If you watched live, you're excused for calling it a night at 11-1. No judgment here. If you stayed up, I'm so proud of you. A week prior, Terry Mulholland tossed a no-hitter against the Giants. For just a 77-win team, a lot of crazy and incredible things happened that season. Maybe it's the years that have passed or the time zone difference, but you don't hear about this one anymore. Certainly not to the extent of The Steve Jeltz Game anyway. But in a lost season, on a seemingly lost night, the Phils did something extraordinary. They snatched victory from the jaws of defeat. So thanks, Carmelo. And Rod Booker. And the other six guys who reached base that inning.

You'll have your moment in a later chapter, Sil.

The In Play, Run(s)

Name: Chad Ogea

Position: Pitcher

Career Record: 37-35; 4.88 ERA (5.00 FIP)

Phillies Tenure: 1999

"Ogea's leaving a lot of pitches up, Pat."

"Ya think?"

Chad Ogea gave up 36 home runs in his one season in Philadelphia. That's not a misprint. Don't go putting my editor on blast (if I had an editor). I considered listing every player who hit a bomb off Ogea in 1999 just to fluff up the word count – like when you increased the margin size of your Word Doc for a high school paper.

Ryan Klesko ...

Orlando Merced ...

Mike Mordecai ...

Pokey Reese ...

The only Phillie who gave up more long balls was bullpen coach Ramon Henderson, who pitched to Bobby Abreu at the '05 Home Run Contest. (The actual single-season Phillies record belongs to Robin Roberts, who gave up 46 bombs in 1956. In Robin's defense, though, he pitched 297 innings and won 19 games). It was an uphill battle for Chad. Unless you're David Blaine and a master of deception, it was tough to sneak an 87-mph fastball past a major league hitter.

If you're too young to remember the righty, just imagine the 2020 Phillies bullpen morphing into Megazord. Home runs didn't *just* clear the wall. There isn't footage of balls sailing just beyond the outstretched arms of Doug Glanville. Maybe if Ron Gant could've been positioned in Section 575, we could've kept the home run tally below 30, but who's to say for certain. Ogea was a prototypical "pitch to contact" guy, which is a generous euphemism for 'lacking an out pitch.'

"If Chad keeps the ball down ..."

Sure, and if Sharone Wright can stay out of foul trouble. We could do this all day. When pitchers can't avoid contact, they have to embrace it. Ogea struck out just 4.1 batters per 9 innings in '99. Now, strikeouts aren't the only indicator of success. Christy Mathewson had the same strikeout numbers in 1911 and won 26 games. He gave up like two earned runs a month. Sure, he pitched in the Dead Ball Era and every hitter was 5'3" and 117 pounds, but still. Christy did it. There was a precedent. Pitchers who rely on guile and placement and sure-handed fielders can have their moments – think the Brian Bannister types – but they need some luck. It's possible, just not necessarily sustainable. Ogea had success at certain points. Just not in Philadelphia.

He came up with Cleveland in 1994 and is part of this incredible Manny Ramirez story that left me speechless.

"When O.J. Simpson had his infamous car chase in June of 1994 and it was being played in the Indians clubhouse that day, Manny wanted to know what was happening. When one of his teammates told him that O.J. was accused of killing his wife, Manny memorably said, "Oh no, not Ogea! I know his wife." Ramirez didn't read newspapers and somehow thought the player meant their Indians teammate Chad Ogea, a pitcher who was not quite as well-known as O.J. Simpson." (Calcaterra 2011).

How can I possibly top that?

From '95 through '97, Ogea won 26 games as a starter. The numbers were ok. He had a lofty 4.99 ERA in 1997, but Playoff Chad was a different animal. He only went 2-3 that postseason, but never conceded more than three earned runs. He beat the Marlins twice in the World Series, even retiring enemy of the state, Jeff

Conine. He also chipped in two hits in Game 6, collecting two RBIs and scoring a run. As crazy as it sounds, he may have been named World Series MVP if Cleveland held on to win the series. (Liván Hernández captured those honors).

A knee injury limited his '98 season, and after Cleveland was eliminated by the Yankees in the ALCS, trade rumors involving the righty swirled. In November, the Phils swooped in and acquired Ogea for reliever Jerry Spradlin, who the *Philadelphia Inquirer* described as, "owner of a blazing, but straight fastball, he often had trouble pitching in tight games." (Salisbury 1998). (Two days later, Ray Rhodes and the punchless Eagles offense lost to Washington, 28-3. Bobby Hoying went 15-31 for 110 yards and 2 INTs. Boniol chipped in a 19-yard field goal).

I loved the trade. It was a great buy-low move! We can rag on all the gopher balls twenty years later, but that's just revisionist history. People weren't second-guessing the move, saying, "Shit, we lost Spradlin? Who's gonna handle the 7th inning now?" I even remember calling my buddy after the fact and saying, "Ogea can even hit a bit!" It was dumb, yes, but I was drunk on October baseball. He hit .091 for the Phillies, but back in November of '98, I was toying with Chad in the eight hole.

Ogea was a postseason hero a year prior, and those late 90s Phillies teams never got *anyone* who made noise in October. Ron Gant? Are we gonna count Norm Charlton's cameo in '95? Is that the list? Am I missing someone? Did Terry Steinbach have a cup of coffee with us? Did Calvin Maduro and Jack Morris anchor the Twins rotation in '91 and it just slipped my mind? Chad Ogea was a name, and hell, all we wanted was a name. Spradlin had a career year in '98, but there were a hundred Jerry Spradlins running around. It was a no-brainer for the Phils. Even Cleveland GM John Hart expressed a bit of uncertainty.

"We may regret trading Chad Ogea to the Phillies when he wins 20." (Skelton 2021).

Looking back, that line was a bit used car salesman-ish – "I can't believe I'm giving you this '94 Ford Escort for only $6,500" – but Phillies fans couldn't be bothered to check under the hood. We got a steal. This guy excelled on the biggest stage. Besides, we'll just give Yorkis Perez the ball in the 7th.

"This guy knows how to pitch," Wade said. "Is he a Curt Schilling? No. But we're trying to build behind Curt Schilling." (Salisbury 1998).

To steal a line from *Swingers*, Chad was the guy, behind the guy, behind the guy. Ogea squared off against Greg Maddux in his first game as a Fightin and got walloped. He was chased after just 3 ⅓ innings, giving up 7 ER and three long balls. One of those bombs came off the bat of Maddux, which really put a dent in my, "Ogea may be the best hitting pitcher in the NL East" narrative. Then he settled down. The Marlin Killer shut down Florida in two consecutive starts and escaped April with a 3.64 ERA.

The weather eventually warms up, though. So do the bats. The ball started jumping. He gave up nine more home runs in May, seven in June, and fast-forward to August, and his ERA was well over 5. On the 18th, the Phils beat the Cardinals despite Ogea surrendering hits to the first five St. Louis batters. He lasted just 1 ⅓ innings.

"I didn't have anything, basically," Ogea said (Salisbury 1999).

After a disastrous start against the Rockies before Labor Day, he was out of the rotation permanently. *The Courier-Post* offered a damning scouting report the next morning.

Ogea doesn't have a single pitch he can rely on for a strikeout. His fastball isn't fast enough to throw by anyone. His changeup isn't different enough from his fastball to fool anyone. And his curveball isn't sharp enough to get a swing and miss (Roberts 1999).

But other than that, though?

He was relegated to mop-up duty for the remainder of the season. On September 4th, the Phils got hammered by the Reds, 22-3. The Phils took a 2-0 lead before Cincinnati countered with 15 unanswered. They bashed NINE homers. Starter Paul Byrd said, "It felt like they were swinging aluminum bats." One fan in the 8th shouted to the broadcast booth, "Hey, Harry, go get loose." (Salisbury 1999).

After Politte left, it was Chad Ogea's turn to join the long-ball lunacy. And no one does it better. Banished to the bullpen less than a week ago, the right-hander was sacked for three homers in 2 ⅔ innings, giving him the major league lead in homers allowed with 35.

"I felt like I had some of my best stuff all year," Ogea said. "It just wasn't a good night to pitch." (Salisbury 1999).

There weren't many good nights to pitch that season. The writing was on the wall. Or over the wall anyway. He finished the year with a 5.63 ERA. It was his last season in the bigs.

The OPS

Name: Michael Martinez

Position: 2B/SS/OF

Career Slash Line: .194/.243/.261

Phillies Tenure: 2011-2013

Of the 428 hitters in team history who accumulated at least 300 career plate appearances, Martinez ranks 425th in OPS (.495). The only players worse than him were Tony Cusik, Frank Ringo and John Vukovich (Stolnis 2013).

Oh, Mini Mart. He had a slash line only a mother could love. A favorite scapegoat of the Twitter bygone era, Martinez somehow got over 200 at-bats for a 102-win Phillies team. It was like the 2011 Fightins were on the penalty kill. Zac Rinaldo just got hit with a 5-minute major so now Martinez has to play second and hit 8th. I don't make the rules. Whenever my dad watches a Phils pitcher struggle, he wonders aloud, "Isn't there anyone else?" In Martinez' case, I guess there wasn't. I guess there literally wasn't anyone else. Mini Mart's shortcomings were amplified by the fact that the rest of the team was so good. It's like leading off every conversation about Hakeem Olajuwon by saying, "Man, he really struggled with the Raptors." Fans were spoiled with Roy Halladay, Cliff Lee, Cole Hamels, and Roy Oswalt, but I swear to god if Manuel makes us watch one more Mini Mart at-bat, I'm buying an Orioles hat.

He was a Rule 5 draft pick acquired from the Nationals in 2010. He wasn't this fast riser through the minor leagues – his numbers down on the farm were pedestrian – but as Nikola Jokic will tell you, the best ability is availability. Mini Mart was standing right there, and that's half the battle. With future hall of famer

Chase Utley beginning the year on the disabled list, the rookie infielder broke Clearwater with the big club. It was easy to harp on the obvious downgrade, until you discovered that Martinez was actually One Of Us™.

Martinez, meanwhile, is a 28-year-old rookie who once idolized Allen Iverson and had hoop dreams, blasphemy for a kid from the Dominican Republic (Brookover 2011).

We're all Michael Martinez. Every kid from the tri-state area who wrapped electrical tape around a corked wiffleball bat and laced up their Reebok Questions was Michael Martinez (jorts optional). Objectively, it was a low risk move. The hit rate on Rule-5 guys is a long shot, but the Phils had caught lightning in a bottle with Shane Victorino a few years prior.

"I like to see who is going to get a chance," Victorino said. "I think it's very interesting. I don't know why all 30 teams don't take a chance on a Rule 5 guy. It's a $50,000 risk. If I was an organization, I would take a guy every year."

Only Washington, with 10 Rule 5 selections, has made more than the Phillies' 9 since 2004 (Brookover 2011).

Martinez was both a victim and beneficiary of circumstance. The Phils loved these Rule 5 dart throws and with some starters banged up, Mini Mart was pressed into action. His versatility was appealing; he could play a lot of positions. He made his major league debut on April 3rd, playing centerfield and BATTING LEAD-OFF. Wilson Valdez hit 8th that day. (I'm assuming that was gonna be your next question). He hung around. The 2011 Phils had an aging lineup. Guys missed time. Utley, Victorino, Polanco, they were all on the wrong side of 30. I used to live across the street from this pizza place that sold $1 slices. They didn't even throw 'em back in the oven for you. Just dumped the slice on a paper plate and sent you on your way. After every cold slice, I vowed never again. They'll never get another cent from me. Until the next time it was 11:00 and I had only $3 on me. That was Mini Mart. He wasn't a great option, but he was an option. The organization had so much money tied into their core. Management had to plug holes with some guys who could handle multiple positions. Ben Zobrists don't exactly grow on trees.

On July 17th, he hit his first career home run off the Mets' Mike Pelfrey. It was like one of the miracles the Catholic Church points to when canonizing a saint. I guess, in this case, it's St. Mike Pelfrey, the Patron Saint of Long Balls. The Phils hit 16 dingers off Big Pelf in his career, easily the most of any team. But outside of that, Martinez really struggled. He hit .196 in '11. Then he *really* struggled in 2012, batting .174 with a .208 OB%. Yama hama. The Mendoza Line may as well have been Stan Musial's 1948 numbers. If only online sports betting was around during the Michael Martinez Era. I'd be anchoring every 6-leg parlay with a "Michael Martinez to record 1+ Hits (+1200)" wager.

"Honey, come in here. Quick! If Mini Mart can leg out a grounder to short, we can pay off our car loan."

He registered just 40 plate appearances in 2013, hitting .175/.175/.175, and, no, I didn't suddenly blackout and hit CTRL-V over and over. He had 7 singles in 40 at-bats. Not a walk or a bloop double in sight.

Perhaps the only player on the roster who has infuriated fans more than Mayberry is Michael Martinez.

The former Rule 5 pick has managed to keep a job because he can play a variety of positions. But Martinez is simply not a major league player: Martinez' .495 career OPS is the 29th lowest OPS since 1900 out of 4,549 non-pitchers with 350 or more plate appearances in that time.

Martinez was outrighted off the 40-man roster shortly after the season, but he's not gone for good until he's released, or another team claims him (Lawrence 2013).

Then a funny thing happened. Just when Martinez was out of sight and out of mind, right when we thought we had seen the last of him, he popped back into our lives like a Zendon Hamilton 10-day contract. Mini Mart was playing in the World Series. He got three at-bats for Cleveland in their match-up with the Cubs and I have to plead ignorance here. I hadn't done my homework on the Cleveland bench. When I heard Joe Buck say, "Michael Martinez now coming to the plate," I just assumed a slip of the tongue. Maybe he meant that former Phillie legend Manny Martínez had made a comeback? Nope. There was Mini Mart, live and in color. It was like watching the Super Bowl and asking yourself, "What the hell is Mike McMahon doing under center? Is he lost?"

He went 0-3 in the World Series, and 0-4 overall that postseason. But good for Martinez. He got there. He stuck in the bigs for seven years, despite what any of us thought, despite any of our objections or angry tweets.

He ended his career with a .504 OPS.

The Prankster

Name: Roger McDowell

Position: Pitcher

Career Record: 70-70; 3.30 ERA (3.73 FIP)

Phillies Tenure: 1989-1991

Let's just clear something up right now. Despite what 9-year-old me may tell you, Roger McDowell is NOT "Black Jack" McDowell, the 1993 AL Cy Young Award winner. How did a former Phillies reliever go on to win 22 games for the White Sox? I don't know. Maybe a more dedicated off-season regimen? I was in 3rd grade. What do you want from me?

(26 years later, I did Google, "Did Roger McDowell go by 'Black Jack' McDowell?" You can never be too sure).

Now that we got that out of the way. If it ever rained during a baseball camp in the 1990s, that camp was contractually obligated to show kids only one of two videos:

1) The 1980 Phillies Video Yearbook

2) Any *Baseball Bloopers* VHS

That's it. That's the entire list.

"But, Dave, I swore I watched *The Sandlot* during some rainy days at baseball camp."

No, you didn't. That wasn't baseball camp. That was "rec" camp run by your township. You didn't play baseball. You played stickball, and the camp had a pool, and a counselor would rub baby oil over a watermelon and chuck it in the deep end. Big difference.

Baseball camps had a video library of two. The rainy day alternatives were working on your bunting stance in the cafeteria or discussing game strategy with a camp counselor, so door #1 wasn't too bad of an option. Every Baseball Bloopers video had three staples. If they didn't have the clip of Paul O'Neill kicking the ball from right field at the Vet, Terry Mulholland throwing his glove to first base, or some Roger McDowell hot foot action, you were watching a cheap bootleg. Return that VHS to the West Coast Video you acquired it from and demand a refund. McDowell was the star of these films. He was the preeminent prankster of the late 80s.

Before a game in Los Angeles in 1987, McDowell appeared on the field wearing his uniform upside-down, pants stretched over his head and shoes on his hand.

Also in 1987, he made light of an administrative crackdown on ball doctoring by conspicuously wearing a carpenter's belt in the bullpen, complete with lubricant, sandpaper, a file, and a chisel.

If there was a slumping hitter in the lineup, McDowell could be counted on to toss a lit pack of firecrackers into that player's slot in the bat rack.

He once got the attention of fans seated around the visiting bullpen at Dodgers Stadium, then threw open a door to reveal teammate Jesse Orosco seated on the toilet (Springer 2021).

Roger was perhaps best known for the hot foot. Hot foot is when you light someone's shoes on fire, which I consider more arson than a prank. Hasn't McDowell seen *Backdraft*? One of his more notorious jokes involved Phils pitcher Tommy Greene after the righty tossed a no hitter in Montreal on May 23rd, 1991.

A brief aside from that game: opposing Expos starter, Dennis "Oil Can" Boyd, told reporters that he didn't see one of Greene's 130 pitches that day. He spent each bottom half inning in the clubhouse smoking cigarettes (Fredericks 1991).

After the game, Greene's wife, Lori, called up to offer him congratulations. This gave McDowell an idea.

A few minutes later, Greene was notified that there was another caller who wanted to speak to him.

"Hello," said the French-sounding voice on the other end. "This is the prime minister of Canada and I just wanted to congratulate you. And I'd like to meet you."

"Yes, sir," said Greene. "I have to check our schedule first."

Green was serious; the caller wasn't. (Carchidi 1991).

Roger had recruited a clubhouse worker to make the call.

McDowell won 14 (!) games out of the bullpen for the Mets '86 championship team, relying on a heavy sinker that opposing hitters pounded into the ground. He followed that up with a stellar 2.63 ERA in '88. Most assumed the popular jokester would be a lynchpin of the Mets bullpen for years to come, but by mid-June of '89 he was gone. In a colossal win for the Fightins, the Phils acquired McDowell and Lenny Dykstra for Juan Samuel and Tom Edens. Roger scuffled in '89 with New York, taking a backseat in the bullpen pecking order behind fellow righty, Rick Aguilera. GM Lee Thomas saw an opportunity.

"We wouldn't be able to get a guy like McDowell if he hadn't been struggling." (Pascarelli 1989).

The Mets were also linked to outfielders Ellis Burks and Joe Carter (never heard of 'em) but had always been enamored by the speedy Samuel (Klapisch 1989). The trade triggered a mixed reaction from New York fans. Some thought Dykstra's attitude had become a problem and liked what Juan brought to the table. Others, like Yolanda S. in a letter to the editor in *The Journal News* argued that, "The Mets ought to be shot for trading Dykstra and McDowell." (*The Journal News* 1989). Juan stole 31 bases in his lone half season with New York but registered a brutal .599 OPS. He would move on to Los Angeles following the '89 campaign. On the same day, Philly also traded closer Steve Bedrosian to San Francisco for Terry Mulholland, Charlie Hayes, and Dennis Cook. Along with Thomas acquiring another integral piece of the '93 team, Bedrock's departure left an opening in the closer role. McDowell delivered. He had a microscopic 1.11 ERA with the Fightins along with 19 saves. He was named the Rolaids Relief Man of the Month for July 1989, and let's be honest, none of you remember any other Rolaids Relief Man of the Month award winners from 1989 because Rog rendered them all obsolete. Looking back, Dykstra and the second coming of Bob Gibson were a pretty nice haul for Samuel and Tom Edens.

In a late September game against McDowell's ex-mates, Roger relieved Jeff Parrett with two outs in the 9th and the Phils holding a 5-3 advantage – trying to preserve the win for starter Ken Howell. Future Phillie Gregg Jefferies was at the plate. Jefferies may be one of the biggest spazzes to ever play in the major leagues. You probably best remember Gregg from slamming his helmet against the Vet turf after every routine groundout. My mom was horrified.

"Oh, that's terrible. Why would he do that?"

"He's a gamer, mom."

There's a thin line between being competitive and being batshit crazy. I loved that Jefferies cared, but I also think that he'd chase you with a 5-iron if your dog ever peed on his front lawn. McDowell induced a Jefferies grounder to second. After the ball hit first baseman Ricky Jordan's mitt for the final out, Gregg half-heartedly touched first then made a beeline towards the closer. Jefferies, who I'm guessing had a strong amateur wrestling background like Bayside's A.C. Slater, got low on McDowell and lifted the hurler in the air. Roger connected with a few right hands on the way to the ground, but the ref awarded Gregg with the two-point takedown.

A nice bonus of bench clearing skirmishes from 1989 is that every player had their name on the back of their warm-up jacket. Made it very easy to identify their role in the melee (MLB 2013).

Jason Grimsley: Peacekeeper.

David Cone: Innocent bystander.

Tom Barrett: Not sure what to do with his hands.

Randy Myers: Deceptively fast.

Bob Ojeda: Seems like a good dude.

Jefferies had his detractors. Despite looking like the congenial Steve Guttenberg, Gregg rubbed coaches and teammates the wrong way.

"[The ending] was all right," Phils manager Nick Leyva said. "[It will] give ESPN something to talk about. I imagine there is some bad blood or something between them from [Roger] being over here. I think the situation was, there were 30 guys on our side rooting for Roger and 20 guys on their side rooting for him." (Jerardi 1989).

McDowell offered a bit of trolling in his postgame comments.

"Gregg's been through some tough times this season. There's been a lot of pressure on him and maybe it all got to him." (Springer 2021).

Roger saved 22 games in 1990, but by '91, the bullpen was now anchored by Mitch Williams. The Phils acquired the Wild Thing from the Cubs right before the start of the regular season and anointed him the 9th inning guy soon after. There were a few reasons suggested about why the Cubs traded Williams. One was that skipper Don Zimmer supposedly told GM Steve Frey that he 'preferred Williams pitch elsewhere this year' (Hagen 1991). I can't believe that worked, because I said the same thing about Willie Green for an entire decade. In July, the Phils traded McDowell to the Dodgers for the light-hitting Braulio Castillo and Mike Hartley. Roger would bounce around a bit before retiring in 1996.

McDowell was the rare bullpen pitcher who gained pop culture fame. Like I don't remember Rod Beck having a recurring role on *Walker, Texas Ranger* or anything. He appeared in an episode of *Seinfeld*, playing the role as "the second spitter." Kramer and Newman accused Keith Hernandez of spitting on them at a June 14, 1987 Phillies/Mets game. (In actuality, the Phils played the Expos that day. Mike Schmidt blasted 3 home runs in a 11-6 win). He also was a star of MTV's *Rock n' Jock Softball*. To give you an idea of what we were working with, MC Hammer led off the 1992 game with a ground ball to the left side, but *Point Break's* Lori Petty's throw was offline. Now MTV just airs *Ridiculousness* for weeks at a time, so I have no idea if Margot Robbie can hit behind the runner, or if Jonah Hill can make the throw from third.

Thanks for nothing, Rob Dyrdek.

The Drive Home

Name: Kevin Jordan

Position: 1B/2B/3B

Career Slash Line: .258/.297/.363

Phillies Tenure: 1995-2001

Jordan heard the crowd of 16,245 at Veterans Stadium call him out for a curtain call, but he wasn't about to respond.

"I wouldn't know what to do," said Jordan, who doesn't even remember hitting a grand slam in Little League. "I've never gone out there before. I didn't want to embarrass myself." (Associated Press 2001).

I didn't have my license for very long. This girl asked me to drive her to prom. To be clear, as her date, not like her Lyft driver. Of course, I told her. Not a problem at all. I didn't actually *have* my license at the time, but that was just semantics. After some parallel parking issues during the first test and a failing grade in physics that required some navigation with my angry parents, I got my license in the nick of time, one day before the big night. Then I got lost on the way home from the dance. Like really fucking lost. It has been twenty years, but I think I started in Doylestown and took Route-611 to like Binghamton? I don't know. It was far. There was no GPS back then. Back then, you had to either dabble in cartography or print out directions from Mapquest. I just kept driving and driving, waiting for the Neshaminy Mall to magically appear.

Spoiler Alert: It never did.

The next time behind the wheel was a week later: April 20th, 2001. My buddies and I were going to the Phillies game, and my dad explicitly told me that I was not allowed to drive. He probably figured I'd end up in Chattanooga or something. I told him I was driving to my friend's and *his* dad was taking us which was a lie. I already had Linkin Park's *Hybrid Theory* queued up in the car. My boys and I were throwing down with the Atlanta Braves, and we were getting to the battlefield via my mom's Nissan.

Omar Daal gave us six strong. His stuff was moving. By the 7th inning, however, I got antsy. I was already one lie into my folks, and my only experience commuting home involved a four-hour ride from New York's Southern Tier. So I made my friends leave in the 7th inning of a 2-2 game. I'm not gonna sit here and defend my actions. It was a mistake. I pulled the same stunt that Alex's mom did. That's not lost on me. While we pulled out of the parking lot, Kevin Jordan ripped a grand slam over the leftfield wall. The Fightins put up 6 runs in the 7th and defeated Atlanta, 8-3. Wayne Gomes, *our* Wayne Gomes, got the win.

There was construction on 95 that night. Like I think PennDOT was building a road from scratch. Only one lane was getting by. It took *three hours* to get home, which was especially frustrating since I lived in lower Bucks County, not Poughkeepsie. A buddy climbed into the trunk of mom's Pathfinder to pee in an empty Snapple bottle, but was overwhelmed by crippling stage fright. He couldn't perform under the bright lights of I-95 traffic. He spent the last two hours in a cold sweat, praying for death. Any track from *Hybrid Theory* still triggers his PTSD to this day. My parents weren't stupid. They called around, discovered I was driving, and waited in Gorilla Position when I walked through the front door at 2:30 A.M. They grounded me for the foreseeable future. The next day, Reggie Miller hit some bullshit three to defeat the Sixers, 79-78, in the opening game of the NBA Playoffs. The Sixers scored 26 points in the second half. It was a rough weekend.

All seven of Kevin Jordan's major league seasons were spent in Philly. It was an unassuming seven years. There was no outrage or KJ fatigue. Nobody came up to my locker in 9th grade saying, "Jordan made the opening day roster again, Dave? Seriously? Can you believe this?" KJ was that jar of whey protein on your kitchen counter. You hadn't been to the gym in years, but you keep lugging it around from apartment to apartment. It didn't bother you. It wasn't a nuisance. Hell, it was part of the kitchen decor at this point. When there was a lefty on the mound in an AL park, you'd dust off Jordan. When there wasn't? Here's Rob Ducey. Jordan was one of those late 90s Phils – Kevin Sefcik, David Doster, etc – that just blended into the background.

"Dude, you know there's someone sleeping on your couch?"

"The couch? Wait, this couch? Oh, right. That's just Alex Arias. Don't mind him."

Kevin has Australian citizenship, making him my favorite Aussie to ever play in Philly behind Jordan Mailata and Mark Bradtke. (I'm writing this after Game 7 of the 2021 NBA Eastern Conference Semifinals). There is a bit of controversy surrounding his citizenship, however. The Australian Baseball site, Flintoff & Dunn, doesn't recognize KJ in their list of Australians to play in the major leagues (Klugh 2018). It's very scandalous. Jordan gained citizenship after marrying a woman from Brisbane, but Flintoff & Dunn aren't letting KJ into the inner circle on a technicality.

To be technically precise, Kevin Jordan did play in the US major leagues as an Australian citizen towards the twilight of his ML career, but we certainly cannot claim him as an "Australian raised" player who reached the US Major League!

Firstly, let us make this crystal clear, 'Flintoff & Dunn' do not in any way decry the baseball talents of Kevin Jordan and we are proud to claim him as a new Australian citizen, especially given his long-standing contributions to big league baseball both here and in the United States of America (Flintoff & Dunn 2021).

Geez, welcome to the spin zone. Jordan may not be a founding member of Midnight Oil, but he is Australian. Do the right thing, Flintoff & Dunn, and pencil him in next to Grant Balfour. We'll be watching. The Phils acquired the Aussie and Bobby Muñoz in a 1994 trade with the Yankees for the ageless Terry Mulholland. Baseball-Reference lists him as a second and third baseman, but I always considered KJ a first baseman. It did take me twenty years to differentiate Brian R. and Brian L. Hunter, so, on second thought, I could just be confusing Kevin with Ricky Jordan. I also thought that KJ mashed lefties, but his .640 career OPS against southpaws suggests that I don't know a damn thing about our protagonist.

There's this nutty story involving Kevin Jordan and his major league debut. He joined the big club in August of '95 after Mariano Duncan was claimed off waivers by the Reds. Hearing stories about Philadelphia and its bad wrap, KJ, and I can't believe this is true, KEPT HIS GIRLFRIEND INSIDE HIS HONDA ACCORD at the Vet parking lot for fear of her safety.

"The only thing I heard about Philly was that it was a dangerous city. I told Nina, who's now my wife, to wait in the car. I didn't think she'd be safe if she got out. Even though it was a hot, muggy August Philly day, she stayed in the car with the windows up and the motor running." (Gordon 2008).

The fuck? Was Nina wearing a Troy Aikman jersey? She would've been fine, KJ. Let the poor girl out of the Honda. Jordan just slid down my Favorite Philly Aussie Rankings. Back into the top-3 you go, Matisse. Six seasons later, on September 26, 2000, Jordan hit an inside the park home run off Jerry Spradlin. Daal got the win in Chicago that day to improve his record to 4-19. (More on Daaly later).

The Phillies broke last night's game open with six runs in the top of the ninth against Jerry Spradlin. Three of the runs came off an inside-the-park home run by Kevin Jordan who circled the bases as left fielder Julio Zuleta frantically searched for the ball in the ivy (Hagen 2000).

I imagine Zuleta searching for the ball like it was a flag covered in orange slime on *Double Dare*. Jordan would hit two more home runs in the big leagues. His 23rd and final career dinger came on that April 20th night.

So I've heard.

The Double Play

Name: Tyler Goeddel

Position: Left Field

Career Slash Line: .192/.258/.291

Phillies Tenure: 2016

"36 games into the season, and they are 13-3 in one run games." (Riccaboni and Corino 2016).

I was dressed to the nines on Saturday, May 14th, 2016. I just can't remember why. I was either at a wedding or a gala (it wasn't a gala), but I was in a suit and tie. You don't forget that. When you wear a suit twice a year, it's easy to pinpoint the exact date and time you dusted off that navy blue ensemble you purchased off the rack at Men's Wearhouse.

The 2016 Phils were an interesting bunch. On paper, they were lousy. On the field, they were also lousy (71-91). But not in May. In May, they were frisky. In May, they were a Pythagorean's worst nightmare. When they lost, they lost badly, and when they won, they squeaked by. The Pythagorean Theorem is a formula that "correlates the number of runs a team has scored and surrendered to its actual winning percentage" (Baseball-Reference 2021). While Bill James was waiting for the other shoe to inevitably drop, I was counting Jeanmar Gómez saves like they were jellybeans in a jar.

"Just gotta get to Jeanmar, Doug."

"Yep, shorten the game ... Lights Out Gómez will take us home."

From May 7th to May 13th, Jeanmar racked up five saves. His only day off was the 11th, when Jerad Eickhoff labored through 4 1/3 innings against Atlanta in a 5-

1 defeat. I caught myself saying old-timey things like, "Mackanin has the guys playing hard," and "Small ball is making a comeback," and "You see that safety squeeze by Cesar last night!" I was a Greg Buckner pass deflection away from turning into Larry Brown. Every fiber in my being knew this team was going nowhere, but 21-15 is 6 games over .500, and not even Bill James could dispute that math.

Tyler Goeddel was another Rule 5 Draft pick that landed in the Phillies outfield. The Goeddels have some strong family genes. Tyler's brother, Erik, also played in the majors, and their father, David, is a renowned molecular biologist who is lauded for his efforts in genetic engineering and the creation of synthetic human insulin, growth hormone, and tissue (Pfeiffer 1999). Much of his breakthrough work was done at the biotechnology firm, Genetech Inc, and before that, he worked at the pharmaceutical company, Devlin-MacGregor, where he helped with the development of the drug, Provasic. He had zero involvement, however, in the switching of any tissue samples or the killing of Lentz.

(I understand that only 5% of you will get that reference, but my backspace button is broken, so in it stays).

People liked the Goeddel selection. Phillies Nation ranked him as the #12 Fightins prospect entering the 2016 season (Floyd 2016). Dan Farnsworth of Fangraphs penciled him at #14, just ahead of Andrew Knapp, who holds the franchise record for 9th inning pinch-hit appearances:

#1: Andrew Knapp (17,971)

#2 (tie): Jason Michaels and John Mayberry Jr. (43)

Goeddel is the perfect type of acquisition for the Phillies. In an organization without entrenched regulars in the outfield, he's the type of fringy-tool outfielder who could play his way into a bigger role if given enough of a chance, which the Phillies should be able to offer him this year. (Farnsworth 2016).

That was the consensus. "Hey, he's worth a look." A little refinement, some regular playing time, and who knows, maybe the Phils could strike Rule 5 gold once more. By May, Goeddel got his chance. On the 14th, while I was at a funeral (?) or the opera (?) – seriously, why the hell was I was wearing a suit – Aaron Nola kept the Reds at arm's length while Tyler reached base three times. Andrew Bailey, in one of his 33 appearances with the club, pitched a scoreless 8th and the Phils clung to a 4-2 lead entering the 9th. There was only one small problem. Even Ol' Rubber Arm Gómez needs a day of rest. With Jeanmar unavailable, Mackanin turned to righty David Hernández.

Things got a bit hairy. The first three Cincinnati hitters reached safely. I pulled into my driveway with the Phils lead shrunk to 4-3 and sprinted inside. With two runners in scoring position, Hernández induced a groundball from Tucker Barnhart. One down. I loosened my tie and rolled up my sleeves like I was John Chaney (R.I.P.) patrolling the sidelines at McGonigle Hall. The Reds' Jordan Pachero then hit a flyball to left, pretty deep. I expected Goeddel's throw to be cut-off. Fox Sports Ohio thought the same.

"High in the air to left. This should get one run in." (Aliaksandr A 2016).

EXCEPT NO ONE TOLD TYLER GOEDDEL. He threw an absolute seed. This wasn't some throw that two-hopped to the catcher, like Mickey Morandini using the Vet's AstroTurf to turn a double play. Goeddel fired a rocket. Cameron Rupp took a shot from runner, Eugenio Suarez, but held on for the 7-2 double play. I jumped into a Jimmy Connors fist pump and shouted the only thing I ever shout after an outfield assist.

"HOSE 'EM! HOSE 'EM!"

I thought, and still think, that Tyler Goeddel was a good player here because I *only* remember that throw. I don't think I'm alone there. Our Goeddel memories are pretty short. Along the same lines, Ronnie Brown could become a future senator, and I'd be like, "The dude who tried to throw a pass at the goal line? That Ronnie Brown?"

2016 was Goeddel's lone season in the majors. The Phils waived him the following spring. He finished the year with a .549 OPS, but I can't recall one at-bat.

Tyler had a cannon. Everything else was just background noise.

The Twin Bill

Name: Mark Parent

Position: Catcher

Career Slash Line: .214/.268/.375

Phillies Tenure: 1997-1998

There is no occupation that is more devoid of talent than the major league catcher. Out of the 7.9 billion people walking this planet, there are, what, like three good catchers? You can't find four people who can both:

A) block a breaking ball in the dirt

and

B) hit .255

Accomplished racehorses retire and live out their days as studs. Secretariat sired over 600 foals, and maybe it's time we consider drastic measures. Should we freeze Iván Rodríguez' sperm to ensure the preservation of the position? We resurrected the American Bison from near extinction in the 19th Century. I'm sure we can put our heads together. In the 1990s, there was Pudge, Mike Piazza, and everyone else.

But what about Sandy Alomar Jr., Dave?

Are you done? Did you get that out of your system?

95% of starting catchers were bleh, and every reserve backstop was 38 years old. That was a prerequisite. You can't run for president or spell Chris Hoiles unless you're north of 35. Backup catchers exit their mother's womb with a five o'clock shadow. Sal Fasano, Steve Lake, Charlie O'Brien, etc., they all got their first razor in 2nd grade, and Google won't tell you this, but Don Slaught was the actual inspiration for Jennifer Garner's *13 Going on 30.* These guys just skipped their twenties. They just woke up one day, and poof, they have creaky knees and can't catch up to a low-90s fastball.

Mark Parent joined the Phils in 1997 at the tender age of 35. Lieberthal was now the backstop, settling into the starting role after Benito Santiago moved to Toronto in the offseason. The Phillies signed three players named 'Mark' in a span of 24 hours, which I'm guessing is a major league record? (Leiter and Portugal were the others). Not sure why Mark Grudzielanek thought he was above it all.

Backup catchers fall into the same bucket of clichés as NBA reserve big men. If you replace "catchers" with "centers" here, It's Ed Stefanski describing Tony Battie.

He will be, Thomas said, "a great influence on our young catchers." (Donnellon 1996).

Parent put up good power numbers before his arrival. In fact, Topps thought his power tool was so potent that in their 1990 rendition, his card inadvertently said he slugged .800% in '87. The actual number was .080. (He went 2-25 that year). That's not quite Billy Ripken's '89 Fleer "fuck face" card but still fun. Mark's numbers eventually improved. He slugged 18 homers in '95 and posted a .500 slugging% the year after. What's the old saying? "Mark Parent didn't get cheated up there." He took his hacks, and there was something noble in that. I liked Parent, but I can't give a concrete reason why. Maybe it was because his last name was also a noun and I found that endearing. Kinda like Pat Borders. Or perhaps it was because he reminded me of my mom. You see, Parent was very proficient at crossword puzzles – maybe the best in baseball, per Ruben Amaro Jr. (Salisbury 1998). Mom has been doing crossword puzzles IN PEN since the 1970s because scared money don't make money. Or maybe my affinity for the backstop was because I recognized that Mark's .150/.198/.177 slash line in '97 allowed a lot of room for growth. I can't pinpoint it, and I know it's bizarre, but I had a soft spot for the grizzled vet. I *did* anyway, until July 24th, 1998 when Mark Parent left me holding the bag.

It was a twin bill at the Vet against the Marlins. Florida won the World Series in '97, and then sold their entire team in route to a 58-104 campaign. Their roster was such an affront to the game that Adam Silver and Jerry Colangelo sat in their cars outside Joe Robbie Stadium itching for Selig to give them the ok to intervene. I was there that day. My two buddies and I watched two consecutive Phils/Marlins games without the aid of the performance enhancement drug, beer. We were just a couple of wide-eyed 14-year-old kids who had Wild Card Fever. Both games went 12 innings. It was over 7 ½ hours of baseball. Mark Parent caught all 24 innings.

Now, I was an admitted Parent supporter, but there is such a thing as *too much* Mark Parent. You can love pasta, but also not be the gluttony guy from *Seven.* Mark struggled that day. Tired knees, tired bat, tired legs. The list goes on. No other Phils backstop would catch both games of a doubleheader until J.T. Realmuto in September 2020 (Shenk 2020). (Realmuto only caught 14 innings that night). A pain in Lieby's abdomen forced Parent to work the double shift (Silary 1998). It was a tough spot for him – who the hell wants to work a double – but the Vet faithful offered little sympathy.

Perhaps kiddingly, perhaps not, Parent said he had not caught a doubleheader "since a lot of these guys were in grade school."

When asked whether he was OK, he forced a smile and shot back: "Not if these fans could have had anything to do with it ... I was a little tired. I couldn't focus on the ball. My eyes kept blurring over." (Silary 1998).

Fans unleashed hell on Parent. My section found their target. I could've tried to quell the angry mob. I could've reminded my section that Mark mashed 16 home runs in 1994; that he just needed to get a few at-bats under his belt, find his rhythm. But those past accomplishments ring hollow when Parent was 0-8 at the time. SEPTA reminds us that if you see something, say something. I did the exact opposite. I sat on my hands and kept my mouth shut. I made a business decision. Nobody was happy with the big receiver. My buddies then started attacking *me*, because my guy was failing time and time again. I backtracked.

"Me? A big Mark Parent fan? Whoa, whoa, whoa. Hold up here. You mean Jeff Parrett. Common mistake. Parrett's my guy. Great off-speed stuff."

But history beckoned. In the nightcap, Mark stepped up in the bottom of 11th of a 5-5 game. The Phils had loaded the bases with one out. No would remember the 0-8 after Parent delivered the game-winning base knock. He was ready to exorcize the demons. Just eight empty plate appearances between friends, water under the Tacony-Palmyra. Any professional at-bat would do: a sac fly, a seeing-eye single, a Texas Leaguer, a Baltimore Chop, a swinging bunt down the 3rd baseline. I wasn't picky. He just had to avoid the double play.

I said he just had to avoid the double play.

As long as he didn't hit into a double play.

Just don't hit into a ---

God damnit, Mark.

Parent hit into a tailor-made 4-3 double play. He was out by ten feet. When you've been behind the dish for 23 innings, I can excuse a guy for running down the first baseline like he had Carlton Loewer in a fireman's carry. Not everyone was as tolerant, though. *The Philadelphia Daily News* said simply, "Parent had a brutal night." (Silary 1998). I had never seen a player, before or since, go 0-9 in one day so I guess I witnessed history? (The Phils would later win on a Brogna single).

1998 would be Parent's last season in the majors, but he did find his way back to the organization. He would manage the Lakewood BlueClaws in 2010 and later the Reading Phillies, before taking a bench coach job with the White Sox. In an August 25th, 2013 contest with the Texas Rangers, Parent was ejected BEFORE the game even started. Crew chief Jerry Layne tossed him out during the lineup card exchange. I respect it. That's the baseball equivalent of calling out of work the morning of – when your PTO request for that day was previously denied. The confrontation with Layne supposedly stemmed over an incident from the previous night's game (CBS 2013). Maybe. Or maybe Mark Parent just wanted a jumpstart on his crossword puzzles.

The Quad Injury

Name: Jeff Manship

Position: Pitcher

Career Record: 7-10; 4.82 ERA (4.45 FIP)

Phillies Tenure: 2014

Sandberg had the option of hitting John Mayberry Jr. with the winning run at third and two outs, but he did not want to tax his tired bullpen any further (Brookover 2014).

I have nothing against Chris Wheeler. Let me put this on record: I'm Pro-Wheels. I love Wheels. He was like a friend of the family who you weren't related to, but you called "Uncle Wheels" anyway.

"Timmy, make sure you write Uncle Wheels a thank you note. He sent you that signed Randy Ready ball. Dad is stopping by the post office tomorrow morning."

"Ok, mom, right after *Denver, the Last Dinosaur* is over."

Uncle Wheels is all class. But – you know there was a 'but' coming – Wheels definitely coddled the pitchers. Wheeler treated pitchers at the plate and on the base paths like they were fine china. I didn't love that. These guys are professional athletes. They were the best players in Tee-ball, Little League, Babe Ruth, high school, wherever. Like there's some guy at a bar right now talking about how Ed Vosberg batted .857 on his U-12 Genuardi's Orioles team. I'm not asking a pitcher to run the Boston Marathon. I just want him to run 90 feet without disintegrating into dust. And if they somehow reached base? Oh, the humanity. Pitchers were handed this bulky jacket, like they were Randy from *A Christmas Story*.

"Is Kent Bottenfield wearing a shawl over there on second base, Beth?"

"Yep, must be a nip in the air."

This thinking was so common. We held our collective breath when a pitcher accidentally reached first. You almost wished for a fielder's choice just so we can get the hurler off the base paths. If that failed, then you NEEDED the #2 hitter to take a few pitches so Amaury Telemaco could recoup.

"Heady move by Rollins here. Seeing a few pitches so Amaury can find his wind in the dugout. That's just smart baseball."

Like how winded was Telemaco, really? By my count, he ran about 94 feet in total. The whole thing seems like one, giant overreaction until you remember Jeff Manship's cautionary tale. Soon, you're sticking pitchers in bubble wrap and petitioning for a universal DH. You're filling a bullpen cart up with Regular Unleaded and ushering these pitchers to and fro. You can't be too careful.

Manship entered the May 31, 2014 extra inning contest against the Mets with a robust 7.53 ERA. He slid into that mop-up duty role, those late inning outings when the Phils are down 5 runs and you flip over to HGTV while the Fightins are in the field. (Oh, like I'm the only one). Does that make me a bad fan? A little fairweatherish? Maybe, but the way I see it, I have two options:

1) I can monitor Jeff's control of his secondary stuff

or

2) See if Tarek and Christina can stay under their $50,000 remodeling budget.

In his 20 career appearances with the Phillies, the Fightins were just 3-17. When Manship pitched, the Phils lost. I'm not implying anything. That's not an indictment, just facts.

The Phils had beaten the Mets the night prior, 5-4, in 14 innings. Six relievers were used to secure the win. Ryne Sandberg's hand was forced. Eventually, the Justin De Fratus well dries up, so the skip called on Manship to begin the 10th. The moment was ripe for my pops saying, "Manship? Come on Ryne! Anybody but Manship! Where's Bedrock!?" but my dad hasn't been awake for an extra innings

Phillies game since Game 5 of the 1980 NLCS.

We all expected the inevitable crooked number from the Mets, but Jeff Manship, the much-maligned Jeff Manship, dominated. He hurled four perfect innings, striking out six in the process. He shouldered the load, while Mario Hollands and co. recharged their batteries. He was terrific and now up at the plate for the second time. In the bottom of the 13th, he was up with two down and Ryan Howard on third, seeking the first hit of his big-league career. He topped a grounder over the mound – a tough play for the charging Ruben Tejeda. Manship busted out of the box. The opportunity was there for the ultra-rare Phillies walk-off infield single by a reliever, a feat not accomplished since Duke "The Dumpster" Sedgwick sank the Brooklyn Robins in 1921 (don't quote me on that).

But Jeff strained his quad (Associated Press 2014). Manship pulled up to first more tentatively than Bobby Abreu near an outfield wall (Settle down. I love Bobby). Somewhere within those 90 feet, the baseball gods intervened. They decided that this hill was too steep to climb; that asking a reliever to run a few seconds scot-free was a check Phillies fans weren't allowed to cash. Manship eventually touched the bag, but not until the ball was safely in the first baseman's mitt. Sandberg's plan was to ride Manship. This vessel had a lot of voyages left in him. Jeff was going to lead us into the wee hours of the night if need be, but plans change. Injuries happen. Ryne had to make a move. Antonio Bastardo took the loss in the 14th and Jeff landed on the IL. He would make just four more appearances with the Phillies.

The Clerical Error

Name: Tony Longmire

Position: Outfield

Career Slash Line: .285/.340/.391

Phillies Tenure: 1993-1995

Anthony Eugene Longmire had a .928 OPS in 1995. That .356/.419/.510 line isn't surprising to anyone, though, because no one, and I mean *no one*, had a nicer swing than Tony Longmire. I'll concede that Ken Griffey Jr. had a prettier swing, sure, but Tony? He swung violently. He swung like you handed him a stickball bat and the only automatic homer was over the telephone wires. He wielded his club like *Golden Axe's* Gilius Thunderhead. Trust the Process? No, Trust the Results. He shifted his weight back in his left-handed stance and let it rip. Years ago, Netflix promoted a show called *Longmire*, and I remember thinking to myself, "It's about damn time Tony got his due," but turns out, the series focused on a Wyoming sheriff. That was deflating.

The '95 Phils outfield had some mileage on them: Dykstra was 32, Eisenreich (36), Van Slyke, Dave Gallagher, and Gary Varsho were all 34. Outside of Gregg Jefferies, and I suppose Kevin Stocker (he had a .578 OPS that year), there weren't any young position players infused into the roster. It was an old team still *technically* defending their NL East crown due to the strike-shortened '94 campaign. There was nostalgia with Dykstra and Eisey, and maybe people had an attachment to Van Slyke because they scooped up his '87 Topps card (the most beautiful Topps set of all time) in a pack purchased over at their local Clover, but no fan was content with the team's future. No one thought the foundation was in place for years to come.

"Heard Gary Varsho's been working with a nutritionist in the off-season, Will."

"Heard that, too. Should do wonders for his knees."

Any 90s kid gravitation to Tony Longmire shouldn't be a surprise. More recently, it happened with Dom Brown, and to a lesser extent, Freddy Galvis. We had no idea if these prospects were any good, but they were young and new, and the shiny object always catches people's eyes. Hell, Gabe Kapler called outfielder Nick Williams "the Phillies closer" and only like 82% of the tri-state area thought that was strange. Fans just want something to cling to – any success by a young player will suffice. I'm writing this chapter in nothing but a Bobby Hoying jersey. I'm just as guilty. Tony Longmire wasn't my favorite random Phillie, but no judgment if he was yours. I get the appeal.

The Phils acquired Longmire via clerical error in 1990. As legend has it, Pittsburgh Pirates GM Larry Doughty accidentally placed Julio Peguero and Wes Chamberlain, the organization's #1 prospect going into the season, on the waiver wire, which is a pretty big accident. (Not quite the same, but I do know of someone that moved Bears RB Adrian Peterson to the top of their queue before they auto drafted, instead of Vikings standout, Adrian "AP" Peterson). Eight teams, including the Fightins, quickly jumped on the oversight and claimed both prospects.

Once he realized his error, Doughty scrambled to put together a deal that brought the Pirates Carmelo Martinez from the Phillies in exchange for the two prospects.

"My wish came true," Chamberlain said. "Even if [Doughty] made a mistake, as all the hearsay says, it was a wish come true."

If Chamberlain harbors any bitterness, it is that the Pirates never explained to him whether the waiver incident was a snafu or deliberate. Chamberlain said he was "shocked" when he learned he was placed on waivers (Halovnik 1990).

How does that happen? Isn't someone in the Pirates organization giving this waiver wire list a once over? Who's in charge of quality control?

"Hey, Sid Bream, you got a quick second? I have these players written down on a sheet of paper. Anything jump out at you?"

"Yeah, looks like you have the organization's #1 prospect on here. Did you mean to do that?"

See? Was that so hard? Along with the 2 for 1 swap, the Pirates threw in a player to be named later. That mystery man was Tony Longmire. He arrived in the bigs in '93 and made the postseason roster (striking out in his only plate appearance in the NLCS). 1994 was a struggle for Tony as he was mired in a long slump, but that .606 OPS was just an aberration. The lefty blew up in '95. Well, when he finally reported to camp anyway.

Outfielder Tony Longmire's days with the Phillies appear to be numbered.

He told the Phillies he wasn't in Clearwater as of Friday's reporting deadline because of a mix-up with his airline ticket and because of an ear infection. Neither excuse was well received.

When asked about Longmire Sunday, Fregosi said, "Who? Is he on this team anymore?" (Holeva 1995).

But when he did show, all he did was hit. Or walk. He mashed the only three home runs of his career that year – all pinch-hit bombs – including an upper deck shot at the Vet that reportedly landed on a snowball previously set aside for Jay Novacek's stupid face. Another came on June 15th when Longmire faced Astros closer, John Hudek, with two on and two outs in the 9th. The Phils trailed 2-1 and needed some late-inning heroics.

"He got behind in the count, so he had to come across the plate with one," Longmire said. (Associated Press 1995).

Yeah, he did. Longmire lined an absolute rocket into the right field bullpen. The time between departure and landing was only a split second. Both home runs were off shoulder-high fastballs that Tony clubbed like a lumberjack chopping down a redwood.

"Swing and a long drive ... deep right ... outta here! Home run, Tony Longmire!

Phils win 4-2 with two outs in the ninth. Man, oh man!" – Harry Kalas (JDP2 2021).

It was Longmire's last year in the majors. His final taste of the big leagues ended with a .356 average. It's rare. No one retires on a high note. You plod your way into your mid-30s until you eventually backup Joel Embiid. Hulk Hogan didn't body slam Andre the Giant in '87 and say, "Yeah, that's enough. I'm going back to Clearwater and getting a desk job." But Longmire's '95 campaign was cut short due to an August wrist injury, and that was it. He couldn't get healthy. That same ailment also cost him the '96 season and a heart condition in spring training of '97 ended his big league career (Holeva 1997).

"If I was the general manager, I'm not sure I would have been as patient with Tony Longmire as they've been," Longmire said. "They were a class act." (Holeva 1997).

He then faded into the background. Outside of the occasional, "Hey, remember Tony Longmire?" water cooler talk, he was out of sight, out of mind. No one heard from him. Life moved on. That was until August 2019. The Fightins were playing out in San Francisco and a Phils fan behind the dugout was giving it to Gabe Kapler. The razzing got so bad that, and this part can't be confirmed, that either Kapler himself, or a player (there's speculation that it was Sean Rodriguez), requested the fan be ejected. Which, ok, fine. A bit strange, but not entirely unheard of. Philadelphians can be a tough bunch. But then you read this:

This stirred Krage to yell, "Hey Kapler, way to motivate your team, you bum."

That's all he said, Krage claims.

It's when Krage noticed a guy sitting across the aisle from him with a huge ring on his hand. Krage, who was wearing his 1993 John Kruk jersey, asked who he was. The guy said he was a teammate of Kruk's on the 1993 Phillies, and identified himself as Phillie alum Tony Longmire, who pointed out Ricky Jordan, sitting two rows down.

According to Krage, Longmire said, "Kapler sucks, I can't believe that he's still part of the team." (Santoliquito 2019).

I have many questions, but I'm going to condense them down to two:

1) Ricky Jordan and Tony Longmire are friends!?

2) Why are we dragging Longmire into this squabble?

Where's the fan/random Phillie client privilege here? What about HIPAA? Ok, that was four questions. That Longmire quote didn't need to be shared. That was just Tony talking shop. You gotta keep that in-house. What if I was boys with Marlon Anderson? I wouldn't go singing like a canary every time he made a remark over coffee about Desi Relaford's double play turn. That's between Marly and me. Although, I suppose *Tuesdays with Marly* does have a nice ring to it.

In 2020, Longmire was a guest on Marcel Johnson's Podcast, *I Am Necessary*. Johnson played Little League with Tony and told this story about a 10-and-under championship game. Longmire's team lost, and when handed the 2nd place trophy, he threw it on the ground before stepping on it. Tony told the master of ceremonies, "I don't want this." (Johnson 2020).

Some people are just built different.

The Monster (Half) Season

Name: Jeremy Giambi

Position: 1B/OF/DH

Career Slash Line: .263/.377/.430

Phillies Tenure: 2002

Once you get past the Phillies-got-the-wrong-brother-again jokes, the acquisition of Jeremy Giambi raises a bunch of interesting questions. Uppermost on the minds of many people was this:

Huh?

An important lesson in life: If something seems too good to be true, it probably is. And this deal looked like a head-scratcher. (Hagen 2002).

The acquisition of Jeremy Giambi is my favorite, inconsequential Phillies trade of all time. It didn't move the needle. They never threatened the Braves, who won the NL East that season by 19 games. He didn't become a building block for the franchise. He wasn't even a Phillie in '03. To the best of my knowledge, there are no Jeremy Giambi jerseys in the wild. No jerseys *not* worn by him anyway. I did find a gorgeous powder blue game-used jersey for $299.99, and you'll find a GoFundMe link at the bottom of this chapter. Please consider donating. No amount is too small. Jeremy played 82 games in Philadelphia and was OUTSTANDING. Whether through shrewd negotiations or dumb luck, the team stumbled upon this super valuable asset. Then the organization moved him for a light return, and you're left scratching your head.

"Wait, he was awesome here, right? Did I imagine that?"

In the last thirty years, Jeremy Giambi put up the best numbers in Philly that no one talks about. Now, I acknowledge that's something someone with a Twitter blue checkmark would say.

@SomeoneWithABlueCheckmark

I feel like we don't talk enough about how good Michael Jordan was

9:03 PM · May 23, 2021

64,523 Retweets 819,378 Likes

But the point remains. Giambi had a monster half-season in Philly that was swept under the rug along with Iverson's second Sixers stint and the nine games the *other* Steve Smith played for the Birds. Giambi deserves his due, and we're gonna give it to him.

Right after we get this out of the way.

Derek Jeter did something in the '01 ALDS. It was a routine play, ok? A dime a dozen. Rich Aurilla has made that same toss a thousand times. Walt Weiss records that out in his sleep. Walt doesn't need to be idolized. Rich doesn't need this never-ending adoration. But because it was Jeter, because it was the Yankees, poor Jeremy can't go five minutes without being reminded that he should've slid into home. Whatever. Besides, we're expected to worship at the altar of Derek Jeter, Defensive Wizard? The guy had less range than Chris Boniol outside 40 yards.

Ok, back to the important stuff.

Jeremy Giambi smoked weed. He got a citation in 2001 after a small quantity was found in his luggage at Las Vegas' McCarran International Airport (Paul 2001). I'm not the pot police but Giambi developed a reputation off the field. *Moneyball* referenced his affinity for the party scene and the Vegas nightlife. (He would also later appear in the Mitchell Report and admit to using steroids). Back in '01, no other team had fully subscribed to the Sabermetrics thinking outside the A's. It was still this underground society seeking mainstream acceptance. Jeremy was a darling of the advanced stats community. Who cares if you spend your Tuesday afternoons making it rain at Spearmint Rhino, when you're reaching base at a .391 clip? Not me. I'd have battled I-95 traffic to shuttle Doug Glanville to and from

Daydreams if he posted anything higher than a .285 OB%.

Which is why the Giambi trade was so goofy. How the hell did the Phils get Jeremy Giambi from the A's of all teams, for – of all people – the light-hitting and base-never-reacher John Mabry? At least hold out for Travis Lee, Billy. If you played your cards right, I'd also have thrown in Doug Nickle. Apparently Beane was in a pissy mode one night and wanted to shake things up (Jaffe 2012). That's the story. That's the reason. And I guess Ed Wade was like, "How about John Mabry?"

Giambi had a .435 OB% with the Phils. MY GOODNESS. When did you get here, Tris Speaker? You find the place ok? Every time I watched a Giambi at-bat, he walked. I know I tend to exaggerate slightly, but I'm telling ya, he was Eddie Gaedel with a softer midsection. Jeremy never swung at anything outside the strike zone. His eye at the dish was elite. Giambi would've cleaned up at Erotic Photo Hunt at your local dive, peppering the Top-10 Leaderboard until some employee unplugged the machine and erased years of hard work (Looking at you, Irish Pol). He also ripped 12 homers in that span and slugged .538. Giambi homered twice in his Phillies debut at Montreal, proving that while you can't sneak weed past customs, you can bring over lumber. In a June 4th game against Florida, he walked four times. Unfortunately, the other Phils couldn't solve the Hansel Izquierdo puzzle in a 5-0 loss.

No one ever questioned his offense or his eye at the plate. The criticism of Giambi always centered around his lack of position.

"He can't play outfield."

"You have to hide him at first."

Who cares? Play him at short. Play him in center. Put him at short field like the one guy on your beer league softball team who wears a knee brace. Giambi had a .974 OPS with the Fightins. Put him anywhere. The 2010 Mariners constructed this roster full of defensive-minded players – guys like Franklin Gutierrez and Jack Wilson. GM Jack Zduriencik emphasized run prevention (you can't lose if you don't concede any runs), which is nice in theory. Here's the problem with starting Jack

Wilson, though. Jack Wilson also gets to bat. Seattle finished 61-101 in 2010. I never subscribed to this emphasis on defense. Giambi being a liability in the field was overblown, but it was clearly on the organization's radar.

After September, the Phillies will have a fascinating decision to make.

Lee's defense or Giambi's offense?

Lee, 27, is one of the best defensive first baseman in baseball, but has yet to live up to the offensive potential many thought he had when he signed with the Arizona Diamondbacks in 1997. He established career highs with 34 doubles and 90 RBIs last season, but is far off that pace this season.

Giambi, also 27, has proved that he has a valuable bat, but remains a man without a position. (Brookover 2002).

Who was Team Travis here? Reveal yourself. I'll wait. I'm guessing the same weirdos who thought Rachel should've ended up with Joey. The Phils eventually went with Option "C" and chose neither. They inked free agent Jim Thome in December of that year to a huge deal ($85 million guaranteed), leaving little use for either first baseman. The crime wasn't the signing, though. It was the return. Nine days after the Thome contract, Wade moved Giambi to Boston for Josh Hancock. Wade would admit after the trade that, "The reality is that he's an American League player." (Brookover and Salisbury 2002). You know, it's ok to get on base in the National League, too.

Hancock would pitch just 12 innings in Philadelphia.

The Clichés

Name: Don Carman

Position: Pitcher

Career Record: 53-54; 4.11 ERA (4.42 FIP)

Phillies Tenure: 1983-1990

1985 – games pitched – 4th (71)

1986 – winning percentage – 8th (.667)

1987 – wins – 9th (13)

1987 – games started – 4th (35)

1987 – innings pitched – 10th (211)

Other career highlights include:

A one-hit, complete game shutout vs. the New York Mets in front of 30,799 fans at Veterans Stadium (September 29, 1987).

A three-hit, complete game shutout vs. the San Diego Padres (May 16, 1987).

A four-hit, complete game shutout vs. the Pittsburgh Pirates (September 15, 1986).

Held All-Stars Craig Biggio, Ken Griffey, Jr., Jeffrey Leonard, Pete Rose, Larry Walker, and Matt Williams to a .025 collective batting average (1-for-40).

All Stars Tony Gwynn, Tony Pena, Darryl Strawberry, Gary Carter, and Tim Raines hit a collective .364 (67 for 184) (Wikipedia 2021).

Who/how/what discovered that Biggio, Griffey Jr., Jeffrey Leonard (!), Pete Rose, Larry Walker, and Matt Williams were a combined 1-for-40 off Don Carman? And who decided this Wiki entry needed to include Tony Gwynn, Tony Pena, Darryl Strawberry, Gary Carter, and Rock Raines' career numbers off Don? We couldn't have left that nugget out? I don't know the individuals on the Official Don Carman Research Team, but:

1) Are you hiring?
2) I think they're a little too good at their job.

My first memory of Don Carman is from *Mike Tyson's Punchout.* As just a wee little 4-year-old, I couldn't fathom that two people could have the same first name, so I legitimately thought Don Carman was that shit talking twerp, Don Flamenco. I didn't understand how the #3 ranked boxer in the Major Circuit on a Nintendo game was also a Phillies hurler, but that wasn't my job to reconcile. Don Carman, as I later learned, is/was an interesting dude, not a 22-3 defensive fighter with 9 measly KOs. There are many layers to Carman. The research of these guys is sometimes draining. It can be a labor of love, but I never got that feeling with Don. I liked uncovering his story; I loved what Carman was putting down. In fact, I plan on sending him a copy of this book. Knowing Don, and I think I do, he may even write back.

Every kid at some point wrote to an athlete asking for an autograph. We all have a story. I picked up a book at a garage sale that listed the physical address of every NBA team. It was paper gold. You want to write to Kelly Tripuka? Send a letter to:

Charlotte Hornets
Attn: Kelly Tripuka
P.O. Box 5557
Charlotte, NC 28130

You always included a card for the player to sign – usually Score, Dunross, or Bowman – something low-brow. This wasn't the time to be slipping in those rookie cards or Stadium Club beauties. The biggest regret in my autograph hunting campaign was a letter to Patrick Ewing. For two reasons:

1) A team's best player never wrote back. This was an amateur move on my part. Who cares if I was 9? I should've known better. A savvy veteran would've played it close to the vest and penned a letter to Herb Williams.

2) I told Ewing that he dominated Shawn Bradley.

To admit that in writing – to betray Bradley's trust like that – I've never gotten over it. Even Benedict Arnold showed more integrity. And for what? A potential autograph that never came? It was a moment of weakness that I've since spent every second of my life trying to atone for. I'm sick to my stomach just thinking about it. Ewing probably never wrote back because he watched in horror as this young Sixers fan turned his back on his favorite team's young center. I don't blame the big fella for the silent treatment.

The math was simple. A lesser-known player got less fan mail, so they were more likely to respond. Carman was always diligent about writing back (Oppedisano 2006). These letters, however, fell to the wayside in '91 after he moved from Philly to Cincinnati (he signed a free agent deal with the Reds that April). Fifteen years later, he was cleaning out his garage when he discovered a box full of unopened letters.

He decided he'd answer each one, paying his 8-year-old son, Jackson, $4 to open and sort.

"He would read the letters, too, and it made him feel great because a lot of the kids were 8, 9, 10 years old," Carman said. "I think it brought to life what it may have been like for me playing. He didn't get to share in any of that." (Oppedisano 2006).

Most of the letters were from kids or card collectors seeking an autograph. Most, but not all.

"One was from a man whose wife I had visited in the hospital," he said. "She had always been a Phillies fan and she was dying. She expressed how wonderful it was I'd been there, and he said what a special time that was.

"I wrote a three-page letter trying to explain why it was late, to catch him up a bit on my life, and to try to tell him how difficult it was to write in the present about something so emotional that far in the past." (Oppedisano 2006).

Carman has always been a bit different. His biggest claim to fame is his list of

37 sports clichés that he taped on his locker in 1990. He had been hearing the same athlete catchphrases over and over since his pro ball career began in 1979. So after a 2-1 win over the Pirates, he posted the list and told reporters to take what they need. A few of my favorites:

8. It takes 24 (25) players.

22. Give the guy some credit, he hit a good pitch (The cousin to the best sports cliché of all time, "Sometimes you just have to tip your cap").

37. I don't get paid to hit. (Unterberger 2009).

Speaking of hitting, Carman finished his career with an .057/.066/.057 line, which begs the question: Who the hell walked Don Carman? That would be Padres pitcher, Eric Nolte, who gave two free passes to Don in an August 1987 game. Smart move. Can't make a mistake middle in to Donnie Baseball. (Carman's first career hit snapped an 0-48 skid).

Author Brad Balukjian wrote a 2020 book titled, *The Wax Pack*. The premise was brilliant and I'm jealous I never thought of it. He opened a pack of 1986 Topps cards and sought to meet every player inside. One card in that pack was Don Carman. The pitcher grew up in a small town in Oklahoma. After high school graduation, he wanted to be pushed, challenged, so he attended Seminole State College where the head coach, Lloyd Simmons, had the reputation of being a cranky blowhard. Carman didn't want to be coddled. He wanted to see if he had the chops to play pro ball and Simmons was a means to an end. Don wanted to be coached tough for one year and move on (Balukjian 2020).

"I went 7-2 and got into the starting rotation. I didn't see him smile all season. I go into the last day of the season and made sure the door was open so I could run. I said, 'I want to thank you. It's been great here for me, but I'm not going to be coming back,'" Don says. "Apparently, he didn't think I would follow through on my promise to leave after one season. He said, 'You'll never step on another field, you piece of shit.'" (Balukjian 2020).

Carman signed with the Phils in '78 and saw his first big league action in a

September promotion for the 1983 NL East Champions. He recorded a save against Pittsburgh in Game 161, pitching to fellow rookie and minor league call-up Darren Daulton. Carman and Daulton became very close friends, staying in touch long after Don left Philadelphia. Dutch passed away from a brain cancer known as glioblastoma in 2015. When his condition took a turn, Don stayed by his side for Daulton's final two weeks. "I'm just glad I could talk to him." (Baseball Happenings 2020).

I think of Don Carman, the starting pitcher, and he was, but not early in his career. He had a huge year out of the 'pen in 1985, going 9-4 with a tidy 2.08 ERA and 7 saves. He was gaining momentum with the Vet faithful as the Robin to closer Ken Tekulve's Batman.

Those delivered-with-gusto boos reverberating through Veterans Stadium in the eighth inning yesterday weren't meant to say "nay" to Kent Tekulve as much as "yeh" to Don Carman.

Don Carman? Sure, the reliever whose nickname among the Phillies soon may change from "Namrac" – his surname spelled backward; self-given in true, wacky lefthander fashion – to "Small Town."

Why that? Blink at the wrong time, you might miss him. (Silary 1985).

Carman threw 86.1 innings in 71 appearances that year. It was short relief – certainly not uncommon in modern day baseball – but more of an anomaly back then (To put into context, Royals closer Dan Quisenberry threw 129 innings that season). Fans wanted more of Don Carman. They didn't want the early hook, and boy, did they get their wish. He would move into the rotation and start a whopping 67 games in '87 and '88. His numbers were decent, but he regressed in '89, going 5-15 with an ERA north of 5. A 1989 season *in memoriam* in Allentown's *The Morning Call* was especially harsh.

Negatives? There was very little to feel good about in the 67-95 mark scratched out this season.

The coroner's report is in and a fatal dose of Starting Pitcher Horrendous –

traced to Bob Sebra, Don Carman, Alex Madrid et al – did this club in.

***Least Valuable Player**: 1) Bob Dernier; 2. Curt Ford; 3. Don Carman* (Bostrom 1989).

He worked out of the 'pen the following season. His numbers improved, but 1990 would be his final year in Philadelphia. After a year with the Reds and one in Texas, he was out of baseball by '93. Carman, though, attempted a comeback one year later. After golfing with Dutch down in Florida, Daulton made a few calls within the organization and got Don an invite to spring training.

Carman hasn't won a big-league game since the Phillies showed him the exit after the 1990 season. That's zero wins in three years.

The writing is on the wall with Don Carman. It's in big, bold letters: GET OUT. QUIT. GO AWAY. YOU HAVE NO CHANCE OF PITCHING IN THE BIG LEAGUES EVER AGAIN.

Carman refuses to wear his reading glasses. (Brookover 1994).

(He made a handful of appearances for Scranton/Wilkes-Barre but never got back to the majors).

On August 20th, 1986, Don Carman carried a perfect game into the 9th inning of a scoreless contest at Candlestick Park. Bob Brenly, who also broke up a Steve Carlton no-hit attempt in '82, hit a double to left center that tailed away from a sprinting Milt Thompson. Juan Samuel would eventually hit a 10th inning home run to give the Phils a 1-0 win. Don called it, "easily the best game I've ever pitched in Little League, high school, the minor leagues or anywhere else." (Ashburn 1986).

The Giants, in turn, offered their own spin on cliché #22 from Don's list.

"You get tired of giving the other pitcher credit." (Schwarz 1986).

Carman is now a sports psychologist working in tandem with agent, Scott Boras.

The Phillie Killer

Name: Jeff Conine

Position: OF/1B

Career Slash Line: .285/.347/.443

Phillies Tenure: 2006

It would be overstating things to say that Conine ended the Phillies' wild card hopes, but not by much. (Sheridan 2003).

Jeff Conine fucked us over and over. Let me be clear here. I don't hate Conine. I don't have a vindictive bone in my body. Jeff Conine hates me. He also hates you. He hates your family, and your friends, and your pets. I don't know if Conine was a distant relative to hitchBOT, but the sole intent of his 17-year career was to stick it to Philadelphia every chance he got. Let's review the videotape:

October 22, 2006

The Birds lose to Tampa on a game-winning 62-yard field goal by Jeff Conine.

February 23, 2009

The Sixers lose a heartbreaker to the Nets at the Meadowlands, 98-96. Jeff Conine hits a lunging half-court heave as time expires.

1998 Eastern Conference Quarterfinals

Flyers goaltender, Jeff Conine, goes 1-4 with an .860 save percentage in a first-round loss to the #6 seed Sabres. He admits to reporters after the series loss that, "I don't even know how to skate."

I was just as surprised as you to see Conine between the pipes.

Anytime something bad happened in Philly, Conine was there. He was like Lee Trevino in *Happy Gilmore*. If my life depended on the Phillies getting either Conine or prime Barry Bonds out, I'd first ask what Bonds has done his last ten games. The term 'Phillie Killer' gets thrown around all the time. It's probably a bit overused, but the premise is real. There are a handful of people whose eyes light up when they see the red pinstripes. Here are my unofficial rankings (all stats *are* official, however):

1) **Jeff Conine:** Career .728 hitter against the Phillies, with 102 home runs.

2) **Brad Wilkerson:** Has hit for the cycle 61 times. 57 of those have come at Citizens Bank Park.

3) **Freddie Freeman**: Has never been retired by the Phillies.

Conine was an All-Star in '94 and '95. He was named the '95 All-Star Game MVP, snatching the award away from winning pitcher Heathcliff Slocumb and planting the seeds for a decade of spiteful vitriol against our beloved Phils. After a lengthy tenure in Florida, Jeff left for Baltimore in '99. Personally, I think he should've stayed there. Baltimore is a lovely town. You like crab legs, Jeff?

The 2003 Marlins were a scrappy bunch. Juan Pierre and Luis Castillo slapped grounders to the left side of the infield and created havoc on the base paths. Mike Lowell terrorized teams. So did Derrek Lee. They went on a tear after interim skip, Jack McKeon, took the helm. They turned a 16-22 record under Jeff Torborg into a 91-71 finish. The Phils and Fish were neck and neck for that NL wild card spot. Florida, wanting some reinforcements, reacquired the familiar Conine on August 31st. What could go wrong?

On September 23rd, the Phils traveled to Miami trailing the Marlins by one game in the wild card standings. In game one of the three-game set, the Fightins had a 3-0 lead entering the bottom of the 7th with ace Kevin Millwood on the bump. Millwood issued free passes to both Lee and Miguel Cabrera to begin the inning. Juan Encarnacion then flew out to center. Next up was Conine.

I was a sophomore in college. Phillies/Marlins games weren't televised on the Canadian border. Canada's The Sports Network (TSN) knew their audience. They weren't superseding curling in primetime to show this NL East tilt, no matter how pivotal. I was in the dark. I followed along on Yahoo, clicking refresh over and over. I held my breath. The Phils HAD to get this one. Don't do it, Yahoo. Don't you dare do it. Don't you -

In Play, Run(s).

Jeff Conine was so thrilled by his home run Tuesday that he pumped his fist, something he said he has done only one other time in a 12-year career.

His teammates were excited, too. They mobbed Conine at the plate to celebrate the biggest hit in the Florida Marlins' biggest game this season (Associated Press 2003).

There is this misconception that Jeff Conine hit a walk-off that night. Time tends to bend the truth. He didn't, but does it matter? Conine was like the old guy from *Thinner*, placing a curse on the Fightins that wouldn't be exercised until Game 162 in 2007. Millwood's fastball clocked in at just 88 mph (Sheridan 2003). That's good enough to travel back in time in a DeLorean, but not nearly hard enough to sneak past Jeff Conine. I stared at the computer screen. There are some bad moments in Philly sports that make you scream – a Carson Wentz red zone interception was my trigger. There are others that debilitate you. Biggio's homer against Billy Wagner in '05 was one. Kawhi's game winner in Game 7 was another. All the life gets sucked out of you. You can't yell. You can't move. You're frozen. Ten years of Phillies futility told me there was no fight left in them. They were cooked. Mike Williams and his 6.12 ERA relieved Millwood after the Conine blast and quickly gave up two more runs. The Marlins would sweep the Phils and go on to win the World Series.

The team acquired the 40-year-old Conine in late August of 2006. I had serious misgivings. This guy had been fucking me since 1993, and now he wants to patron my local Wawa? I'm supposed to be ok with this?

"You hear the Phils brought in Conine, Liz?"

"For what? To try him for war crimes? He did it. He's guilty of everything."

"I hope it's good," Conine said of his anticipated reception there. "Hopefully, I

can reverse the killing this time." (Parent 2006).

I suppose he said the right things when asked about his Phillie Killer past. *He was just doing his job. It wasn't personal*, blah, blah, blah. I've watched The Red Wedding at least three times, so excuse me for being a bit skeptical. Besides, doesn't anyone else remember Al Horford's one season here? You can't trust anyone.

Jeff was ok. He didn't do anything egregious that triggered my Spidey-Sense anyway, and believe me, I was looking. I swore we had a turncoat in our midst, but the evidence was lacking. He homered against his ex-mates in an 8-6 Phils win (lulling us into a false sense of security?) and posted a modest .280/.327/.390 line. Conine never lost a playoff series in his career, and that clean slate remained intact as the Phils again missed the postseason. After the acquisition, GM Pat Gillick confirmed that Conine was part of the team's future plans, but that was not to be (Hayes 2006). He moved to Cincinnati and finished the 2007 season in Queens after an August trade. He got to witness the Mets epic collapse firsthand. It was a strange end to a terrific career. Maybe it was just happenstance. Or maybe this was Conine's parting gift to us, an olive branch of sorts. Maybe he figured we Philly fans deserved this; that we had suffered long enough.

Or maybe the Phillie Killer just finally got what was coming to him.

The Power Beard

Name: Ken Ryan

Position: Pitcher

Career Record: 14-16; 3.91 ERA (4.30 FIP)

Phillies Tenure: 1996-1999

Overheard at The Princeton:

Date: June 2nd, 1996

Time: Approximately 10:57 P.M.

"You see Ken Ryan lowered his ERA to 1.80 tonight?"

"Pretty cool, right? When is Mr. Greengenes supposed to go on?"

There are two different Ken Ryans. There is the bearded version, the one who dominated in 1996 and helped anchor a solid Phillies bullpen. Then there is the clean-shaven, baby-faced one; the Ken Ryan who I barely recognize. I've erased the latter from my memory. When I pulled up Ryan in Google Images and saw this youthful, clean-cut reliever staring back at me, I was caught off-guard.

I thought Mike Mimbs was taller?

Ryan was one of my guys. His name was like a hybrid of Ken and Ryu from *Street Fighter.* If I get confirmation that his mother's maiden name was 'Balrog,' he'll jump Chase Utley as my favorite Fightin ever. Did 12-year-old me ever shout, "Hadoooooken," when Ryan fired a mid-90s fastball past a hitter? I wouldn't tell you if I did. I choose not to acknowledge the '97-'99 version of Ryan, a disappointing stretch where he was plagued by a string of elbow issues. 1996 Ken Ryan was lights out. His two-seamer generated its power from a NE Philly neckbeard that said, "Yeah, I can rattle off each cross street of Roosevelt

Boulevard. What's the big deal?" Ken earned my trust – and aside from every Eagles team who won their first preseason game – I don't trust easily. I wasn't a Ken Ryan believer from Day 1, though. Certainly not after being acquired for another one of my favorites.

It only seemed to take longer to complete than the Blue Route.

After nearly two weeks of speculation, the Phillies received outfielder Lee Tinsley, righthanded reliever Ken Ryan, and minor league slugger Glenn Murray for Heathcliff Slocumb (Hagen 1996).

NOOOOO! Not Heathcliff!

The move was confounding. Slocumb was an All-Star the season prior, notching 32 saves and a 2.89 ERA. His numbers tapered off a bit in the second half, but when the team finishes 69-75 after a 38-21 start, you tend to gloss over the closer's full body of work. There is a deemphasis on the saves category today, but not in the mid-90s. Closers were still very much *en vogue*. Case in point: The Red Sox would flip Heathcliff Slocumb to Seattle a year later for Derek Lowe and Jason Varitek. So why did the Phils settle?

The Phillies tried shopping Slocumb for a front-line starting pitcher at these meetings, but "that animal's not out there," Thomas complained Wednesday night. (Stark 1996).

Lee Tinsley swiped 18 bags for Boston the year prior, but all signs pointed to Ryan being the prize of the deal. The Phils had been big fans of Ryan's arsenal for years and planned to use him in a set-up role to new closer, Ricky Bottalico (Stark 1996). Ryan closed a bit in '94 (13 saves) but bounced back and forth between Boston and Pawtucket the following campaign. The Phils traded their current closer for a reliever who would set-up the new closer who was already on the roster. Why not just keep Slocumb? Hang tight and see if the starting pitching market improves? I don't think Heathcliff Slocumb, Clubhouse Cancer, was a thing. Or maybe the Phillies brass jumped at the deal because they expected Glenn Murray to drive in 100 RBIs (he didn't). Everything about the trade seemed redundant.

Ryan got roughed up in spring training, allowing 21 hits and 13 walks in 14 innings (Hagen 1996). But it was common knowledge that Ken Ryan was a slow starter, like Styx's "Come Sail Away." Once our boy got going, though? Look out. Ken found his sea legs once camp broke. He and Ricky Bo were terrific – it was piecemealing the other seven innings that was the challenge (the team collectively had a 4.48 ERA). He didn't concede a run in his first seven appearances, even collecting two 3-inning saves which is almost as rare as the drop kick attempt after a touchdown.

The Colorado Rockies were built to play here. No matter how many runs their pitchers give up, the lineup was carefully constructed to always have a chance to come back.

The only hitch is, in order to take advantage of the Coors Field jet stream, the Rockies have to hit the ball up into it. Yesterday, down 5-1 with Ken Ryan on the mound against them, the Rockies didn't have a chance (Sheridan 1996).

A regression was to be expected. Ryan eventually did allow a run (on May 1st to be exact) but logged 89 innings and recorded a pristine 2.43 ERA. The '96 Phils were a train wreck, but at least we had a reliable bullpen arm for the next few years, right?

From 1947-2021, here is the list of highest ERAs by a Phillies pitcher in a single season who threw at least 20 innings:

1. *Bob Miller (1958): 11.69 ERA*
2. *Gavin Floyd (2005): 10.04 ERA*
3. *Ken Ryan (1997): 9.58 ERA* (Boye 2021).

Ok, so there was a slight jump in ERA from '96. Elbow tendinitis delayed his '97 debut. He returned in May to, um, sub-optimal results and landed back on the IL in June with a sprained ligament (Fernandez 1997). He had reconstructive elbow surgery in the fall of that year and didn't make his first appearance in '98 until August (Salisbury 1998). He joined the big club to start the year in '99, but by mid-

May, he was optioned. A 6.32 ERA ended his Phillies tenure, and ultimately, his major league career. A promising future in Philly torpedoed by a mountain of injuries. His last major league appearance was a May 15th game against the Mets. In the top of the 6th, he faced Mike Piazza with runners on first and second and nobody out. Piazza lined into a triple play. It was the final batter Ken would face in the majors.

The Other Free Agent

Name: David Bell

Position: Third Base

Career Slash Line: .257/.320/.396

Phillies Tenure: 2003-2006

"I don't know where you have any argument. Frank [Robinson]. You're down 14 to 5." - Harry Kalas, June 28, 2004 (MLB 2018).

There are a surprising number of David Bell shirseys in circulation. Mike Lieberthal, though? None. Abreu? Nope. Millwood? Negative. Where did they all come from? Who was mass producing David Bell t-shirts? Was FlynnO'Hara behind this? It's like there was a promotional David Bell t-shirt giveaway and it drew a crowd of 3 million people. So I called up the Philadelphia Department of Records (it's called research, folks) who verified that the top-3 biggest outdoor events in the city's history are:

1) Pope Francis' visit in 2015
2) Phillies vs. Expos: David Bell T-Shirt Giveaway Day
3) Live Aid

All tees have been relegated to gym or lounging around the house status. You don't see Bell shirts at the Bank – not even in an ironic sense. It's too risky. Bell was *not* popular here. Like I'm not strolling up to the Linc in a Nnamdi Asomugha jersey; I got a family. I'd get eaten alive. I was at a Planet Fitness in 2007 and saw – no lie – four different people wearing a David Bell shirsey. One other guy was wearing a No Fear shirt, because I can only assume his Bell tee was in the wash. But if you consider where the Phils were in 2003, it makes sense. Bell was a victim of expectations, an ok player who was under the microscope because of a renewed, fanatical interest in the team.

"These are not your traditional Phillies. They have been the most aggressive team going into the free-agent season." (Gammons 2002)

Citizens Bank Park opened in 2004. Entering '03, management looked to make a splash before the change of scenery and the subsequent windfall of cash. The Phils were linked to every free agent in the '02 offseason, after seemingly not being connected to anyone since the Danny Tartabull debacle. (I'll give you Jose Mesa, if you insist). Along with the bats, the Fightins were tied to both Tom Glavine and Jamie Moyer (talks with Glavine were more substantial). Neither obviously signed, but one was an eventual World F'n Champion. The other got fileted by the Marlins in the final game of the '07 regular season. The Fightins had a few holes in their infield, and there was a belief that landing Bell could help recruit Jim Thome, the prize of the '03 free agent pool.

"I talked to him three or four times over the last month," said Bell, a friend of Thome's from his two stints with the Indians in 1995 and 1998. "My gut feeling is he's going to make a good decision and the right decision." (Maaddi 2002).

David's gut really went out on a limb there. But Bell's influence shouldn't be overstated. This wasn't signing Thanasis Antetokounmpo. It's not like befriending some kid in your English Lit class just because you want to date his sister. Bell had just put up a respectable .762 OPS with San Fran, including some timely hits in the '02 NLCS and World Series (The Giants lost to the Angels in 7). But even if your opinion of Bell wasn't high – and you considered the 4 year/$17 million dollar deal a reach – the risk was worth the potential reward. If the third baseman played even the slightest role in acquiring Thome, the closest equivalent to Paste in *Bases Loaded*, then it was justified. Philly was not an attractive destination for free agents. Scott Rolen told us to go screw. J.D. Drew wouldn't sign. '93 may as well have been 1893. The Phils landed Bell, Thome, and Millwood (via trade) that offseason. The foundation already included Abreu, Rollins, and Lieberthal. The talent was there. All we needed from Bell was to field his position and not completely shit the bed on offense.

In the Phillies clubhouse Thursday afternoon, David Bell said he felt closer to where he wants to be than he had in weeks.

Bell had started the day with just two hits in his last 26 at-bats (.077) and just five in his last 46 (.109). (Zolecki 2003).

He started his Phils tenure by reaching base his first 13 games, and then nose-dived through Memorial Day Weekend. On June 9th, he was hitting .197. It was a tough look. Did Bell ultimately help influence Jim's decision to sign with Philly? Perhaps, but it didn't matter by June 9th. Western University boosters greased the wheels for Ricky Roe by purchasing his father a tractor. All David Bell did was make a few phone calls.

"He's hitting below the Mendoza Line, John!"

"But he helped recruit Thome!"

"He called him like twice!"

The honeymoon was over.

Bell will be a fixture in the Phillies lineup for the next four years. Phillies fans haven't quite warmed to that idea yet. So far, Bell is getting more than his share of boos. In a stunning bit of bad timing, he's hitting just .143 at Veterans Stadium this season.

"I appreciate the fans," Bell said. "I take their passion as a positive." (Roberts 2003).

At least he appreciates us. You reading this, Scott Rolen? Using the benefit of hindsight, Bell's struggles were magnified by the fact that 1) the Phils finished so close to the Wild Card despite his shortcomings and 2) the team could've promoted a young Chase Utley and moved Polanco to third. Yes, I'm making a few leaps here, but you're allowed that *carte blanche* when writing about David Bell in 2021. Utley did come up in '03 and registered just a .696 OPS, but compared to Bell's .579, he was basically Eddie Mathews. David's struggles could be traced to a back injury which sidelined him in mid-July (Roberts 2003). He and the team hoped two weeks of rest would suffice, but Bell wouldn't return to the lineup until September 23rd against the Marlins – better known as, "The Jeff Conine Game." That – that is bad timing.

Bell was much better in '04. Healthier and free from the shackles of the Vet, he registered a career-high .291/.363/.458 line, including hitting for the cycle against Montreal on June 28th. But that Monday night wasn't without its controversy. Needing only a triple when he faced Expos reliever Rocky Biddle in the 7th, Bell ripped a drive to center. A fan leaned over the railing, attempting to catch the ball with their hat. And let's just say it, that's a copout in my book. The callouses on my hands are from catching foul balls, not years of carpentry. The ball caromed off the wall as Bell rounded into third. Review wasn't a thing back then. Montreal skip Frank Robinson protested the triple, claiming the ball hit the fan's arm or hat, which would've made Bell's drive a ground rule double. Expos outfielder and fellow cyclist Brad Wilkerson pedaled in from center, also claiming fan interference. The umpires convened for a few moments, but the call stood. He remains the last Phillie to hit for the cycle. You'd think a J-Roll or an Utley type would've repeated the feat, but David Bell's reign of terror lives on.

He struggled again in '05 and was moved to Milwaukee in the middle of '06 for Wilfredo Laureano. Fans had tired of Bell. If he signed here in the mid or late-90s, people wouldn't carry the same venom. Expectations were nil back then. Like who spends their days trashing Todd Zeile? Life's too short. He just would've been another average player passing through the city, another forgotten name from years past.

"Remember David Bell?"

"Who? You mean Juan Bell?"

But he was a key free agent in a very important offseason for the organization. The '03 – '06 teams were good, though never great. They were talented, yet infuriating, and the only thing that Philly fans love more than the backup quarterback is a scapegoat. We like to condense the blame to one person, if possible. It's cleaner that way. Of course, Bell wasn't the sole reason why those Phils never grabbed an NL East crown or a wild card berth. There was a myriad of reasons why that stretch of teams never got over the hump – it wasn't just the play at third. But Bell was there for all the close misses. He outlasted both Thome and Millwood. He became synonymous with these teams that just weren't quite good enough. Fans were ready for change. They demanded an upgrade.

They got Wes Helms. (More on him in a bit).

The Clubhouse Cancer (Depending on Who You Ask)

Name: Tyler Houston

Position: 3B/C

Career Slash Line: .265/.312/.423

Phillies Tenure: 2003

"It's all crap," Houston said, "and I'm sick of seeing these lies. They're covering it up with something about me not being happy with my role." (Hammond 2003).

"He's a loser," said Bowa. "You can put 'loser' in the paper with his picture." (Roberts 2003).

I've worked *a lot* of yard sales in my day. My parents were downsizing and had a basement and a garage and closets jam-packed full of odds and ends. Calling 1-800-GOT-JUNK? was the easy way out. That wasn't in my mom's DNA. They instead had yard sale after yard sale. I'd recognize the same items over and over.

"No takers on these gently-used school folders yet, huh?" I'd say, before stamping a $.25 sticker sale price on them.

I respected my mom's hustle but trying to sell this Huey Lewis and the News cassette tape in 2018 was a tall task. And make no mistake about it, I was the Head of Sales. Every time I showed up at the house, I expected to be manual labor – move a few tables, lift a few boxes – but nope. Yard sale shoppers are incredibly prompt. If doors open at 8 A.M., they're there at 7:30. Now punctuality was *not* my mom's strong suit. It'd be 10:00, and she would still be rifling through the basement looking for product. She was nowhere to be found. Meanwhile, I'm in the driveway trying to convince this prospective buyer that her sunroom décor wouldn't be complete without this broken ham radio. Mom would hand me a coin-filled fanny pack like I was a pro wrestler from 1997 and tell me to do what I do best: peddle these VHS copies of *Powder* and *Con Air.*

There was one true staple of the yard sales – one item(s) that got lugged back and forth from the garage to the driveway, from the garage to the driveway, over and over and over. Mom was selling ten (10!) bowling balls. She would have me stage the balls in the "Sporting Goods section" and I'd reposition some wooden tennis rackets and my old soccer shin guards to make room. They were a headache. How does one go about acquiring ten bowling balls? Did she loot a Brunswick Zone? I had a lot of questions, but 7 A.M. sneaks up on you fast. My investigation got put on hold. As the hours passed, my Sporting Goods section remained unscathed (not a lot of sports fans, I figured); that was until the three-legged dog appeared.

"How much are the bowling balls?" a woman asked, holding the leash.

Huh? These bowling balls? How should I know? I'm just the Head of Sales. We never bothered to actually price the bowling balls. Pops and I figured we'd move them back into the garage for the next inevitable yard sale six weeks from now. But, hey, I had an interested buyer here. I couldn't let her go. I had to think fast.

"Um ... how about this? If you let me pet your dog, I'll give you the bowling ball for free?" She laughed.

"Well, I'm interested in all of the bowling balls."

The fuck? What is your intention with all these bowling balls, ma'am?

"All of 'em? For real?" What was the going market for ten used house balls? *I was asking $5 a ball, but I'll give you the entire lot for $30?*

I was at a loss. This was unchartered territory. My college business classes never covered this. We just read *Rich Dad, Poor Dad* and talked about Southwest Airlines. So I scratched her dog's ears (it was a very good dog) and gave her ten bowling balls ON THE HOUSE. After helping load her car (door to door service), I took $20 from my wallet and slid it into my fanny pack. It was a small price to pay; these bowling balls weren't our problem anymore. I was trying to make a statement. Let my parents know that every Saturday in the fall couldn't be dedicated to another yard sale. It was ok to move on. My message was intended to be subtle. The Phils front office and Larry Bowa would choose a much louder approach.

Long before Tyler Houston was involved in one of the most heated feuds in franchise history, he was the #2 overall pick of Atlanta in the 1989 draft (The Phils selected outfielder Jeff Jackson #4, ahead of a guy named Frank Thomas). There were big hopes surrounding the high school catcher. Houston secured a then-record $232,500 signing bonus, which surpassed Andy Benes' $230K the previous year (I lovingly called him Andy "Beans," just like Bernard Aranguren from *Even Stevens*). Even with the record-setting contract, Tyler's father wondered if they left some money on the table.

"You always wonder if you could have gotten this much more," said Houston's father, Sam, holding his fingers inches apart (Associated Press 1989).

I get it, Mr. Houston. I gave away ten bowling balls for free. And, yes, I noticed his father's name was Sam Houston, but, no, I couldn't find any reactions from Tyler's Uncle Jake the Snake. Houston never reached the lofty expectations bestowed upon him, but he did have a decent eight-year career. He found his footing with the Cubs in the late 90s and developed the reputation as a dependable bat off the bench. He bounced around the NL before inking a one-year deal with the Phils in 2003. Before the calendar hit September, Houston took his occasional hacks in relative obscurity. He was best known for dying his hair blonde, along with fellow bros, Pat Burrell, Jason Michaels, Tomás Pérez, and Todd Pratt.

Now, few would call Larry Bowa a player's manager. Known for his animated personality, fair or not, the book on Bo was that his players eventually tuned him out. He wears on them. The manager wasn't oblivious to his reputation.

"He knows the ESPN cameras love him and admits that a quarter of his own players loathe him because of his dugout histrionics. (The Phillies' broadcast

network, Comcast SportsNet, bowing to a request from the club, has curtailed the use of its Bowa-cam) (Verducci 2003).

That's not to say Larry wasn't successful. He recorded a 337-308 record as Phillies skip, but the expectations of the '03 team were taking its toll. The pressure mounted. A 4-0 defeat in Montreal on August 28th was their 6th consecutive loss and left them 15 games back of Atlanta. *The Philadelphia Inquirer's* headline the next morning read, "Bowa Goes Ballistic After Sweep."

It will be interesting to see how the clubhouse responds to Bowa's blowup. Players have had a prickly relationship with the manager over the years, and there have always been rumblings that they tire of his abrasive personality. In June, Phillies GM Ed Wade met with Bowa and told him to be more positive in the dugout after management had sought out the opinions of players.

One had said Bowa's demeanor had become a problem. (Sheridan 2003).

After leaving Montreal, the Fightins headed to Queens for a three-game set. Pat Burrell homered in game one and snubbed Bowa after trotting back to the dugout. Instead of going in the home plate entrance where Larry was standing, Pat bypassed his skip by using the center of the dugout for entry. Houston would later call it a "staged thing." (Verducci 2003). The coaches were livid.

They suggested to Wade that Houston, a close friend of Burrell's, had become a bad influence on the under-achieving slugger. (Salisbury 2003).

The next day, Tyler Houston was cut.

After the debacle at Olympic Stadium, the Phils rattled off nine wins in their next ten. While many pointed to Bowa's tirade as the motivating factor, Houston told the *Courier-Post* after being released that the team held a player's only meeting on the ride to the Montreal airport. And hell hath no fury like a bench bat scorned. Houston emptied the skeletons in the closet.

"Everyone feels the same way about Bo – he doesn't give a crap about anybody in there. He doesn't give a crap about his players. Bo only cares about himself." (Roberts 2003).

And from a piece in *Sports Illustrated*:

"Bo's meeting was the last straw with Bo. We had to have a players meeting because of him. A lot of guys felt like he was giving up on them. So the players decided to win for ourselves."

Bowa calls the discussion on the bus "their little meeting," adding, "If that meeting ignited [the players], I'm glad. If it took my meeting for them to have a meeting, I'm glad. I just wonder why it took them so long to have a meeting." (Verducci 2003).

The Phillies' company line was that Houston was released because he was unhappy with his role. According to Bowa, he called Tyler in his office in July and told him that Polanco was moving to third and rookie Chase Utley would man second with the injury to David Bell. Houston's alleged response to the lineup change was, "It's a joke." In that same interview, Bowa reminded reporters that Tyler had played for "seven teams in seven years" (Eichel 2003).

Houston refuted the team's story. He told reporters that he never had an issue with his role. He was just the fall guy for Burrell's home run snub. It made sense. The Phils couldn't cut the young bat in the middle of the lineup, but there was insubordination in the clubhouse which had to be addressed. It was much cleaner to make an example of Houston. There was a precedent here. Seven years prior, Hunter Hearst Helmsley took the heat for the famed "Curtain Call," not WWF Champion Shawn Michaels. Houston is Helmsley. Helmsley is Houston.

"I fully accepted my role as a pinch-hitter," he said to the Inquirer. "I was trying to be the best pinch-hitter in the league. This is the way they want to say it went down, because they can't run their own clubhouse." (ESPN.com News Services 2003).

Houston was very successful in his role. He went 13-for-29 for a .448 average in pinch hit appearances that season. Tyler expressed concern that management was trying to blackball him; that Bowa publicly disparaging his character and attitude was preventing his ability to make a living (Roberts 2003). Reading Larry's words, it's tough to dispute that.

"He'd better hope no manager calls me and asks about him," Bowa said. There's a reason he's with a different team every year." (ESPN.com News Services 2003).

The team replaced Bowa with the amiable Charlie Manuel in 2005. Tyler Houston never played in the major leagues again.

The Ten Days

Name: Ricky Otero

Position: Centerfield

Career Slash Line: .256/.320/.326

Phillies Tenure: 1996-1997

"You've got to be excited about that little guy in centerfield," he said. "He didn't seem nervous. He swung the bat well. We're excited. I think this is one guy our fans are going to want to watch."

Easy, big fella. Fregosi, of course, remembers as well as anyone that after Lenny Dykstra's wrist was broken on Opening Day 1992, Ruben Amaro went on a one-week tear. The talk shows wondered why the Phils didn't just trade Dude while they had a chance. Amaro ended the season batting .219. (Hagen 1996).

I'm bald. Have been for years. Today, it's much more common. People have embraced the shaved head. When I first shaved my dome (I was 21), the only products for bald/balding people were Rogaine and Hair Club for Men. The only products on the market said, "You can't be happy, right? You don't like looking in the mirror, do you?"

Now, there are razors and shaving creams and lotions specifically designed for the shaved head. There's a whole market dedicated to it. I ordered a bunch of shaving creams and aftershaves from this company called Bee Bald. My wife saw all these bottles and tubes one day and wondered why our dining room table had turned into a vendor booth. I explained that I was an influencer in the bald head community – "It's no big deal" – and this company asked me to try out their products.

"The bald head community? That's a thing?"

"Oh, it's a thing."

Truth was, if I spent $18 more, I got free shipping. Bald guys now are a dime a dozen, but not 15 years ago. Not when you're in your early 20s. I was the only follicly-challenged show in town, and when you're the only person without hair, you get compared to *every* bald celebrity. It came with the territory. I don't look like any of these people, but in the 2000s, I was one of only five bald people on earth.

"Anyone ever tell you you look like Moby?"

Ugh. That's kinda insulting, no? I'm 20 years younger and a former athlete (see: U-12s Hoop It Up participant). I'm only wearing these black-rimmed glasses because I can't see five feet in front of me, not because I collaborated with Gwen Stefani on the hit track, "South Side."

"You remind me of Stanley Tucci a bit."

I'll take it! A very distinguished actor.

"You probably get this a lot because you play tennis, but anyone ever say you look like Andre Agassi?"

And the bushy eyebrows to boot.

"Dude at the urinal looks like David Cross."

Geez, no chill. I got that comp at an Eagles game. Can't you let me pee in peace? Give me a "Go Birds" and keep it moving.

"Dave does look like Pitbull."

I was in Vegas years ago for a bachelor party and we decided to wear these goofy suits called OppoSuits (Don't start). My twin brother, Pitbull, was performing on the Strip that weekend and the groom's brother had this idea. We took a picture together and he posted it on Facebook.

"Ran into Pitbull in Vegas! Super nice guy!"

The very first comment – THE VERY FIRST COMMENT – didn't question Pitbull's identity, or the authenticity of the photo. This person didn't consider that the groom's brother was posing with an imposter. The poster didn't even give a generic, "haha." The very first comment?

"Wow! I didn't realize Pitbull was so short."

tl;dr: I'm short and bald.

I've always gravitated to the shorter athlete. Greg Grant was one of my guys. Michael Chang, too. I'd even welcome the diminutive cheater, José Altuve, into my clubhouse. If you ain't cheating, you ain't trying, right? Dominique Moceanu was my favorite of the Magnificent Seven and I still believe in Gizmo Williams' ability in the open field. The list goes on and on. But the 5'5" Otero was in a class of his own (Baseball-Reference says he's 5'7", but everyone knows that if you say you're 5'7", you're really 5'5). Editor's note: I'm also 5'7". Ricky Otero is my favorite player in this book. In late 2008, I wrote the first of these essays, starting with Charles Shackleford. A few former Sixers followed. Otero was the first Phillie ever covered.

How much do I love Ricky?

Put it this way: Two days from now, the Birds are gonna go on the road to Arizona, beat Kurt Warner and the Cardinals, and advance to the Super Bowl. Yet, all I can think about is Ricky Otero.

Still holds up. There was no other Fightin considered. I was like Kevin Costner in *Draft Day*: "Ricky Otero no matter what." For one week in 1996, I was in love. I witnessed the heir apparent to Lenny Dykstra. I watched the greatest Phillie centerfielder since Richie Ashburn. I once saw some thread on Twitter, where the poster asked you to name a player that you were wrong about. Name a player that you were convinced was going to make it but didn't. My head says Tim Thomas. My heart is going with Ricky Otero.

The Phils acquired Ricky from the Mets in December of '95 for minor leaguer Phil Geisler. In 51 at-bats with New York, he recorded an OPS of .362, which is basically the 400 points you get on your SATs just for spelling your name correctly. The Mets saw a lost cause. I saw a reclamation project. Centerfield was a thin position – among many – for the '96 Phils. The 33-year-old Dykstra ended up on the DL. His 1996 campaign would be his last. Newly acquired from Boston, Lee Tinsley hit just .135, before he was traded *back to the Red Sox* in early June. He generously gave the Phils seven singles and a .135/.196/.135 line before his exodus.

Otero made his Fightins debut on May 28, 1996 and collected three hits in a convincing 9-3 win over the Dodgers. He walked three times the next night and swiped two bags. He reached base five times a few days later in a 9-8, 12-inning victory over the Padres. The #1 song on June 2nd was by Bone Thugs-n-Harmony, and they weren't the only ones at a Crossroads. Was Ricky Watters no longer my favorite Philadelphia athlete? I had a lot to digest, but I did know we had a star on our hands. I was convinced that a godsend had just fallen into our lap, ala Trevor Ruffin. The easy explanation for the Ricky Otero phenomenon was small sample size, but I'm going to let you in on a little secret. Small sample size doesn't apply to your new favorite player. Cody Ross went buck wild in the 2010 NLCS. Now, THAT was a case of small sample size. Ricky, though? He had a .467 OB% after that Padres victory, and as far as I was concerned, that was as sustainable as clean energy.

It was around this time that Delaware Valley kids started lobbying for a Ricky Otero jersey. What a tall task. You couldn't insert your AOL "100 Free Hours" CD and do a little online shopping. I could hear my amazing mother calling sporting goods stores on the downlow – dragging the phone extension cord from the kitchen into the dining room – waiting for some Modell's associate to "check the back," as if the Otero jerseys were just misplaced behind some Flyers sweaters. The other important note here is that even if a Ricky Otero jersey did exist (it doesn't), my mom would *never* have just given me the pinstriped beauty. You had to earn it, like a rookie trying to crack Joe Girardi's line-up. She would've hidden that gorgeous Phillies kit in the attic until just the right time. She also would have purchased an XL because I'll "grow into it," even though I was a 72 lb. sixth grader. I'm still swimming in a Jerry Stackhouse jersey twenty-five years later.

The next night at Wrigley Field, he hit his first career homer. I remember this game vividly, because it was my first distinct memory of the Phils playing a night game at Wrigley. I jumped off the living room floor as the ball landed in the right field basket.

"Otero! Otero! Yeah, Ricky!"

What couldn't do this man do? Getting on base at almost a .500% clip and now sprinkling in some pop? It was like giving Wolverine Nightcrawler's teleportation powers. Otero ended the night with a .921 OPS.

"Lee Tinsley who?" I told my pops on the way to school.

"Thanks for '93, Lenny," I said to my mother before emptying the dishwasher.

There was always a point in a VH1's *Behind the Music* when the band's success story is about to take a turn. It was inevitable, and usually around the half hour mark.

"After the break ... a concert in Connecticut would change Milli Vanilli's career forever."

Otero's numbers dipped and dipped quickly. Three weeks later, his .238 average left me wondering if Wendell Magee Jr. could adapt to NL East pitching. Entering the '97 season, Ricky seemed like a longshot to make the opening day roster.

Like [Kevin] Jordan, Otero also has an option remaining and likely will be sent to the Red Barons before camp breaks. He sees the demotion coming his way like a high, inside pitch.

"No one has told me anything," Otero said. "But it doesn't look too good." (Holeva 1997).

In an early April Red Barons game, Otero suffered a gruesome injury while sliding into home. He caught his fingers in the catcher's shin guard. The game was stopped for 22 minutes as Ricky laid across home plate. Bone was sticking out from Otero's fingers as he suffered compound fractures and dislocations of the middle and ring fingers, along with a dislocation of the pinky. Manager Marc Bombard called the injury "one of the worst he's seen in 26 professional baseball seasons.

He's probably going to be out for the year." (Sokoloski 1997).

Bombard was a touch conservative with his diagnosis. The official timetable was 6-8 weeks, but Otero was back hitting eleven days later. He was activated not even three weeks after the incident.

"This is my year," Otero said. "I'm not getting sent down no more. That's why I wanted to come back quick and play. I wanted to come back here and stay the whole year." (Roberts 1997).

Ricky joined the Phils again in mid-May, but this time, there was no magic. He was sent back to the Red Barons eleven days after being called up. He returned in June and labored to a .657 OPS. You wonder if Otero came back too quickly, if he felt his big league footing slipping away due to a fluke injury and pushed too much. Or perhaps the injury wasn't a reason for Ricky's struggles at all. When he wasn't up with the Fightins in '97, Otero hit .331 for Scranton/Wilkes-Barre. So maybe the answer is right there in front of me. Despite my better 12-year-old judgment, despite what I wanted to believe, Ricky was just a fringe major leaguer, a AAAA player, who for ten days, was anything but.

The King of Long Relief

Name: Clay Condrey

Position: Pitcher

Career Record: 18-12; 4.10 ERA (4.47 FIP)

Phillies Tenure: 2006-2009

"Oh, meant to tell you. I saw that Phillies reliever with the goatee on South Street."

"You're gonna have to be *way* more specific."

I read this story on Deadspin about reporter, Nick Canepa, who once made a draft selection for the Clippers.

I think it was the draft where they drafted [Terry] Cummings. I think it was the '82 draft. This is the honest to God's truth, there were a lot of rounds in the draft then, not two like there are now. I think they were up to like, the seventh round. And I'm sitting in Silas's office, and you know, he's looking at these sheets, and he goes, "I don't know Nick, you pick somebody."

I'm saying, is Eddie Hughes gone yet? Eddie Hughes was a little guard who was just a rocket at Colorado State. I'd been covering San Diego State basketball before that. ... One of the fastest players I've ever seen. [I said] "Is Eddie Hughes from Colorado State gone yet?" And he says, "No." So they drafted him. I drafted a guy. (Ley 2006).

Clay Condrey wasn't a 7th round pick. He was drafted in the 94th round of the 1996 Draft. Yeah, you read that right. The 94th round. How many rounds are there exactly? I thought there were like 30 in the MLB Draft, and now I'm discovering there are 64 ADDITIONAL ROUNDS? By the 12th round of a fantasy draft, I'm exhausted. I just double up on kickers and defenses. Half my roster has the last name 'Gramática'. How are teams managing this draft pool? Who's maintaining the Excel doc? Who is even left to draft? Little Leaguers? Dead people? Was I picked at some point? Did some team select me in the 81st round of the '02 Draft, but my mom never gave me the message?

"Dave, the Kansas City Royals are on the line asking for you."

"Not now, mom, I'm playing *Twisted Metal*."

You're telling me I could've been cutting my teeth at High-A ball with the Wilmington Blue Rocks, but I was too busy fucking around with Mr. Grimm?

Condrey was selected #1728 out a total #1738 picks (Baseball-Almanac 2021). Mr. Irrelevant was Aron Amundson out of Eastern Oklahoma State College – no relation to Lou it appears, but the 23andMe results are still pending. On March 28th, 2004, the Phils acquired Condrey from San Diego for minor league infielder Trino Aguilar. The Sixers loved the deal. It deflected some of the attention away from their 89-65 (65!) loss at Boston that night. And listen, I know I already wrote a book about the Sixers and this isn't the proper forum, but the Black Shirts had 23 points *at half*. They scored 9 in the 2nd quarter. John Salmons went 1-13. Greg Buckner and Zendon Hamilton played a combined 23 minutes and neither scored.

Where was I?

Oh, right. Condrey joined the big club in 2006. For four years, he was the (channeling my Mikey Miss) the preeminent mop-up and long relief man in Major League Baseball. That's not bullshit. I'm being sincere. We took it for granted. We took Condrey's effectiveness for granted. He kept opponents at bay. If Clay entered the game in the 4th with the Phils trailing 5-1, he left in the 6th with the Phils trailing 5-4. What a concept! For the last ten years, I've watched reliever after reliever walk from the bullpen with a can of gasoline, pour it over the mound, light a match, and then walk to the clubhouse. They didn't say a word. They didn't even throw any warm-up tosses. They'd just pull a BIC lighter from their back pocket and whoooosh! Flames everywhere.

"Juan Soto has broken this game wide open."

Thanks for the update. I missed that. At the behest of the Fire Marshall, my section was walking single-file out of the stadium like the kids from *Kindergarten Cop*. Condrey did his job. He was an unsung hero. In three of four seasons in Philly, he posted an ERA under 3.26. He was everything you wanted in a long relief guy. If you dug deeper, he may have been a bit lucky here or there – the strikeout numbers were lacking – but Clay and I will not apologize for trusting the guys behind us. If Ben Francisco told us he was he shaded towards left center, then we pitched to Cristian Guzmán accordingly. The big man was an athlete, too. In a testament to his agility, Clay was able to keep his center of gravity despite stuffing 13 lb. of chew in the left side of his mouth. My sciatica flared up just thinking about it. I got fired from the Dollar Tree in high school (long story) and grabbed a pack of strawberry bubble tape gum on my way out the door for services rendered. That's six feet of bubble tape, but mere child's play for the Texan, who every outing shoved a wad of dip the size of a Granny Smith apple inside his cheek.

As a World F'n Champion, I assumed Condrey would command a bit more reverence than the average reliever of Phillies past. For example, I can see a 2041 roundtable discussion among Birds fans fondly remembering Corey Clement as the second coming of Marshall Faulk. But maybe I'm naïve. Twitter searches of Clay Condrey paint a different picture. He's the outlier of the '08 team, the baseline for middling relievers.

"Even Clay Condrey would close for this Phillies team."

Stuff like that. Maybe we fans are evolving, and the past is just the past. People's visions are no longer clouded by nostalgia. I tend to prop these former players up on these pedestals. Hell, this is the second book I've written on this exact premise. But maybe Twitter is right. Maybe Clay Condrey was just a middling reliever on a really, really good baseball team. Or – hear me out here – maybe Clay Condrey was just fucking awesome.

The Long Ball(s)

Name: Steve Jeltz

Position: SS/2B/3B

Career Slash Line: .210/.308/.268

Phillies Tenure: 1983-1989

Mike Schmidt evidently felt Jeltz could improve his hitting also. Schmidt told Phils president Bill Giles he would work with Jeltz for $100,000 and that if Jeltz didn't hit at least .250, Schmidt wouldn't take a cent. Needless to say, the deal wasn't resolved (Ashburn 1988).

I've always heard about the Steve Jeltz Fan Club. I don't know if it's an inside joke or a tangible organization, but either way, I want in. Where can I send my membership dues? Do you need help with recruitment, because I got ideas. A friend of mine was in the Lance Painter Fan Club (seriously) because – honestly, I don't know why – but he got an autographed card and a placard full of Lance Painter fun facts. I was jealous. Was I not worthy? Was my resumé not up to snuff? Put me through rush week. Brand my thigh with a hot iron, whatever you gotta do. I want to be part of *something*. If I find out any of you are in a Dickie Thon Fan Club, I'm going to be pissed.

Even with a .210 career batting average, Steve had a pizzazz about him. He rocked a Jheri Curl that would impress even 1980s Michael Cage. You don't have locks like that and hide them under a catcher's mask. Jeltz was a shortstop who looked the part. But as years passed, Steve has been unceremoniously crowned the posterchild of light-hitting middle infielders.

"Name a – "

"Steve Jeltz."

"No, no, I was gonna say name a Spin Doctors song."

"Oh. Well, the song about buying flowers then."

The thing is, no middle infielder could hit back then. It was contagious. As Jason Kelce said, "It was the whole team. It's the whole team." In 1976, Larry Bowa hit .248/.283/.301. If an everyday player put those numbers up today, I'd be holding a boom box outside Pedro Florimon's bedroom window. But in '76? That was good enough for Bo to make the NL All-Star Team. Jeltz wasn't exponentially worse than the merry-go-round of infielders who played during these times. I just think he did enough cool things to stand out from the crowd.

(Another shortstop from that era was Garry Templeton. Regarding the 1979 All-Star Game, he *allegedly* said that, "If I ain't starting, I ain't departing." Larry Bowa was named the NL starter. Templeton was selected as an All-Star reserve but didn't go).

Steve leads all French-born MLB players in games played, at-bats, runs, hits, doubles, triples, RBIs, and walks, which cements his status as the greatest French athlete not billed from Grenoble in the French Alps. The French-leader in career home runs is actually Bruce Brochy (26) whose father was stationed overseas in the U.S. Army. Jeltz is second on the list, but please don't mistaken him for a power hitter by trade. From '85 through '88, Steve hit zero homers, a cold streak not seen since my single buddy moved to Salt Lake City. He hit 5 long balls in 2,041 career plate appearances, meaning .0024% of his PAs ended with a round tripper. Two of those five bombs were hit on the same day. I tried to calculate the probability of Jeltzy smacking two homers in the same game, but it hurt my head and math isn't my strong suit. So let's just say it was improbable.

Steve played his college ball at the University of Kansas. The Jayhawks have been good to us. First, they gave us Wilt, then Steve, and later Rex Walters. I think this Embiid kid may pan out, too. Jeltz first joined the Phils and the Wheeze Kids in '83, when the team brought him up in July after moving utility infielder Larry

A gift for you

Hopefully you don't already have this
From Brian D'Alesandro

Order of December 21, 2022

Qty.	Item
1	**A Phillies Odyssey: Exploring the Forgotten Players of Fightins Yesteryear** Rueter, Dave --- Paperback **1735637025** 1735637025 9781735637020

Return or replace your item
Visit Amazon.com/returns

0/Xs09flgFh/-1 of 1-//ACY9-CART-B/second/0/1226-22:30/1223-23:27

A2-
M2

amazon Gift Receipt

Send a Thank You Note

You can learn more about your gift or start a return here too.

Scan using the Amazon app or visit **https://a.co/d/dGKHiXO**

A Phillies Odyssey: Exploring the Forgotten Players of Fightins Yesteryear

Order ID: 112-6228871-8496212 Ordered on December 21, 2022

Milbourne to the Yankees (Associated Press 1983). He hit .125, but in only 8 at-bats, so we're not going to hold that against him. It's like your first few shots in an open gym. You need to acclimate yourself with the rims and the shadows and whatnot. No one walks right on to the court and hits that initial elbow jumper. Jeltz split his time between Philly and the minors, before seeing regular playing action in '85.

I really dig his '85 Dunross rookie card. For starters, it has the gorgeous and iconic "Rated Rookie" design in the bottom right-hand corner. The most valuable lesson that Dunross ever taught me was that all rookies are rated. If you stumble upon an *unrated* rookie, that's when you should tread carefully. The card also features Jeltz in a retro batting helmet. Helmets back then didn't have ear flaps, so it looks like he's wearing a mini helmet that concession stands serve ice cream in. I *know* it's a normal-sized helmet, but when you've been staring at this card as long as I have, your mind starts playing tricks on you.

"Maybe Jeltz just has a really tiny head?"

The '87 Phils started 1-8, so the *Lancaster New Era* gave a forum for readers to offer their explanation for the Fightins struggles. And, boy, did people have opinions.

Axe Jeltz

1. *Get rid of Steve Jeltz. He can't hit, and doesn't field well enough to carry his bat in the lineup.*
2. *Team is pressing, due to too-high expectations. Team is not good enough to catch Mets, even without Gooden, due to improvement by Cards, tougher Cubs with Dawson, and even improving Bucs. Only Expos are weaker than last year.*
3. *Get rid of Steve Jeltz.*
4. *Phils need another pitcher badly.*
5. *Get rid of Steve Jeltz.*
6. *Pick up another catcher so Russell can be used in left or to pinch-hit.*
7. *Give Easler two at-bats, then get him out of left, no matter what.*

8. *Get rid of Steve Jeltz.*
9. *Get rid of Steve Jeltz.*

- *Fred W., Lancaster* (New Era Sports Poll Letters 1987).

In that same piece, another reader suggested the Phils "trade or buy with cash someone like Mookie Wilson or Barry Bonds for centerfield," and *New Era* subscriber, James M., stole my thunder, but I couldn't agree more (New Era Sports Poll Letters 1987). Steve's average crept up to .232, up from .219 in '86. So maybe there was reason for optimism? Or maybe Schmidt just wanted a hundred grand. In early April of '88, the shortstop made headlines at the expense of the Mets, and even noted Jeltz-hater, Fred W. of Lancaster, could get behind that.

The Mets were a tired bunch before the game, having arrived from Montreal at 4 A.M. because of delays at American customs. One Met, Gary Carter, got caught napping to end the game on perhaps the game's most unusual play – the hidden-ball trick. (Marcus 1988).

The Phils were up 5-1, and Bruce Ruffin was on the bump in the 9th trying to secure the complete game. Carter was on second when Howard Johnson roped a liner that was caught by right fielder Glenn Wilson. Glennbo then fired the ball back into short. Jeltz gave a half-hearted tag, but Carter was back safely. Nothing to see here. The camera panned to HoJo who was trotting back to the dugout. A split-second later, the screen flashed to second base umpire Doug Harvey emphatically calling Carter out (MLB 2018). Gary had strayed off the bag (Carter disagreed) and Steve nabbed 'em. The post-game reports implied that the slick shortstop tipped off Harvey ahead of time. Even with an *alleged* co-conspiracy looming over his head, Steve was no snitch.

Jeltz refused to admit he had the whole thing planned. Only his wry smile gave him away.

"I wasn't trying to trick him," Jeltz said of Carter. "I just saw him go off the base." (Marcus 1988).

It was an impressive display of gamesmanship by Jeltz, but the real hero here is second base ump and esteemed Mets Killer, Doug Harvey.

"I said to Carter: you're out and so am I." (Corbett 1988).

Fuckin' ay. Drop that mic, Doug Harvey. While Jeltz' hidden ball trick still gets the occasional play on social media, it's what he did a year later on June 8th that everyone remembers. The Pittsburgh Pirates were in town and put a 10 (10!) spot on the Phillies in the top of the 1st inning. (A few years prior, the Fightins defeated the Mets, 26-7. LOLMets, am I right? They were up 16-0 after two. Von Hayes hit two dingers in the 1st inning and later named his boat, "Two in the First," in homage).

Back to the Pirates game. Phillies starter Larry McWilliams recorded – let me check my math here – one out. He got one batter out. Reliever Steve Ontiveros didn't fare much better. The Phils clawed back and with help from a five-run 8th inning, defeated the Bucs 15-11. Pirates broadcaster, Jim Rooker, told viewers on air that, "If we don't win this one, I don't think I'd want to be on that plane ride home. Matter of fact, if we don't win, I'll walk back to Pittsburgh." (Lalli 2011). To his credit, Rooker did eventually make the 300-mile trek back to Pittsburgh in the name of charity. The journey was dubbed, "Jim Rooker's Unintentional Walk." The trip took twelve days, beginning at the Vet and ending at Three Rivers Stadium (Cohn 2014). There was this famous two-part *Boy Meets World* episode titled, "A Long Walk to Pittsburgh," where Topanga's family is moving across the state, leaving she and Corey's relationship in jeopardy. I'm convinced this episode, and the title of this episode, was an ode to Jim Rooker's walk. *Boy Meets World* was based in Philly after all. So, I wrote to Matt Nelson, the writer of that episode, to confirm my suspicions, but he did not respond by the time of this book's publication. (But that's just a formality. I know I'm right).

Steve Jeltz, power-hitting Steve Jeltz, mashed two of his five career homers that night. He hit a round tripper from each side of the plate, becoming the first of only four Phils to accomplish that feat. It would later be done by Rollins, Tomás Pérez, and Freddie Galvis. The Phils comeback over the Bucs isn't a deep cut. Everyone knows the story. The two bombs by Jeltz, Jim Rooker's famous quote, etc, etc. Time won't erase that Fightins win. But what I didn't know, or what I had forgotten anyway, is that Steve didn't even start that night. He replaced potato chip mogul, Tom Herr.

Jeltz entered the game in the top of the second in place of Tom Herr, who was playing with a sore foot. Leyva frankly admitted he thought the game was out of reach and wanted to give Herr a rest. (Bowen 1989).

Steve did all his yard work that night off the pine. The light-hitting infielder was the unlikeliest of heroes. It's difficult to fathom, hard to process, until you remember that Steve Jeltz is the greatest French baseball player of all time. Then it suddenly all makes sense.

The Hugger

Name: Mike Sweeney

Position: 1B/DH/C

Career Slash Line: .297/.366/.486

Phillies Tenure: 2010

Philadelphians have opened their arms to Mike Sweeney. He couldn't be happier about that.

If you didn't get a hug from Sweeney on Sunday, you were one of the few. (Gonzalez 2010).

When guys hug each other, they usually adhere to the same basic three steps.

1) A handshake that shifts to a 12 o'clock position.

2) While making a fist with your opposite hand, the handshake is followed by a two-count rhythmic pat on the dude's back.

3) Always ass out.

Guys hug each other ass out and I think it's because they're afraid of stumbling into a game of tummy sticks. That's the best explanation I can offer anyway. Mike Sweeney didn't observe these social norms, though. When he hugged you, he put some oomph behind it. As my wife would say, "squeeze if you mean it." There was this endearing, authentic quality about Sweeney. He was a popular figure wherever his career took him – first Kansas City, then Oakland, Seattle, and finally Philly. He was known as one of the "good guys" in the game, like former Reds first baseman, Sean Casey, who was dubbed, "The Mayor," due to the friendly conversations he had with baserunners. (No relation to Steve Mix, however). There wasn't a Phils fan who hated the mid-season acquisition. You didn't hear anyone call the 36-year-old bench bat washed or cooked. Sweeney had this infectious personality that made him impossible not to like. Fans adored him. He was embraced instantly yet hit just .231 in 58 plate appearances. A lot of players have come and gone through this city hitting below .235. We're familiar with that type of production. We're not usually that tolerant. But none of those guys were Mike Sweeney.

He earned his stripes with the Royals. From 2000-2005, he was an All-Star five times. He hit a gargantuan .340/.417/.563 in '02, a massive season that has all but been forgotten because he played for KC – and some really bad KC teams at that. Kansas City was a lot fun in PS2's *MVP Baseball*, though, because they made Angel Berroa way better than he really was and Zack Greinke threw like a 51-mph curveball. My buddies that came in cold off the street were pure fastball hitters, the Greg Dobbs of video games. They expected to raid my parents' cupboard for some ACME Shark fruit snacks and pummel the Royals into oblivion. Instead, they were ten minutes early on Greinke's 12 to 6 Uncle Charlie. They still ate the fruit snacks, though.

Mike's first taste of the big leagues was back in '95. He was a September call-up all the way from Single-A. Sweeney was grabbing dinner with some teammates when he was told there was an urgent message for him back at the stadium. He rushed back to manager John Mizerock's office.

On the desk, Sweeney recalled, was a can of Copenhagen tobacco, a pouch of Levi Garrett tobacco, a cup of coffee, and a shirtless Mizerock was smoking a cigarette and drinking a cup of beer from a keg in the corner of his office. (Grathoff 2020).

Sweeney was not a drinker, but his skip insisted. Holding a Dixie cup full of beer, Mike then asked about the urgent message.

"Is grandma sick? Is it family? What's the emergency?"

Mizerock then told Sweeney he was going to the Royals and would play in a doubleheader against the Blue Jays at Kauffman Stadium. Sweeney said he later heard that the Royals wanted to call up Sal Fasano but couldn't reach him (Grathoff

2020).

A lot to take in here. I respect that Mizerock had a keg in his office, but can we get him a sleeve of red solo cups? Dixie cups? What are we doing here, Miz? Dixie cups are reserved for mouthwash and Jell-O shots. And Sal – where was Sal? WHERE WAS SAL? Pager didn't work? Couldn't one of Sal's Pals track him down?

Sweeney would appear in a 1997 *Saturday Night Live* skit along with Gregg Jefferies, Scott Rolen, Todd Zeile, Cliff Floyd, Jeff Fassero, Marty Cordova, Mark Wohlers, and a host of others ball players. Jefferies, Rolen, and Zeile – but no Kevin Stocker? NOW WHERE WAS STOCK? He must've had the same shitty pager as Fasano. The skit had a lot going on. Sweeney walks into Chris Kattan's room holding a keg. Wohlers calls Kattan a homophobic slur (the fuck?). Helen Hunt hosted. Hanson was the guest performer, and I'm assuming they played "MMMBop."

Sweeney would eventually move from the catcher position to first base and a DH role. By '99, he was up in the bigs for good. Given the success of those Royals teams – or lack thereof – Sweeney's most memorable moment in Kansas City didn't involve a game-winning hit or a walk-off homer. In a contest with Detroit in '01, his fists, not his bat, delivered the comeuppance.

Certainly, this was out of character for Sweeney, known as an outgoing clubhouse leader who courts fans, hugs babies, and leads Bible studies in Baseball Chapel.

"I don't care what your reputation is," [Tigers manager] Garner said. "That was totally uncalled for." (Kaegel 2001).

That wasn't him. That certainly wasn't Sweeney's personality. In fact, it was the only time he was ever ejected. But everyone has a breaking point – even the most good-natured of men. Someone calls you a word or a phrase and it really rubs you the wrong way. It triggers something. It has you seeing red.

Tigers pitcher Jeff Weaver called Sweeney a "fucking pussy." (Galloway 2015).

Mike had requested the lanky pitcher move a rosin bag he felt was too close to the mound. Weaver declined, then hurled some obscenities towards home plate before uttering those two magical words.

As Weaver turned toward center field, Sweeney charged the mound, eluding [umpire] Fichter's attempt to haul him in. He chucked his helmet at the startled starter, threw a few jabs and finished with what would be considered a flawless cross body block in the world of professional wrestling. Sweeney got a few more shots in before one of his favorite teammates (and the man who would replace him after his ejection) swooped in to pull him out of the human wreckage (Galloway 2015).

Weaver should've known that the nice guys are the ones you don't mess with. That's Scrap 101. The people that constantly chirp are non-threats. Like has anyone seen Kevin Garnett actually throw a punch? Jeff thought he could mutter a few insults and live to tell about it***. Nope. In the waning moments, and a testament to his otherwise friendly demeanor (or naivety), he grabbed his helmet and tried to get back in the batter's box (Timothyhellman 2008). Sorry, Mike. You don't get to whip Jeff Weaver's ass AND bat. It's one or the other.

***The Philly sports site, *Zoo With Roy*, dubbed the *Care Bears* theme song over this brawl. It's a nice way to spend fifty seconds (Zoo With Roy 2013).

Up until 2010, the only thing Sweeney hadn't experienced in his decorated career was postseason baseball. The Phils scooped him up in early August after Ryan Howard went on the injured list. Before the acquisition, the alternative was the ol' Ross Gload/Cody Ransom platoon, and Manuel was quick to sever that two-headed monster. The former Royal saw steady at-bats for close to three weeks until Howard's return. The numbers weren't great, but it didn't matter. Everyone loved the dude.

Out in California, everyone from Dominic Brown to Jimmy Rollins felt Sweeney's sweet embrace. If the Gatorade cooler had limbs, Sweeney would almost certainly have made the inanimate object hug it out and bring it in for the real thing.

"I'm just embracing being [with the Phillies]," Sweeney told The Inquirer. No word on whether he then hugged the baseball beat writers who made the trip to

the Left Coast (Gonzalez 2010).

He had only one postseason at-bat in his 16-year MLB career. In game 2 of the NLDS against the Reds, he ripped a single off Aroldis Chapman in the 7th. I watched this half inning on delay. My wife had the gall to send me out mid-game to pick up dinner from – of all places – California Pizza Kitchen.

"Dave, we've had this California Pizza Kitchen gift card sitting on the counter for nine months."

"It ain't gonna walk out of the apartment. Can't you see we got this Reds bullpen on the ropes? Let's just fix some sandwiches."

Well, we had pizza that night. I eventually saw Jay Bruce lose a Jimmy Rollins liner in the lights. Never had a slice tasted so good. Mike Sweeney would retire the following spring with a career playoff OPS of 2.000. That May, he came back to the city and paid a visit to his old teammates. He was asked by reporters if it was difficult; if it was hard being back in the Phils clubhouse.

"Nope," he said. "My heart is here." (Housenick 2011).

The Streak

Name: Matt Beech

Position: Pitcher

Career Record: 8-22; 5.37 ERA (5.07 FIP)

Phillies Tenure: 1996-1998

Matt Beech, his left arm encased in ice, was sitting alone in the clubhouse when Rockies third baseman Vinny Castilla tapped a grounder to third. Scott Rolen picked up the ball and threw to first.

Game over.

Beech sighed deeply, tilted back his head and smiled a radiant smile. (Hagen 1997).

I played in a hoops league at the Healthplex in Springfield (shout out to my Delco crew). A buddy from work organized a team and he needed a steady point guard to run the offense. It just so happens that I was free on Sunday nights. Now my friend, Mike, has a lot of strengths but one glaring weakness.

Strengths: Smart, nice, great father.

Weaknesses: Horrible talent evaluator.

We were rotten. In two seasons, we finished a combined 0-25. GM Mike would bring in these jabronis mid-season and talk them up like they were difference makers.

"Steve averaged 12 and 8 in the Haverford YMCA League back in '93."

"When he was 9?" I asked.

New Steve rolled up in cargo shorts and Airwalks and complained about his shin splints. It was like telling Matt Klentak we needed bullpen help, so he goes out and gets Brandon Workman and Heath Hembree – hypothetically speaking anyway. The baby blue team beat us by 65. We lost a few times by 50. We trailed one game at half, 31-8, and two guys argued over who had more points. Each player finally agreed they both had 2. The highlight of my two-season tenure was breaking my wrist mid-game. I was able to walk right down the hall to the emergency room – very convenient – and got to miss four contests (all losses).

I was very excited to discover a MattBeech.com, a one-stop shop for all my Beechy news. But that Matt Beech does oracle readings and runs mystical workshops. I was intrigued, but the forum didn't offer any insight on how to approach Ryan Klesko. If you needed to get Klesko out (a career .000/.083/.000 line against the lefty), you called the OG Beechy (Stathead 2021). If you needed to get anyone else out, maybe phone someone else. Beech had his struggles here in Philly. It would be disingenuous to say otherwise. There's a YouTube video called, "Barry Bonds CRUSHES a homerun off Matt Beech, Phillies," and after watching the clip, I can vouch for the title. Bonds hammered one into the upper deck so high and far that all Chris Wheeler could muster was, "Oh, baby." (Baseball Roski 2021). That July 22nd, 1997 loss dropped the Phils to 29-68. (One 7-3 mark on the next home stand, however, and they're right back in it).

Playing for the Bridgeport Bluefish of the Independent League in 2007, Matt was attacked by a bat-wielding José Offerman after hitting the infielder with a pitch (José homered off Beech in his first plate appearance). I don't condone this ex-Phillie on ex-Phillie crime. I'd be just as upset if I found out Joe Thurston roped Eric Milton into a Ponzi scheme. The attack made national headlines. When I first heard about the incident, my initial reaction was, "Wait, *our* Matt Beech?" like 90s Phillies pitchers were kids and we were all co-parents.

"Can you pick up Little Paul Quantrill today? I got a work thing."

Bluefish catcher John Nathans suffered a concussion from the incident. Beech broke a finger. The former Fightins infielder was charged with two counts of second-degree assault and Nathans would be awarded $940,000 in a lawsuit seven years later (Associated Press 2014).

Matt Beech wasn't considered a top prospect on the Phillies farm. In a 1996-preseason ranking by *Baseball America*, Matt sat outside the top-10. For context, and a trip down memory lane, here's the list:

1) *Scott Rolen*
2) *David Coggin*
3) *Marlon Anderson*
4) *Reggie Taylor*
5) *Mike Grace*
6) *Bobby Estalella*
7) *Carlton Loewer*
8) *Wayne Gomes*
9) *Larry Wimberly*
10) *Wendell Magee Jr*. (The Baseball Cube 2021).

Beech was an able body, though. He received an August promotion that year and won his first career start, outdueling Greg Maddux while throwing 7 innings of one run ball. Fregosi was impressed with the young lefty, comparing Beechy to "a young Rick Honeycutt." (Carchidi 1996). Which seems like something *I would* do – comparing one random player to another random player you haven't thought about in twenty years. Either Fregosi stole my shtick, or I stole his. Then Beech hit a cold streak, like the 2012 Eagles red zone offense cold. He went 0-4 in his next seven starts to end the year with a robust 6.97 ERA.

He started the '97 campaign in Triple-A, but an injury to Mark Portugal put Beech back into the rotation in early May (Roberts 1997). Then he did this:

No decision against the Cardinals (Phils lost).

Lost to the Reds.

Lost to the Mets.

No decision against the Pirates (Phils lost).

No decision against the Expos (Phils lost).

No decision against the Red Sox (Phils lost).

No decision against the Braves (Phils lost).

Lost to the Braves.

Lost to the Orioles.

No decision against the Marlins (Phils lost).

Lost to the Expos.

No decision against the Giants (Phils lost).

Lost to the Dodgers.

Lost to the Cardinals.

We're in August now. We just rattled off 2 ½ months of starts. Schilling, Mark Leiter, and pray for rain wasn't a sustainable business model. The team had no one else. Every fifth day, Beechy got the pill. Every fifth day, the Phils lost. Now to be fair, not every start was a stinker, but even Kyle Abbott scratched out a win in 1992. After the loss to the Cards (he pitched well, it should be noted), Beech took the bump at home against Houston on August 7th. For most, it was a random, meaningless game in another lost season. But for me? It remains my greatest unsolved mystery.

In my first book, I discussed a 2007 Alan Henderson trade. The sources that I primarily used spit out conflicting information. The Sixers traded Henderson to the Jazz, but he never suited up for Utah. Then like a month later, he was back on the Sixers. It was all weird and confusing and sent me down a two-week rabbit hole, but I eventually cracked the case. I always solve the puzzle. Except this one. I'm just as stumped today as I was in 2010 when I wrote about this on my blog. There is this infamous line that has haunted me for almost 25 years that seemingly I'm the only one on the planet who heard.

"Not even Dr. Kevorkian could help this team."

Whitey said this. Well, I'm almost certain he did. I remember it vividly. Or I thought I did anyway. I can put myself in that moment. I was playing Sega in my room – around this time, it was probably *Triple Play '96* – while listening to the

Phils on a boom box that sat next to a nightstand that housed no less than three Matt Christopher books. Here is what *I thought I* remembered about this night.

1) The Phils were playing the Astros at home.

2) Matt Beech gave up a crooked number early (He gave up 4 ERs in the 2nd inning).

3) Whitey said this, not realizing they were back on the air. There was an awkward pause, then a stumbling of words, before the broadcast resumed with the play-by-play.

For the younger folks, Dr. Jack Kevorkian was a pathologist who gained notoriety for his work with terminally ill patients and their right to a physician-assisted suicide. He was convicted of second-degree murder in 1999 and spent eight years in prison. The line certainly qualified as dark humor; I just could not and cannot verify it. Despite all the tools at my disposal, the internet can't corroborate my story. I've devoured countless newspaper articles. I've done more Google searches on this topic than I care to admit. I've recruited help on Twitter, but nada. I'm on an island. You don't write a gazillion essays about random Philly athletes without giving your memory the benefit of the doubt. Like you wouldn't question Beano Cook's recall of the 1966 Rose Bowl, would you?

Having no evidence of this is a huge bummer, but using the information available, I can't contribute that line to Richie Ashburn. So maybe Whitey didn't say it. Maybe Matt Beech wasn't even on the bump that night. Maybe the Astros were actually in St. Louis for a three-game set. Who knows? Maybe I've lost a step. Next, I'm going to find out Willie Burton's career-high is actually 27, not 53. I don't know what I know anymore.

And the Phils won that night! A two-run homer by "The Wonder Dog" Rex Hudler in the 7th and a Stocker single an inning later sealed the comeback victory. Dating back to '96, it was the first Beech start in 15 tries that produced a Phillies victory. His next time out, he threw 7 shutout innings at Coors Fields and got his first win in 369 days. The headline in the *Philadelphia Daily News* the next morning read, "Beech Gets Annual Win." (Hagen 1997). It wasn't quite the Mets' Anthony Young's 27 straight losses, but Beech's 22 consecutive starts without a victory was still an eyesore. He finished the '97 campaign with a 5.07 ERA and made 21 more starts in '98 to lackluster results. The Phils gave Beechy 53 starts in three seasons. I suppose the obvious question is "why?" Why did management give him the pill on 53 separate occasions? For a rotation that was riddled by injuries, the short answer was Beech's arm was properly attached to his shoulder. That went a long way. There's something admirable about Matt's career, though. Even as the losses piled up and the results weren't there, he still took the ball. He was always ready when called, and you couldn't say that about everyone.

But more about Pat Neshak in another chapter.

The Run Saver

Name: Rico Brogna

Position: First Base

Career Slash Line: .269/.320/.445

Phillies Tenure: 1997-2000

Rico Brogna saved 100 runs a year with his glove.

That's not exaggeration or hyperbole. I don't need to cite my sources or offer a link or show my work like a 5th grade math word problem.

"100 is the correct answer, Dave, but how did you get there?"

"That's none of your business, Sister Mary Claire."

Rico Brogna saved 100 runs a year with his glove. That's a fact. If anything – if I allowed room for the tiniest margin of error – it's that I was too light, too conservative with this number. Maybe the actual count was 102, maybe 104 runs a year. You see, Chris Wheeler told the viewing audience that Brogna saved 100 runs a year with his glove and that's all I needed to hear. Wheels would never lie to us. Wheels was the head of Quality Control. For four seasons, the Phillies essentially trotted out Ozzie Smith at first base. I called Rico "The Power Glove" because he had some pop and flashed some leather. It had nothing to do with the fact that I've seen *The Wizard* a million times. He was a walking Web Gem. Brogna personally kept Carlton Loewer's ERA under 10.

Fans of crappy teams live in their own bubble, isolated from the rest of the world. When I started my campaign to get Clarence Weatherspoon to the All-Star Game in late '93, I conceded one singular roster spot to Shaq. That was it (Jordan was playing baseball then). The other eleven spots were in play. No one else was even in my peripheral. Spoon's case was open and shut. He averaged a double-double. The only reason he wasn't an All-Star, I figured, was due to a *blatant* Anti-Spoon bias from the national media. I was like every Jazz fan cherry-picking stats to help my guy's cause.

"Rudy Gobert leads the universe with a +76.1 STARPOINTS rating. Do you know how *valuable* that is?"

No one else is gonna go to bat for your favorite guys, so you have to. Mark McGwire slugged .752 in 1998, but as far as I was concerned, my favorite squad rostered the only first baseman who could pick a bad throw from across the diamond. Jeff Bagwell recorded a .304/.454/.591 line in '99, yeah, but factor in the 100 runs a season Rico saved, and the proof is in the run prevention pudding.

"Bags is the better hitter, Sarah, but Rico is the better PLAYER. How did you do on the social studies quiz?"

Brogna was a first-round pick of the Tigers in the '88 Draft. The Phils selected pitcher Pat Combs #11 overall that year. (Combs' name is synonymous with the bright red 1990 Dunross set and his "Rated Rookie" card is still ingrained into my brain 30 years later). Rico recorded just 29 plate appearances with Detroit. That number was cut short in part due to an August 14th, 1992 game against the Rangers. Brogna was the Tigers' designated hitter but was pulled in the *first inning* for a pinch hitter by manager Sparky Anderson.

Rico eventually established himself in New York. The Phillies acquired the first baseman from the Mets in '96 for relievers, Toby Borland and Ricardo Jordan. There were several trades between the Mets and the Phillies back then. It's an unwritten rule that you don't trade within your division (the revenge factor is real), but the Phils and Mets swapped relievers like a swingers party documented by HBO's *Real Sex*. The trade was a win for the organization. No one looked back and said, "Damn, I can't believe they let Ricardo Jordan slip through their fingertips." Brogna was entering his prime at the age of 27. It was a low-risk move for a Phils team, who primarily utilized an injury-plagued Gregg Jefferies and

Kevin Jordan at first the season prior.

The Fightins didn't enter the '97 season with high expectations, but I was talking division. April optimism is a helluva drug, and after Curt Schilling dealt 8 scoreless in an opening day win at Dodger Stadium, my only question was whether Derrick May would be a suitable DH against lefties in the World Series. But Danny Tartabull took a foul ball off his foot (and was never heard from again), the Dodgers chased Calvin Maduro out after 4 innings the following day, and that was that. So I spent my summer watching *Monday Night Nitro* and counting Rico Brogna extra base-hits. When your team is bad, you grasp at straws.

"Wheels just said that Brogna is 5th in the NL in doubles by a first baseman, Mom."

"That's nice, Dave. Sounds like he is having a nice season."

"Yeah."

The broadcast would feed you these inane stats, a half-hearted attempt to prop up these average players on these bad teams. I ate it up. What other choice did I have? Was I some turncoat who switched over to the Superstation for a 7:05 Braves start when times were tough? Oh, hell no. I had self-respect. Besides, Kalas just told us that Rico Brogna was 11th in the NL in sacrifice flies post-All-Star break, and I COULD WORK WITH THAT. You'd also be reminded time and time again that Rico was a terrific quarterback in his past life, like how Jeff Samardzija played wide receiver at Notre Dame and Chris Hogan was a Penn State lax bro. You couldn't get through one Brogna plate appearance without hearing that he was basically Steve Young.

His best campaign came in '99 when he put together a .790 OPS. He also crossed that magical 100 RBI threshold for the second consecutive year, which morphed Rico from "Run Saver" to "Run Producer." It was exhausting. Now I was tallying Doug Glanville stolen bases *and* Brogna ribbies. I didn't know much, but I knew I needed a bigger notebook. The Phils were 13 games over .500 on August 6th. The team's success was just the narrative I needed for my Brogna Silver Slugger

Award crusade. In fact, I may still have a campaign button or two lying around if you're interested.

(The Phils beat the Diamondbacks that night on a walk-off home run by Domingo Cedeno. They then lost 9 of their next 12).

Rico became the first Phillies first baseman to register back-to-back 100 RBI seasons (Hagen 2016). By 2000, however, a May forearm injury paved the way for top prospect Pat Burrell (Bostrom 2000). His playing time decreased drastically upon his return, and Brogna, disgruntled with his lack of at-bats, wanted out. In late July, the Phils acquired fellow slick-fielding first baseman Travis Lee in the Schilling deal, which further muddied the waters. When a proposed trade to Boston fell through at the trade deadline, Rico expressed his disappointment.

"I thought very seriously about calling the bellman and telling him to come get my luggage and then flying home," Brogna said as he nervously spit tobacco juice into a plastic cup. "In my initial state of mind, I was considering doing that." (Brookover 2000).

Without any viable offers, and unable to make a deal, Ed Wade put the first baseman on waivers after the deadline. The Red Sox quickly scooped him up, ending his tenure in Philly. Rico bridged the gap between John Kruk and Jim Thome (and later Ryan Howard), two of the most popular first basemen in team history. He was decent, perfectly adequate, but an afterthought compared to his other first base contemporaries. His offensive numbers pale in comparison, but after accounting for the 100 runs a year Rico saved with his glove? The difference was negligible.

The Pride of Bucks

Name: Jeff Manto

Position: 3B/1B

Career Slash Line: .230/.329/.415

Phillies Tenure: 1993

On all sides of Jeff Manto, nothing but brake lights. A complete stop. He had decided to quit baseball, and now, in March 1994, driving home from Florida to his beloved hometown of Bristol, PA, he was stuck in an 8 A.M. beltway traffic jam.

The baseball career of Jeff Manto, as mystifying and frustrating as it had been to him, was over. New York's Dallas Green had just become the latest manager to cut him, and Manto figured, "Well, if I can't make the Mets, as bad as they are, it isn't meant to be." (Olney 1995).

I've done my fair share of bowling at Bristol Lanes, so I understand better than anyone the pressures of being under the lower Bucks County microscope. Every person, every small business that sits alongside Route 13 is watching you. It's daunting. Jeff Manto and I are cut from the same cloth in a lot of ways. He had a nine-year major league career and was one of the greatest baseball players to ever come out of Bucks. I once drank three Cherry Cokes and rolled a 183. Manto's big league numbers weren't bad. He had some pop, including an epic three-game stretch in Baltimore (more on that in a bit). It was then, back in 1995 with the Orioles, where I thought his minor league bus trips were in the rearview. He just needed consistent at-bats; Manto just needed an opportunity. But his time in Baltimore didn't last. Less than a year later, he was in Japan, then back in the States bouncing from team to team. I think everyone expected the hometown guy to stick. Instead, Jeff had to settle for one of the most decorated minor league careers of all time.

He quarterbacked the Bristol High football team and was an all-area guard on the hardwood. He hung 31 on Jenkintown in a 110-67 victory in 1982, which was no easy feat (Philadelphia Inquirer 1982). As someone who has watched a lot of Bicentennial Athletic League (B.A.L.) basketball, it usually takes a team six hours to break 50. (Institute a shot clock already, PIAA). He also had a 90-plus mph fastball that attracted scouts. He struck out 17 against Morrisville in a 3-1 loss, and I don't want really to call out the Bristol High 1982 baseball team on this platform, but can my guy get a little run support (Kern 1982)? Manto parlayed a terrific high school career into a scholarship at Temple. He was as "one of us" as it gets. He probably worked in the Oxford Valley Mall food court for all we know.

The Owls captured two A-10 championships during Manto's run. One of Jeff's teammates was former MLB catcher and *Phillies Post Game Live* contributor, John Marzano. Marzano holds the Cherry and White record for career batting average, fractional points ahead of Manto who is #2 all-time for the Owls with a .412 average (Owl Sports 2021). Jeff was a 14th round selection of the Angels in the '85 Draft. There were a lot of big names that year. B.J. Surhoff went #1 overall. Will Clark went #2, and some guy named Barry Bonds went #6. The Phils selected Trey McCall at #16, because I guess they didn't have Rafael Palmeiro (#22 overall) high on their big board. Manto would reach the bigs in 1990 with Cleveland, before the Phils signed him in late '92 (The Birds would clinch a playoff berth a few days later with a 17-13 win over Washington. Heath Sherman ran wild).

Local roots be damned, Jeff had his skeptics within the organization.

One Phillies scout said that Manto was the first major league player he had ever seen with five negative tools: couldn't run, couldn't throw, couldn't field, couldn't hit or hit with power (Olney 1995).

But Jeff feasted on AAA pitching, a common theme for him, before he received a June call-up. The promotion was just a pit stop, though. He was sent back down a couple weeks later with only one base hit in 15 at-bats. He appeared in exactly one other contest for the '93 team. On September 28th, the Phils defeated the Pirates to sew up the NL East crown. I couldn't watch the game because our power went out. (PECO still owes me one). I was listening to the game on a handheld radio while studying with a flashlight for a science test the next day. I know Mariano Duncan hit a grand slam in the 7th and a little less about sedimentary rocks.

Once a team clinches, they all go out and get bombed. It's a rite of passage. When the Birds won the Super Bowl, I dumped the first bottle of champagne on my buddy's head. I didn't have one sip. Wanna know why I didn't take a sip? Because I didn't know what the hell I was doing. Act like you've been there before, they say. Well, I had never been there before. I wasted an entire bottle of champagne. I should've dumped a Bud Light Lime on my friend's dome. Once a team clinches, though, the regular season doesn't just stop. There are still games left to be played. The amazing Phils outlet, *The Good Phight*, called it "The Hangover Lineup." (Klugh 2018)

1) Ruben Amaro
2) Mickey Morandini
3) Tony Longmire
4) Ricky Jordan
5) Jim Eisenreich
6) Todd Pratt
7) Kim Batiste
8) Jeff Manto
9) Kevin Foster

How did Mick and Eisey draw the short straws? Two years later, the local guy landed in the AL East and had the best season of his career. Jeff recorded an OPS of .817 and mashed 17 long balls in just 89 games. He out-homered Brady Anderson, who would go on to hit 50 the following year. In early June, Manto went deep in four consecutive at-bats, which ties an MLB record. A pesky pop-up against

Seattle's Rafael Carmona ruined his chance at history.

June 8th: Homered in the 3rd. Pop-up in the 6th. Homered in the 7th.

June 9th: Homered in the 2nd. Walked in the 4th. Homered in the 6th. Walked in the 7th.

June 10th: Homered in the 2nd. Walked in the 4th. Flied out to center in the 6th.

If I told you these series of plate appearances happened in June 1921, you'd assume I was talking about the Babe. Manto hung around for five more seasons, jumping from Boston to Seattle, then Cleveland, the Yanks, and finishing his career with Colorado. Within that span, he continued to lay waste to the minors. In '97, while playing for the Buffalo Bisons, he homered 20 times in 54 games. Why wasn't anyone pitching around him? Why was he in AAA in the first place? Why did the '97 Phils make me watch Mike Robertson and Rex Hudler?

Jeff's jersey has been retired by half the International League. I know an inordinate amount of people who own Manto bobbleheads. Mom owns two, and they were NOT available for purchase at the yard sales. He was loved, and that's not surprising, because Philly has always loved their own. Jeff's final minor league tally was .276/.396/.504, along with 243 home runs and 920 RBIs.

He currently manages the Trenton Thunder of the MLB Draft League.

The Phenom

Name: Delmon Young

Position: Outfield

Career Slash Line: .283/.316/.421

Phillies Tenure: 2013

I remember when my mindset shifted. I was reading a 2007 ESPN chat with Keith Law, and someone asked about two rookie NL starters, Kyle Kendrick and Tim Lincecum. I'm paraphrasing here (Law put it much more eloquently), but he said Lincecum was very good and Kendrick, well, wasn't. He used stats like K/9 (strikeouts per nine innings) to support his argument. The logic made some sense, but I was still *Mad on the Internet*. I fired off responses from my couch, click-clacking away on the keyboard, waiting for Law to acknowledge my rebuttal.

"Lincecum's record is barely over .500!!! Kendrick won 10 games!!!! K-Squared has composure on the mound. He pitches his way out of trouble!!!!%$"

I may have thrown in a "Hey, numb nuts" as well. A week later, I was at the Bank and watched Kendrick give up back-to-back bombs to Troy Tulowitzki and Matt Holliday in the first inning of Game 2 of the NLDS. Holliday's blast landed in the parking lot of the Camden Aquarium and Lincecum went on to win consecutive Cy Youngs. I have an open mind. So I read *Moneyball* that winter. I adopted OB% as my go-to statistic. Slugging% replaced RBIs, wins and saves were now useless, etc, etc. The mainstream acceptance of advanced stats and Sabermetrics coincided with the birth of Twitter. Anytime a sportswriter dared to reference wins or RBIs, or opened an article with, "WAR, WAR, what is it good for … absolutely nothing," Twitter attacked like a pack of hyenas. They were relentless. I was afraid to tweet about Nintendo's *R.B.I. Baseball* for fear of *ribbie* backlash, and I loved *R.B.I. Baseball*. But you can't be too careful.

There were three players that Baseball Twitter loathed: Jeff Francoeur, Yuniesky Betancourt, and Delmon Young. The Phillies employed two of 'em. They were the antithesis of advanced stats. They took less walks than someone on house arrest. It was social suicide to have your favorite team sign one of these guys. You cringed, not because of the player, but because of the social media fallout. It was like your mom commenting on all your Instagram photos. And just when the aftermath of the signing subsided, and you were ready to move on with your life, Murray Chass or someone would pen an article about Frenchy's locker room presence, and you were forced to relive the nightmare all over again. The SIGNING of a Betancourt or a Delmon Young was much, much worse than watching them play. I didn't care if he struck out on a ball out of the zone. I've seen a gazillion bad swings. I just didn't want a Mets troll to remind me Delmon was the Phils' starting right fielder in the first place.

Young, though, had the pedigree. He was the #1 overall pick by Tampa Bay in the 2003 Draft, selected ahead of guys like Rickie Weeks (a stud in PS2's *MVP Baseball*), Aaron Hill, and Chad Billingsley, who was a Phillie not that long ago but 95% of the city has already forgotten. Young was considered a 'can't miss' prospect, but his brief tenure with the Rays was tumultuous and even that's a gross understatement. *Baseball America* named him the #1 prospect in '05, but a lack of promotion to the big club that year – and a perceived lack of communication from ownership – led to a public spat between the player and the team (Carter 2005). His agent, Arn Tellem (the same thing Ric Flair used to say before handing the mic to The Enforcer), released a statement in September of that year.

"The facts are as follows: There was never a meeting with Delmon and his family, and no one communicated a thing to Delmon or to me about why the best player in minor-league baseball was not called up in September. The lack of communication is mind-boggling, unprofessional, and something I have never

experienced in my 25 years in this business." (Carter 2005).

Rays management disputed Tellem's side of the story. In response, Delmon turned down an invitation to be recognized for the *Baseball America* honor at a Tampa home game. An early call-up in 2006 was likely, but then derailed, however, when Young was suspended a whopping 50 games for hitting the umpire with a tossed bat after a strike-three call in AAA. In Young's defense, and I'm not offering much of a defense here, but the pitch *was* outside. It was a liberal zone for Pawtucket's Jon Lester.

After the suspension, Delmon dug an even deeper hole after an interview with *USA Today.*

"I don't know what they're waiting for," Young says. "They're what, 30 games (actually 20) out of first place? They think we're going to mess up their clubhouse chemistry. B.J. [Upton] should be up there. What are they waiting for? They always have excuses." (Nightengale 2006).

That could be a quote from Young or any WIP caller.

"Let's go to Shawn in Roxborough."

"Last caller kinda stole my thunder, Ang, but I don't know what they're waiting for. They're what, 30 games out of first place? They always have excuses. Bring the young kids up already."

See? Can't even tell the difference.

Young did eventually get the call. He had a nice inaugural campaign, finishing second in the AL Rookie of the Year voting behind Dustin Pedroia. He also cursed out Rays manager Joe Maddon twice, displaying his versatility. Tampa shipped Delmon off to Minnesota after his first full season in the bigs. He was a headache, a talented headache, but a headache, nonetheless. An article in the *Tampa Tribune* covering the transaction ended succinctly with, "He's someone else's problem now." (Henderson 2007). He moved from Minnesota to Detroit, where he won the 2012 ALCS MVP. He torched the Yankees in a four-game sweep, raking two homers and collecting 6 RBIs in the series victory. But even after the postseason fireworks,

Delmon wasn't in high demand. His 18 home runs and 74 RBIs were overshadowed by a disgusting off the field incident. He pleaded guilty to aggravated harassment, stemming from an ugly physical altercation in New York City that involved his use of an Anti-Semitic slur and it makes you wonder why the Phils even bothered.

It's not clear that Delmon Young should even get a Major League contract this winter. He definitely shouldn't be anyone's starting DH next year. He's basically a platoon player at this point in his career, and as a right-handed bat, that means he should play a couple of times per week. (Cameron 2012).

Young was somehow only 27. When the Phils signed him to play right field in 2013 (seriously, why?), I thought he was *way* older. I swore he was rounding out the Tampa lineup with Jose Canseco and the Crime Dog, but maybe I was confusing him with Greg Vaughn? He homered in his Phillies debut, a 14-2 loss at Cleveland. A day later, he took a walk. Not like from his hotel room. But a base on balls. His occasional successes were empty calories, though. Fans didn't watch him lay off one breaking ball and think, "Maybe he turned a corner? Maybe we have something?" Any Young base hit or R.B.I. was like a tax refund. The extra couple of bucks were nice, but you still didn't love the I.R.S.

The Delmon Young Experiment, and the 2013 season in general, was more a sad footnote than anything else. Two years prior, the Fightins won 102 games. Now, the season video yearbook was titled, *A Game of Adjustments*, which is the most depressing thing I've ever heard. May as well name it, *Welp* or *Crap* or *Remember '08: That Was Fun, Right?* I had never seen *A Game of Adjustments* (who has), but now I was really curious. Was Delmon's two home run game in Miami in late May memorialized? Any Pete Orr at-bats I could show my future grandkids? I figured it would be an easy pull – it was only eight years ago – but assuming someone both purchased *A Game of Adjustments* AND uploaded it to YouTube was a tall order.

The MLB Shop was selling the 2013 DVD for $9.99. A bit steep, no? Maybe it's time to move this piece of history to the clearance rack, MLB Shop? Or at least throw-in a Papelbon shirsey. I considered splurging (Hell, I'm the guy who bought a Greg Graham jersey while writing my last book), but then I'd need a DVD player, too. It would be like buying an Acura Legend Coupe, just so I could listen to my MC Hammer *Too Legit to Quit* cassette tape. While the *A Game of Adjustments* contents remain a mystery, I did track down some highlights from the season. And, you know, it wasn't all bad. Dom Brown had a huge first half. Erik Kratz and Freddy Galvis went back-to-back against Aroldis Chapman for a walk-off win. John Mayberry Jr hit a walk-off grand slam against the Marlins in 11 innings. Michael Young had a couple of seeing-eye singles.

The season had its moments. But Delmon's time here? His tenure?

Bleh. He was released in August of that same year.

The Wing Man

Name: Jason Michaels

Position: Outfield

Career Slash Line: .263/.335/.407

Phillies Tenure: 2001-2005

A contrite Michaels was in uniform for Sunday night's game with Atlanta.

"The bottom line is that I would love to talk to you guys about this, but I've been advised by my attorney not to say anything," Michaels told the media. "If you guys want to talk to him, I have [business] cards." (Bostrom 2005).

Jason Michaels' numbers were much better than I remembered. It's usually the opposite. Usually I'm reading about, say, Ricky Ledée, and thinking to myself, "Wait, Ledée didn't hit 30 homers in '02? Who was I thinking of?" I've propped these players up. I've painted this rose-colored picture, where every marginal Phillies player had their career year on my watch. Baseball-Reference and ESPN and Baseball Almanac are just wet blankets really, coolers sent in by the pit boss to knock me down a peg.

"See that guy in the David Bell shirsey? No, not that one, the other guy. The one wearing the Chuck Taylors. He swears up and down that 38-year-old Kenny Lofton swiped 57 bags in '05. Baseball-Reference, would you mind taking this one?"

"Yeah, I got 'em. I'll put him in his place."

Off the field, Michaels was best known as Pat Burrell's wing man. In fact, Jason Michaels was *everyone's* wing man. I met a guy named Brendan, and honest to god, he met his wife through a Jason Michaels trade report, which is the most inexplicable way I've heard of a couple meeting since my boy from Delco married a girl from Myspace. (They both shared a love for Good Charlotte). J-Mike was *Singled Out's* Chris Hardwick, uniting love-starved folks from all over the globe. Brendan was wearing a Phils hat at a bar and a beautiful woman approached him and asked, I shit you not, "Did the Phillies trade Jason Michaels?" They struck up a conversation and have been together ever since.

I love it. Fortune favors the brave. I've used the, "Do you think Willie Green can make the leap to the next level?" icebreaker countless times but the best response I could ever solicit was, "I have a boyfriend."

Burrell and Michaels loved the Center City nightlife. The Bash Bros closed more Rittenhouse Square establishments than a health inspector, but J-Mike's propensity for the party scene got him into some serious trouble. In early July of '05, he was arrested for punching a uniformed police officer outside an Old City bar (Bostrom 2005). While I would've put my money on Plough & the Stars, research shows it was 32 Degrees. The incident took place at 3 A.M. Sunday morning, but I don't know how that's possible because the final stop of every Old City bar crawl is always Paddy's. No exceptions.

Blender magazine had rented out the club in tandem with the Live 8 concert that took place earlier that day (Kim and Gross 2005). Live 8, if you recall, was a series of synched up benefit concerts that took place on July 2nd, spread across ten different international cities. (It was the 20-year anniversary of Live Aid, which had concerts in two locations, Wembley and Philly's JFK Stadium). Every teenager and early 20-something in the Delaware Valley headed down to Live 8 with the same basic strategy – throw vodka in a Deer Park water bottle and overwhelm SEPTA's regional rails.

Most Live 8 stars, however, left town immediately after the concert. The biggest names at the party were Josh Groban, Kaiser Chiefs, rapper MC Lyte, and a squad of pro baseball players.

Just before 3 A.M., Phillies outfielder Jason Michaels left the club with several women, according to a witness, and was walking in a crowd along 2nd Street just south of Market when police officers told the group to disperse. (Kim and Gross 2005).

J-Mike did not disperse. He was arrested and released from headquarters about eight hours later. The prompt release after assaulting a cop led to Police Commissioner Sylvester Johnson ordering an inquiry into the arrest. This internal investigation was triggered by officers flooding the Commissioner's phone line and inbox with complaints about the perceived preferential treatment for the Phillies outfielder (Egan 2005). Further complicating matters was that Michaels was deemed available to play the next day. Charlie Manuel told reporters that Jason "is a good guy. He's not a troublemaker. Sometimes trouble kind of finds you." (Kim and Gross 2005). He did not get in the game on July 3rd but started the following contest (Michaels and Kenny Lofton were in a centerfield platoon). The optics weren't great, and in a bizarre footnote to this story, Michaels appeared in a celebrity dating game a couple of weeks later.

Jason Michaels, currently accused of reverse police brutality, is up for grabs in a celebrity dating game tonight at Grape Street (4100 Main St.) in Manayunk.

"Survivor" alum Gervase Peterson hosts the game, which also offers dates with NBC-10 traffic dude David Gunning and Doublemint twin Pam Moore. (Gross 2005).

Thinking maybe the organizers should've called an audible – dialed in a favor to Kyle Korver or something – but knowing Michaels' matchmaking reputation, I'm guessing both Gunning and Moore found their soulmates that night. The internal investigation concluded that the outfielder did not receive special treatment. There was an implication that his paperwork was processed more quickly than other offenders, expediting his release, but a department spokesman chalked it up to "a slow night. There were only a couple of prisoners." (Associated Press 2005). Michaels would avoid going to trial. He was placed on six months probation and ordered to complete 100 hours of community service (Salisbury 2006).

The incident is why I did a double take after seeing Jason's numbers. Fans don't remember '03 J-Mike, the guy who hit a whopping .330/.416/.569. They only know the Jason Michaels who punched a cop; the guy whose hobbies on his AOL profile included, "Center City Sips."

"Remember when J-Mike hit that big 8th inning double against the Cardinals?"

"Not really. He was the dude who wrestled the policeman, right?"

Fair or not, that story is his legacy. If James Thrash DDT'd a fireman, we'd remember that, not his inability to get off the line of scrimmage against Carolina in the NFC Championship (1 catch, 9 yards. 6 targets). Michaels hit a grand slam on September 9th, 2003 at Atlanta. A year later to the day, also at Turner Field, he had a notorious defensive gaffe. Charles Thomas hit a deep fly to center. Untouched, unaltered by a human being, the ball would've landed at the front of the warning track. Instead, Michaels bobbled the catch. The ball then popped in the air, and J-Mike bobbled it again. This time, the ball sailed over the wall for a home run. (It wasn't as bad as the homer that doinked off Jose Canseco's head, but Jason's misplay ranks up there). The Phils won regardless, but the blunder made headlines. Rollins and Polanco went back-to-back to start the game, but you don't see those home runs on social media twenty years later.

On January 27th, 2006, the team moved Michaels to Cleveland for the ageless Arthur Rhodes (Arthur had a 2.08 ERA in '05 but struggled in his lone season here). You assume the Old City incident expedited J-Mike's departure. Across town, legend has it that Brendan's future wife wasn't even gonna go out that night. The original plan was a quiet night at home, workshop some more pick-up lines for the upcoming weekend.

"You hear the Birds may move Ryan Moats to safety?"

"Heard a report that Mo Cheeks ended practice early. Wants to keep the guys fresh for the back-to-back this weekend."

But plans change. Fate intervened. Brendan's wife decided to shoot her shot.

The Scapegoat

Name: Wes Helms

Position: 3B/1B

Career Slash Line: .256/.318/.405

Phillies Tenure: 2007

I'm not proud of this story. It doesn't reflect well on me, but you have a right to know. I was at a local bar celebrating my 30th birthday. I put a $20 bill into the jukebox and was headed right to my go-to: Kansas' "Carry On Wayward Son." I made one small detour though. While shuffling through the tracks, I found another one of my favorites: "Fast Car" by Tracy Chapman. So I played it. Then I played it again. I played "Fast Car" forty consecutive times ($.50 a song). It was an out of body moment. Like have you ever been in a car and got to your destination, but don't remember driving there? I committed the act. My fingerprints were all over the TouchTunes, but it was like another force summoned "Fast Car" over and over. Still, that's no excuse. It was excessive. I get it. I get the disgust. I confided in my buddy, who was surprisingly receptive.

"Well, this should be interesting," he said, before ordering another round.

By the second time through, you heard the murmurs. People wondered aloud if the jukebox was frozen or "stuck" or "jammed." Others laughed. By the third runback, however, some people were really pissed. Two guys went on the warpath.

"Who the fuck keeps playing this song?" one screamed. My friend and I looked at each other. It was an unspoken understanding. We weren't going to 'fess up. These guys either hated Tracy Chapman's entire catalog, or they'd have preferred "Give Me One Reason" instead. They interrogated the other patrons, one by one.

"Was it you? Was it you? Do you know who did this? Do you know who played this shit?" They then approached my buddy and me, giving us the same third degree.

"We don't know who did it," my friend said. "But my boy Dave and I are going to find 'em."

We needed a plan, but working at a convenience store and managing to save just a little bit of money wasn't gonna suffice here. Let me emphasize: these dudes were pissed. A confession and buying them a Bud Light weren't going to smooth things over. At this point, we were on our fifth, sixth consecutive runback. I stopped singing four plays ago for fear of my life. Soon, the entire bar was staging a mutiny. They implored the bartender to intervene.

Bebop and Rocksteady made their rounds again. They wanted answers. They wanted someone's head on a stick.

"Whatcha find out," they asked my buddy.

"We heard that group at that table behind us laughing," my friend said. "But they just took off a few minutes ago. It had to be them. Those motherfuckers."

"Fuck," they said in unison.

We had to get the heat off us. We needed a scapegoat.

On the heels of the NLDS sweep at the hands of the Rockies, the overwhelming opinion was that Wes Helms had to go. This isn't to say that Wes in any way was to *blame* for the sweep – he registered just three plates appearances in the postseason – but people were over the Wes Helms Experience. It was like Peter Engel force-feeding us the Zack/Tori romance on *Saved by the Bell*. Why did this girl enroll at Bayside six weeks before graduation? Did her credits even transfer? Where was Kelly and Jessie during all of this?

"Let's go to Al in Media."

"I'm disgusted, King. I'm not gonna lie. I'm disgusted. This Wes Helms has to go. He has to. I can't look at him on my TV anymore. Muffing that punt yesterday in the 4th quarter at Lambeau was the final straw – a complete embarrassment. I'm sick to my stomach. I'm sick, King. Just want to get your thoughts on that."

"Al, Al, I think you mean ... the muffed punt ... that was J.R. Reed ..."

"Oh? Well get rid of him, too."

The Phils played musical chairs over at third with Helms, Greg Dobbs, and Abe Núñez. Dobbs could hit but the glove didn't translate. Núñez could defend, but really, really couldn't hit. And Wes was somewhere in the middle. Helms was a highly regarded free agent brought in that offseason. There was never supposed to be a platoon. In 278 plate appearances the year prior with the Marlins, Wes registered a massive .965 OPS. He followed that up with a .665 OPS in Philly, which can only mean he was on Jeff Conine's payroll. Bailing on Helms after the '07 season wasn't some grassroots campaign kickstarted by fans. We were aligned with the front office.

On third base: "We need to improve," said GM Pat Gillick. (Miller 2007).

The name being floated around to replace the three-headed monster was Mike Lowell (Cooney 2007). (It ended up being Pedro Feliz). Lowell was with Boston at the time, but formerly with the Marlins, so he probably would've turned into mush here, too. The Phils dodged a bullet really. After the '06 season, fans wanted someone at third who wasn't David Bell. By the summer of '07, I was stalking Bell's Tumblr and reminiscing about the good times we shared.

Besides, if there has been a storyline to this season, it has been the superior performances by the low-paid backups while the millionaires have underachieved. Kyle Kendrick, Carlos Ruiz, and Greg Dobbs have given the Phillies much more than Jon Lieber, Rod Barajas, and Wes Helms (Sheridan 2007).

My research for this chapter led me to a season preview in the *Philadelphia Daily News*.

The other corner will be manned a majority of games by Wes Helms. The righthanded power hitter has logged – no pun – 305 games at third during his seven-and-a-fraction seasons (Conlin 2007).

I read the above and immediately thought, "'Logged – no pun'? Is there a Wes

Helms poop story I should know about?" Is Wes Helms Najeh Davenport 2.0? Am I missing something? So I hit the archives. I did my homework. My research came up empty but I did find this from Reddit, which has since haunted my dreams, and now may haunt yours, too.

Wanted to share a story about Greg Maddux

With r/Braves being somewhat slow lately, I thought I'd share this story I heard about Maddux from talking with Wes Helms once.

So after games, the players will throw all their clothes into the laundry and have it taken care of for them. Whenever their clean clothes were brought back to them, there was always just a disgusting smell in the basket. As the players would dig out for their clothes, someone would always come across a sock with feces on it. No one ever admitted to it and no one said how or why it got there.

I forget how, but Wes said that eventually Greg admitted to it. When he would go to the bathroom in the clubhouse, he would bring a sock in to use instead of toilet paper, throw it into the clean clothes when nobody was looking, and pretend to be just as surprised as everyone else. (Mrb1946 2014).

WHAT? Who hurt you, Greg Maddux? Jamie Moyer would never. If this serial wiping accusation is true, pull Maddux's bust from Cooperstown immediately. Please keep me abreast of the investigation, Rob Manfred.

It wasn't all bad. He was involved in a cool moment on August 10th, when he homered in a 5-4 victory over Atlanta. Helms wore #18, the same number as John Vukovich, who was posthumously inducted into the Phillies Wall of Fame that night (Juliano 2007). It was one of Wes' five home runs that season. But it was that lack of power which was so concerning. Helms was never mistaken for Brooks Robinson over at the hot corner, but the team figured his bat would cover his inefficiencies in the field. He had just a .368 slugging%, though, a far cry from the .575 he collected with the Florida Marlins. But if you look at his career numbers, 2006 was the outlier. Not '07. It was overambitious to expect a repeat performance. The Phils didn't get a Down Year Wes Helms. They just got Wes Helms.

The Muscle

Name: Russell Branyan

Position: 3B/1B/OF

Career Slash Line: .232/.329/.485

Phillies Tenure: 2007

The Yankees are Branyan's 17th stop. That's two more stops than Matt Stairs made, and one more than Terry Mulholland made. This is sort of staggering when you consider that Branyan is only 35; Stairs was famously nomadic (I once asked an agent whether he'd ever had a player tell him to just sign with whomever offered the most money, no matter where it was. His response: "Yeah, Matt Stairs.") and played until he was 43 years old, and still Branyan already has him beat. (Miller 2012).

Who is the strongest man you know? Is it your father? Ken Patera? Mark Henry? Fletcher Cox? The guy at the gym who walks around with two water jugs because one jug just ain't enough to quench his thirst? I'm sure whoever that person is they're very strong – quads like tree trunks, biceps that could stop traffic, etc, etc. They're incredibly powerful. I won't argue that. They're just not Russell Branyan. They're not country strong like The Muscle. This chapter took me three months to write because I spent the first 2 ½ watching Branyan bombs on YouTube.

"Dave, Dave. Come upstairs! Quick! There's footage of Damian Lillard touring Malvern Prep."

"Just a minute. I'm watching this Russell Branyan 2004-2005 video montage."

He reached the 4th deck at Yankee Stadium. He hit one into McCovey Cove. He drilled the Home Run Apple at Shea. He sent an 89-mph offering from Jon Lieber to the Citizens Bank Park centerfield bullpen. Russell also has the longest home run in the history of Miller Park, a 480-foot missile off Greg Maddux (Baseball-Reference 2021). Legend has it that Maddux was so upset he pooped in *two* tube socks that night.

Smart baseball folks loved Branyan. While some talking heads would tell you that Jahil Okafor could roll out of bed and give you 20 and 10, the advanced stats community pointed to something more tangible. All Russell did was produce an OPS over .800. It didn't matter which team he was playing for, or in which park, or in which league, or which position he was occupying at that time. The Muscle may not make contact for a month, but then he'd a launch a ball into the Monongahela River to push his OPS to .804.

I suspect a lot of you do, too, because Russell Branyan might very well be the official mascot of the Baseball Prospectus era. I used to list Russell Branyan on my Friendster profile, under "Who You'd Like To Meet." In the silly Us vs. Them paradigm that made 2002-2006 so much fun, Branyan was the perfect player for Us. He was always unwanted, his skills were underappreciated, he was stupid strong, and he most likely played for each of our favorite teams at some point (Miller 2012).

Branyan was a Three True Outcome Guy. He either walked, struck out, or hit one across state lines. I'm obsessed with those types. Joey Gallo is one. Jack Cust and Mark Reynolds were others. I know it's not the prettiest baseball. Sometimes you need to move a runner or hit a sac fly. The barrage of strikeouts takes their toll. But then these guys hit a ball to Mars and you're like, "Oh, damn. I'll have what he's having." Branyan played just seven games for the Fightins. He only had nine at-bats. But you don't produce a .222/.222/.889 line without sending a couple deep into the night (hat tip to Joe Buck).

Only one year (2009) did he record more than 500 plate appearances and he promptly smashed 31 homers. I'm not sure why the entire league blackballed Branyan. Was he hitting the ball too far? Were his home runs *too* massive? That's like sitting Michael Vick in *Madden '04* because he was just a bit too quick. Or maybe the reason a team never committed to Russell was because he couldn't see?

For Russell Branyan, the secret to landing an everyday major-league job might have literally been right before his eyes.

The journeyman slugger had crossed paths for a decade with Chicago ophthalmologist Dr. Barry Seiller, or one of his colleagues in major-league clubhouses. But Branyan never took Seiller up on his offers to try the computerized vision-training program he had pioneered in the sports world.

Branyan, now the Mariners' first baseman, had dabbled with the CD-ROM software produced by Seiller's company, Vizual Edge. But it wasn't until spring training with the Milwaukee Brewers last season, when Branyan's up-and-down career was headed for the minors, that he finally embarked on a full-fledged eye-training program (Baker 2009).

I understand Branyan's plight. I was a butcher in left field – historically inept – for my softball team and got demoted to second base. I couldn't pick up the ball. I had horrible depth perception. I'd run in twenty feet, and the ball would sail over my head. Think Dave Kingman without the power tool. Half-way through the season, I got a pair of glasses. Eureka! I just couldn't see anything. That was the problem. I still got tagged with a -14 UZR (Ultimate Zone Rating), though, easily the worst rating among all qualifying beer-league outfielders.

The Phils brought Branyan over in August, and he made his first appearance in massive RFK Stadium. The Nats clung to a 2-1 lead in the top of the 8th when Manuel tapped Russell with his five fingers to pinch-hit for Antonio Alfonseca. With Ruiz on first and Jon Rauch (like there was anyone else) on the bump for the Nationals, The Muscle sent a 1-0 offering over the right field fence. Brett Myers struck out the side in the 9th for the save. My roommates and I were watching at our place in Manayunk. We weren't some geeks off the street. We knew Russell's potential range of outcomes. One of us even said, "Make a mistake, Rauch," which was an important distinction. You never say, "Hit a homer." It's like a no-hitter in that regards. You don't mention it. You don't talk about it. Kids do it all the time because they don't know any better.

"Hey, Ryan Howard, hit a homer!"

But once you're past the age of 8, that's not allowed. That's *faux pas*. Did I want Matt Stairs to send a Jonathan Broxton fastball into the stratosphere? Of course. I just wouldn't dare say it out loud. When you're watching the Birds defense, you don't ask for a turnover. You politely request a tipped ball at the line of scrimmage. Otherwise it comes off as greedy. We're not greedy. We're good people. We asked Jon Rauch to make a mistake and mistakes were made. Our request was honored. It was one of the most memorable (and underrated) nights of that '07 season.

Branyan's only other hit in a Fightins uniform was, naturally, a home run. The Phils then traded him. Three weeks after his acquisition, Russell was moved to St. Louis for a player to be named later.

"The Phils expect to know the player to be named by Oct. 15." (Zolecki 2007).

One small problem. I don't think the Phils ever got a player. I think St. Louis still owes us one. It's like we lent the Cardinals $20 and they just ducked us until we inevitably forgot about the money.

"Oh man, sorry, dude. Can you break a $500 bill? It's all I have on me."

Does stealing sit right with The Best Fans in Baseball? Are they comfortable with this thievery? I want that return. I was promised a player to be named later and it's way past later.

Russell Branyan finished his career with 194 home runs. All 194 were moonshots.

The Bounce Back

Name: Omar Daal

Position: Pitcher

Career Record: 68-78; 4.55 ERA (4.45 FIP)

Phillies Tenure: 2000-2001

"I feel sorry for those guys who get all the way to 19 – they might as well take the final step and lose 20 because [they have] all that frustration and then never be talked about," Kingman said (Lemire 2011).

I called my best friend. Whenever there was a huge signing or a big trade, I called BK. BK and I agreed on everything. We were also wrong about everything.

"Coffey is gonna put the Fly Guys over the top, buddy!"

"We're gonna pour coffee in that Cup!"

"Tartabull should hit 30 in the National League!"

"At least! Maybe 35 if teams don't pitch around him."

"I see a lot of Byron Evans in this Barry Gardner, Dave."

"I'm surprised he slipped to the second round to be honest."

Whatever reservations I had about trading Curt Schilling were washed away after a five-minute phone call. BK and I ran through each of the players in the D-Backs return one by one.

"Daal won 16 games last year. That's nothing to sneeze at."

"Yep, just been unlucky this season. I've also heard a lot of good things about this Figueroa kid."

"Definitely. I've heard he's a control pitcher. He trusts the defense behind him. That keeps his teammates engaged."

"That's a great point. Also, Travis Lee may be the best defensive first baseman in the league."

"A real cool customer, I heard. A slick fielder. And if that bat gets going ..."

"And people love this Padilla guy's stuff."

"'Electric' is the word I've heard."

BK and I threw around 'people say' or 'I've heard,' as if we had any sources of any kind. I didn't have any sources. BK was my source. We were 15, 16 years old discussing prospects on our parents' landline. We didn't read anything online. In the summer of 2000, the extent of the internet was AOL chatrooms and Cindy Margolis pictures. We didn't have regular check-ins with scouts. We didn't go to school with a kid whose neighbor's uncle was Mike Arbuckle. I don't know where we pulled these scouting reports from, but it took just a few minutes to talk ourselves into this massive haul for our star pitcher without the slightest hint of irony. What's better than one ace, we reasoned? Three aces and Travis Lee.

My buddy and I were most excited about Daal for the simple reason that we had heard of him. Omar had been in the majors since '93. He was established. My concern wasn't the team's outlook five years from now. I was thinking that if Ron Gant and co. could give Daaly some run support, we could sneak up on the 4th place Expos in the NL East. What kind of stuff did Omar have? Let's turn it over to Wikipedia:

Daal threw a deceptive fastball that rarely exceeded 85 MPH, a good changeup, and a decent curveball. When he had both control and command of his pitches, he could be difficult to hit (Wikipedia 2021).

I hope you have your ad blocker enabled, because that's straight junk ball pitcher porn.

"Deceptive fastball?" Talk dirty to me, Wiki.

"Rarely exceeded 85 MPH?" Did E.L. James write this smut?

In 2000, however, Daal's fastball lacked that trademark deception. He was 2-10 with a 7.22 ERA before the trade. The peripherals were better in Philly, but his record wasn't. By mid-September, Daal Watch was on. He was knocking on the door of infamy, staring a 20-loss season square in the eyes. Philadelphia Quakers hurler John Coleman holds the record for losses in a single season with 48 in 1883, but in his defense, JC started 65 of the Quakers' 99 games. (His 4.87 ERA was also the best on the team). In more modern times, a pitcher hadn't lost 20 games since Oakland's Brian Kingman. Daal's late season outings became a spectacle that garnered national attention.

Daal's no decision allowed Kingman to at least temporarily retain his title as the last man to lose 20 games in a season. It's one he adores so much that he felt the need to cash-in some frequent flier miles, travel across the country from Los Angeles, then drive from Baltimore just to be at the Vet last night.

"I felt like I suffered so much to do it," said Kingman who was 8-20 for the 1980 Oakland A's. "It has lasted so long and has been so fun. I want to get all the mileage out of it I can." (Brookover 2000).

I'm conflicted. On one hand, I can't fault Kingman for squeezing out a few extra minutes of fame. But following Omar Daal across the country like a groupie is a little skeevy, a little too much '72 Dolphins for my taste. Daaly's trying to finish the season strong. He's a professional. He doesn't need the hoopla. He doesn't need Mercury Morris and the boys hauling a cooler full of champagne from city to city. On a September 21st start against New York, he pitched well. He threw 6 innings and gave up just one earned run for a no decision. It was his sixth consecutive quality start. Omar, to his credit, took the attention in stride. When asked about Kingman sitting in the stands, he replied:

"I think he has to fly to Chicago now," Daal said. "He doesn't want to see me lose, so that's good." (Brookover 2000).

Daal won his next start in Chicago, pushing his record to 4-19. He scattered 10 hits across six innings to avoid history for another five days. Kind of. Omar aggravated his quad running down the first baseline after a bunt and Terry Francona shelved him for the remainder of the season. He was scheduled to start once more in the season finale in Miami.

"He's not going to pitch again," Phillies manager Terry Francona said. "I talked to him when I took him out of the game, and I told him I was proud of him. I told him if he was ok with it, I wasn't going to start him again. He was ok with it."

"I didn't do this for Brian Kingman," Francona said. "I did it for Omar." (Brookover 2000).

(Francona was fired a few days later).

Fans rolled their eyes when new skip, Larry Bowa, tagged Daal as his opening day starter in '01. The jokes wrote themselves. But then something crazy happened. Daaly's fastball rediscovered its magical deception. Like Lazarus rising from the dead, Omar Daal was back. He cleared May with a 6-0 record. At the All-Star break, he was 9-2. He was an obvious All-Star snub. The voters couldn't separate an unlucky 2000 from this newfound dominance. The loyal and underrated 'Daal House' fan club, who before would've been justified if they wore paper bags over their heads, were now collectively giving Brian Kingman and all members of the national media a giant middle finger. Go find a new punching bag. Be gone, haters. Tickets for the Omar Daal Revenge Tour were invite-only. If you didn't love Daaly at his worst, then you don't deserve him at his best.

BK knew what was up.

"Daaly is back! The best is yet to come!"

"Preach, BK! Our guy is dealing!"

Like I said, BK and I were wrong about everything. Daal finished with a 13-7 record, but his ERA from the middle of June through a September 9th start spiked to 6.02. Bowa lost faith in the crafty lefty. The '01 Phils finished a feisty 86-76. Wanting to maximize the outings from his best hurlers, Larry skipped a Daaly start so Robert Person, Randy Wolf, and Brandon Duckworth could take the bump in a critical September series against Atlanta (Hagen 2001).

Daal expressed his discontent at the time. Sources say that came after a shouting match between the pitcher and manager that was sparked by Bowa's decision to pull Daal out of a game earlier than Daal thought was appropriate (Hagen 2001).

Despite the difference of opinions, the Phils picked up Daal's option in the offseason, much to the chagrin of Omar's camp.

"Omar was probably surprised when the option was picked up. And disappointed," agent Peter Greenberg said yesterday. "He definitely wanted to know he was going somewhere else. There's no reason to hide that." (Hagen 2001).

The Fightins eventually moved on from the disgruntled pitcher, trading him to the Dodgers in November for Jesus Cordero and Eric Junge.

"At least we still have Nelly, Lee, and Padilla," I told BK after the move. "It was still a good trade. I stand by that."

"Yep, definitely. Wade and the scouts did their homework."

Travis Lee and Nelson Figueroa were gone the following year.

The (Sinker) Baller

Name: David Herndon

Position: Pitcher

Career Record: 2-8; 3.85 ERA (4.27 FIP)

Phillies Tenure: 2010-2012

I was in class with David Herndon in college. It was a community college at the time. The professor had each student stand up and say where they thought they would be in 5 yrs. He said the Indians or the Royals. I thought "this freaking guy." Joke was on me (BravesDugoutPod 2020).

Every kid has a full complement of pitches in his arsenal. There isn't anything a 9-year-old can't throw. We didn't know *how* to throw any of these pitches, but we had them in our bag regardless.

"Here comes my circle change!"

Slows their arm speed to a grinding halt

"Here comes the knuckleball!"

Proceeds to shotput a ball that lands 15 feet in front of the plate

Oh, you want a slider? No problem. Watch me drop this shoulder and flip a submarine-style frisbee ala Byung-Hyun Kim over the outer edge. Before I shipped my buddy back behind the plate (and by 'plate,' I mean a miniature orange soccer cone), I'd run through the signs.

"1" is fastball.

"2" is curveball.

"3" is change-up.

"4" is circle change.

"5" is slider.

"6" is knuckleball (I was the third Niekro Brother).

"7" is knuckle curveball (shout out to Tyler Green).

"8" is sinker.

"9" is screwball.

"10" is palm ball.

"11" was the forkball, but I couldn't throw that for strikes. My batterymate never called anything #6 - #10, which was frustrating because those were my out pitches. My knuckler danced. My screwball screwed. When I confronted him, when I asked him why he didn't call one palm ball during our five-inning simulated game, he assured me he had. He'd also been calling for the screwball and the knuckle curve. I just couldn't see how many fingers he was flashing inside his catcher's mitt. While I had ten legitimate pitches in my back pocket, David Herndon only needed one. He had the power sinker.

After his first outing in the spring, catcher Carlos Ruiz came to Herndon in the clubhouse and told him his sinker was the best he'd ever caught. Five games into spring training he hadn't surrendered a hit, much less a run (McCann 2016).

Herndon had some buzz. When he made the Fightins as a Rule 5 draftee in 2010, you saw these then foreign stats like GB% (groundball %) thrown around social media.

"David had a 58% GB rate for the Double-A Arkansas Travelers."

Huh? Is that like ERA or something? I didn't get it. I had only discovered on-base% like two years ago. My tiny head could only comprehend so much. But what I am, folks, is a follower. I spread that shit around like it was a Richard Gere gerbil rumor.

"Herndon had a 58% GB rate in the Texas League. That translates at any level."

"That's great, Dave. Did you drop off our rent check yet?"

I became David Herndon's biggest advocate, the Paul Heyman for extreme groundball pitchers. Every base hit he conceded was "bullshit" and "fluky." Every out he recorded was his supreme GB% vanquishing another foe. In 2010, the opposition hit .321 off David, which wasn't ideal, but I had a "David Herndon - Weak Grounders That Found Holes.xlsx" spreadsheet saved to my desktop and there were *a lot* of rows.

"David Herndon is just unlucky" became my battle cry. My weapon of choice was BABIP (Batting Average on Balls in Play) regression. I didn't know what BABIP was – or what it stood for – but a lot of smart people swore by it. Now so did I.

What do we want?

Regression to the mean!

When do we want it?

Now!

He threw 2 1/3 clean innings in the infamous Wilson Valdez Game. Later that season, on September 28, he pitched a scoreless bottom half of the 13th to register his first and only career save. The Phils victory eliminated Atlanta from the postseason picture and ensured a first-round date with the Cardinals. (I wasn't a big baseball fan then. I'm guessing the Phils swept St. Louis? I'm honestly not sure. I was going through an Angry Birds faze).

"I had to face Chipper, Uggla and Freeman. It was one of my favorite moments because so much was on the line. We set a franchise record for wins. We didn't want to face Atlanta again. It was (manager) Charlie Manuel's most wins. He's like an old grandpa you had.

"I punched out Chipper. The next year he sees me and says, 'Where do I know you from?'" (McCann 2016).

(Earlier that month, Herndon had a 7-walk outing in Miami. 5 of the 7 free passes he issued in 3 2/3 innings of work were intentional, and holy hell, why we were so terrified of Emilio Bonifacio).

It was a mixed bag for Herndon. Arm injuries would derail David's 2012 campaign and the Phils would waive him in October. The excitement for the sinker baller waned by year three. People gravitated to other exciting, new players: Darin

Ruf, Freddie Galvis, Jake Diekman, 33-year-old Chad Qualls, whoever. The tweets I saw from 2012 compared to two years earlier don't reference BABIP or GB%. Those later tweets aren't nearly as kind. Fans had made up their minds. Like Chip Kelly's offense, Herndon and his power sinker were ruled a failed experiment. Now, I don't remember David being ostentatiously good or bad. Not compared to other contemporaries anyway. I remember his half goatee, like I was drawing David Herndon but suddenly ran out of ink. But the reliever? His performance on the bump? That's a blur. Herndon stood out from the other bullpen arms because of that one pitch. He was the power sinker guy. That's what people remember. But when you leave that sinker up in the zone, when your flyball % is suddenly mortal, you become just like everyone else.

The Earwig

Name: Sil Campusano

Position: Outfield

Career Slash Line: .202/.260/.324

Phillies Tenure: 1990-1991

"Between Campusano and Ron Jones, the Phils got some heavy artillery off the bench."

"Definitely, Joanne. It's an embarrassment of riches really."

Everyone throws a no-hitter nowadays. It's the most watered-down feat in professional sports. In the first six weeks of the 2021 season, six no-hitters were hurled, seven, if you include Madison Bumgarner's 7-inning outing. I couldn't tell you who threw any of the six. It was probably some 5th starter for the Angels, or maybe Brett Tomko or Pat Rapp was brought in for a spot start. Beats me. It's inconsequential. The Mariners got no-hit twice in two weeks. It's commonplace now. There used to be these "no-hitter alerts" back in the day that would scroll along the bottom of your TV.

"ALERT: Eric Milton is perfect through 7 2/3."

It meant something. You were like, "Shit, Eric Milton must be dealing." Do no-hitters even lead the top of *SportsCenter* anymore? They're probably sandwiched in between some college hockey highlights and Roy Firestone's exclusive interview with Jim Courier. With the reliance on launch angle and the home run ball, strikeouts are way up. If I had a nickel every time I heard Tom McCarthy tell me, "That's the 15th strikeout by Phillies hitters tonight," I would have about $610.20. Everyone swings from the heels, regardless of the count. Kevin Stocker used to choke up on his bat like he was holding Donatello's bo staff. Now? A player guesses off-speed and lets it rip.

Silvestre 'Sil' Campusano was nicknamed 'Earwig,' for – as one site even admits – "obscure reasons" (En Academic 2021). The genesis of the moniker is a mystery. I couldn't find anything on Ol' Earwig, and even Baseball-Reference, the foremost authority on player nicknames, is sitting this one out. For those not well-versed in entomology, an earwig is a nocturnal insect with pincers. There is a myth about the bug that they crawl into your ears and FEED ON YOUR BRAIN, which makes sense because no one has forgotten about Sil Campusano. Earwig *literally* has been living rent free in your head for thirty years.

Campusano made his major league debut with Toronto on opening day 1988 in the shadows of a disgruntled superstar. George Bell, brother of former Phillies shortstop Juan Bell, had won the AL MVP in '87, but was mad. To avoid some wear and tear on his knees, the team planned to move Bell to the DH role and George had zero interest in placating. The opening in the outfield provided an opportunity for the rookie Campusano who beat out future/former/future Phillie Rob Ducey.

(The Phils famously traded Rob Ducey to the Blue Jays, and then reacquired the left-handed hitter in a span of ten days. It's my 5th favorite moment in Philly sports history, just behind the Birds beating the Falcons in the NFC Championship).

Back to George Bell. He told the media, "If they want to win, they'll play me in the outfield. If they want to lose, they'll play me at DH. They'd better leave me alone." (Fung 2021). GM Pat Gillick fired back with the tried-and-true "stick to sports" response, a reliable retort normally reserved for athletes and beat writers with dissenting political views.

"George better stick to playing baseball and not worry about a lot of other things. ... I don't think anyone wants to go out there (on the field) and make an ass of himself. ... As far as I was concerned, there was no misunderstanding," general manager Pat Gillick said after Bell arrived in camp (Fung 2021).

Sil steered clear of the drama. When asked by reporters about the volatile situation, he responded diplomatically, "All I do is look at the lineup, and if my name is there, I play." (Associated Press 1988). On opening day in Kansas City, Campusano played centerfield and went 1-4 in the 9th spot. Bell begrudgingly batted clean-up in the DH role and hit three home runs off Royals starter Brett Saberhagen. A half-decent start, George. Bell's time in the DH role was brief, however. He moved back to LF in mid-April, in large part due to the massive struggles of Campusano who was benched just two weeks into the season. Sil hit just .218/.282/.359 for the year. It would end up being the highest OPS of his career. The Jays gave up on Earwig and the Fightins scooped him up in the 1989 Rule 5 Draft.

Due to Lenny Dykstra's strained right torso, Campusano was the lead-off hitter to begin the 1990 campaign at Wrigley Field (Bamberger 1990). It was short-lived – Dykstra was a starter in that year's All-Star Game – and Sil only recorded 18 hits that season. But, man, one of those hits was a big one.

Pittsburgh's Doug Drabek was fantastic. Winner of the NL Cy Young, he went 22-6 with a 2.76 ERA, staring down hitters with a moustache that would make Alan Jackson tip his cowboy hat. On July 29th, Drabek gave up two hits to the Phils in a 2-1 complete game victory. He walked 7 batters. He threw 150 (!) pitches that day. Jesus, Jim Leyland. Could you get Bill Landrum or Stan Belinda loose in the pen? Five days later, Doug again squared off against the Fightins – this time at the Vet. Any hope that a tired Drabek would be ripe for the picking was fool's gold. Phils starter Bruce Ruffin didn't have his best stuff on this night. He lasted just 1 ⅓ innings. Don Carman and Jeff Parrett didn't fare much better. The Pirates pillaged the Fightins staff, tuning them up for 11 runs through five. John Kruk walked in the 5th, but that was it. Drabek was dealing. The local nine entered the bottom half of the 9th trying to avoid infamy.

1990 was an anomaly for no-hitters. Seven were hurled that season (second behind 1884's 9 no-nos) and by big names, too. Nolan Ryan tossed two. Randy Johnson, Dave Stewart, Fernando Valenzuela, and Dave Stieb each had one. Terry

Mulholland would throw one a couple weeks later for the Phils (Baseball-Almanac 2021). The Phils, though, remained above the fray. They hadn't been no-hit since the Cardinals' Bob Forsch blanked them in '78. Sure, they were a breeding ground for ineptitude in the early 1900s (Frank "Noodles" Hahn and George "Hooks" Wiltse's stuff were moving), but they had a clean sheet in the 1980s. That streak, though, was in peril on August 3rd.

Charlie Hayes led off the 9th with a groundout. Ricky Jordan then struck out swinging. Next up was Campusano. He didn't start the game. He entered after Dykstra was pulled due to the blowout. He had never faced Drabek. In fact, he would never face Drabek ever again. I watched that game with my dad and brother. My pops gave his standard, "Can't anyone hit this guy?" line after each out, which is what every dad over the age of 45 says during a baseball game. That and, "Can't anyone get a bunt down?"

I was lying on my living room floor, a pillow underneath me, eating a pretzel and chip sandwich. You got a bag of chips and a bag of hard pretzels. Grab one of each, and ta-da. You have a sandwich. My position gradually changed. Kids move closer and closer to the TV as the anticipation builds. By the time Ricky Jordan walked back to the dugout, I was the girl from *The Ring*.

"3-2 pitch, swing and a line drive hit to right centerfield – I can't believe it!"
- Harry Kalas (Wuench 2021).

"I wasn't nervous at all," he said afterwards. "I didn't feel any pressure. You either get a hit or you don't. It's no big deal." (Carchidi 1990).

That's exactly something a guy who entered the game 9-48 with a .188 average would say. Anyone with a half a brain knows that Sil loves the ball up in the zone. Doug didn't do his homework and paid dearly. He settled for a complete game shutout. Big whoop. They're a dime a dozen. Now, there was a bit of controversy surrounding the hit. Some fans *booed* after the Campusano base knock. They wanted to witness history. (I'm horrified).

Some of the Phillies came out of the dugout and made angry gestures at their fans.

"It was a little discouraging," said Tom Herr. "It's kind of frustrating when the fans are rooting against the home team. The guys weren't real happy about it." (Carchidi 1990).

That was the peak of Sil's tenure. His most notable moment in 1991 was his late arrival to spring training. Visa problems delayed his trip from the Dominican Republic, and manager Nick Leyva expressed his disappointment before delivering this back-handed compliment.

Leyva said there's a possibility Campusano will make the Phillies as an extra outfielder. "It will probably be him or John Morris," Leyva said. "But Sil is the kind of guy who can come off the bench, and I think he's at a stage in his career that that's the type of guy he's going to be." (Brookover 1991).

Campusano was released following a disappointing '91 campaign where he hit just .117 in 35 at-bats. But put aside the struggles. *Everyone* remembers Sil's big hit. No one recalls the 27 outs Doug Drabek recorded. Just the one he didn't get.

The Trade Return

Name: Phillippe Aumont

Position: Pitcher

Career Record: 1-6; 6.80 ERA (5.26 FIP)

Phillies Tenure: 2012-2015

"The Phils traded Cliff Lee."

"Huh? For who? For what?"

"I don't know yet, Ricky Watters. My mom texted me."

When you think of awful Philadelphia sports trades, the Cliff Lee deal to Seattle isn't the first one mentioned. It's not even First Team All-Crappy Trade. May not even be Second Team. The move was horrific; don't get me wrong. It's just not top of mind. When you're asked to name an awful move in the city's history, it's the Moses for Jeff Ruland deal, or the Barkley trade, or flipping Larry Bowa and a young Ryne Sandberg for Iván DeJesús. For me, it's the Barkley deal, and that's my go-to because the Sixers were so wretched post-swap. Few fans consider the Lee trade the city's worst, because the Fightins were so good regardless. The Phils traded Lee for pennies, but they acquired Roy Halladay, so who cares, right? It's like if I won $1 million dollars and then paid $25,000 for a Milt Thompson rookie card. It's a bad investment, yeah, but I still have $975,000. The December 2009 move has been scrubbed from our consciousness because two more NL East titles were right around the corner. And hell, 364 days later, Lee was back anyway.

Cliff just went on sabbatical for a year. That's how I choose to remember it. At my college, a lottery system was used to select upperclassmen housing. The on-campus apartments were the prize jewel. The lower the number, the greater the odds of getting an apartment. Well, my *sophomore year*, I got written up for something silly. The school added like 40,000 points to my lottery number. If you had a lottery number between 1 and 300 you were guaranteed an apartment. My lottery number was like 48,236. All that was left was the upperclassmen *dorms* in the bone zone. Nobody knew where these dorms were located, because no one ever had a reason to go there. It was like asking me to point to Manitoba on a map.

"No, Dave. That's Utah."

How should I know? Do I have Winnipeg Jets season tickets? Anyways, I did my one-year sentence in the upperclassmen dorms and was reintegrated with society my senior year. Fans didn't see a point in harping over the gap year. We were just happy to have our Cliff back. The decision to move Lee was triggered by financial reasons (Divish 2009). The organization said they couldn't afford both pitchers, but the implication was that they couldn't afford to roster both pitchers in 2011 and beyond. So they chose Doc. Lee was set to only make $8 million in 2010 but was in the final year of his contract. The team correctly assumed Cliff would command a monster pay raise, except the Phillies were the team who ended up giving Lee that money anyway. It's like drinking White Claws on the beach because you're counting carbs, but then ordering funnel cake on the boardwalk after you've had eight Claws.

In addition to the financials, the team figured they could replenish a depleted farm system by moving the lefty. That thought process is common. It's just usually the lousy teams moving stars for young prospects – not the defending NL Champs. The Phils gave up Kyle Drabek, Michael Taylor, and Travis d'Arnaud for Halladay, and Carlos Carrasco, Jason Knapp, Jason Donald, and Lou Marson for Lee in '09.

"If we had just acquired Roy, and not moved Lee, we would have been in position to have lost seven of the best ten prospects in our organization," Amaro said. "That is not the way you do business in baseball." (ESPN.com News Services 2009).

I understood the financial aspect. Actually, I didn't understand the financial aspect. It wasn't my money. Keep 'em both. And besides, do you remember how rabid the Phillies fanbase was in '09? People would have walked in traffic for Clifton Phifer. Send us a link to a GoFundMe, and fans would've raised all the money the organization needed by lunchtime. I would've sold that Milt Thompson rookie I bought for $25K. I'd have taken a bath on it, but it was for the greater good. The return for Lee – Aumont, Tyson Gillies, and J.C. Ramírez – was met with a collective 'meh.' "Underwhelming" and a "win for Seattle" was the consensus and a lousy way to kick off the holiday season. Like most, my original Christmas plans involved caroling and capping the Rutgers/UCF St. Petersburg Bowl Game. Instead, I was forced to pivot. I scoured the internet for Mariners prospects rankings. I tried sneaking behind ESPN's paywall to get Keith Law's thoughts. None of it was encouraging.

Buster Olney

One veteran talent evaluator's take: Only clear winner in the deal is Seattle. Prospects sent to Philly iffy, Blue Jays got OK haul. (Olney 2009).

ESPN's SweetSpot

Dave Cameron really, really, REALLY *likes what the Mariners seem to be doing. The big finish:*

"This is, quite frankly, a heist. The Mariners are getting a Cy Young caliber pitcher for some decent-but-not-great prospects. They aren't giving up Morrow. They aren't giving up Saunders. They aren't even giving up Triunfel." (Neyer 2009).

FanGraphs

The Cliff Lee to Seattle portion of this trade just seems very light in return for the Phillies. They're getting two power arms with a lot of questions marks and a speedy center fielder without a lot of power. None of these guys are top tier prospects. This is the best Philadelphia could have gotten for Lee? Really? A pu-pu platter of interesting, high-risk guys not really close to the majors for a Cy Young-quality pitcher who is already well on his way to Type A free agency?

And, even if that's true, why clear $8 million from the books by trading Lee?

Surely, you could have moved Joe Blanton without eating any of his salary, even if you didn't love the deals being offered. Or, how about this – don't sign J.C. Romero, Brian Schneider, and Ross Gload, whose 2010 salaries are about equal to Lee's. (Cameron 2009).

The reaction wasn't pretty. I wrote something similar about the Sixers selection of Kenny Payne in the 1989 NBA Draft. Draft grades and instant trade analysis aren't the end-all be-all, but it's nice to have a pundit in your corner. After Chip Kelly selected Marcus Smith, the reaction was, "Who the hell is Marcus Smith?" You needed something to hang your hat on, some anonymous scout who praised Smith's high motor, or a blogger who thought he'd be an instant contributor on special teams. You aren't picky. A seven-second YouTube clip of Smith stuffing a running back from Eastern Kentucky would do. Nobody was in Ruben Amaro's corner. No one endorsed the return.

The consensus was correct. Aumont was the most successful of the three prospects by default. Tyson Gillies never reached the majors, and J.C. Ramírez pitched just 18 games for the Phils, registering a mammoth 7.50 ERA. Phillippe made 46 appearances spread across four seasons in Philly. His big fastball was accompanied by serious control issues. Aumont didn't concede a home run in his first two seasons in the league (34 innings), but it's tough to square one up if nothing is around the plate. The team sent him down to AAA in July 2013 and you could feel the exasperation as Rich Dubee discussed the big righty.

"I think he's got one ground-ball out this month," Dubee said. "He should be a sinkerball, ground ball machine. His fastball has been flat."

"Whether he thinks Triple-A is not challenging enough to him or he has to pitch here, whatever," Dubee said. "I think he has to do some self-evaluation after every game. How did he throw the ball and where the ball was in reference to the strike zone? Was it knee high or above? Was it sinking?" (Housenick 2013).

He never did figure it out. Aumont split time between the minors and Philadelphia. He made sporadic appearances for the Phils in 2014 and 2015, pitching 9 2/3 innings total and registering a 19.06 and 13.50 ERA respectively. The Phils released him in July of that year. 2014 was Cliff's last year in the majors and by '15, the team was barely recognizable. They were a shell of their former selves. I didn't see fans, though, using the Aumont release as another opportunity to mourn over the Lee return. There weren't harbored feelings of opportunities lost. Everyone had moved on. Why focus on the bad, people reasoned, when 2007-2011 was so good?

The Ageless One

Name: Fernando Valenzuela

Position: Pitcher

Career Record: 173-153; 3.54 ERA (3.61 FIP)

Phillies Tenure: 1994

"I spent a little over ten years with Dodger blue. I hope I can start a new career in red." (Associated Press 1994).

It was a one-for-one deal. My friend Jay and I had agreed to trade Sega Genesis games for two weeks. I was lending him my *World Series Baseball* for his *WWF Raw*. Saving games or seasons or missions or whatever was much simpler back then. You moved the cursor to 'save' and pressed 'C.' When Nintendo 64 and PlayStation were introduced, they pushed these memory cards, these silly add-ons meant to massage a few more dollars from your pocket. Or your parents' pocket anyway.

"Oh, you weren't gonna play this entire season of *NCAA Football '99* in one sitting? You don't have 32 hours blocked off? Well then. You better get mom to take your ass to GameStop and pick up a memory card."

(My PlayStation talked to me. I thought it was weird too). At the time, I was *deep* into a *World Series Baseball* season with the Brewers. The entire city of Milwaukee, nay, the entire state of Wisconsin rallied behind my Brew Crew. We had an 18-game lead over the White Sox. Robin Yount discovered the Fountain of Youth. Greg Vaughn was driving the ball to all fields. Cal Eldred and Ricky Bones had solidified the rotation. Things were clicking. The team was loose. The town was buzzing. Two weeks later, when Jay returned the cartridge, there was no 18-game

AL Central lead. Greg Vaughn *didn't* have 42 bombs. Ricky Bones *wasn't* having a breakout campaign. Jay erased my season. I went down to season mode, and what's this, a 2-1 Phillies team on ROOKIE Level? Excuse me. Do my eyes deceive me? First off, how did you lose a game to the CPU on Rookie level? And two, where the hell did Greg Vaughn's 42 home runs go? It was bad form by Jay, horrible decorum. He should've called, asked if he could override my season. I would've said no, but I'd have appreciated the gesture. Play some exhibition games, Jay. Do a home run derby; I don't care. But he had no right. He had no claim. You can't just go and upend someone's life like that. If I borrow my friend's car, I can't just go and paint it purple. It doesn't work like that. But you know what's crazy? When I presented this story to Twitter, some of you animals sided with Jay! Some of you thought it was in his right! That my poor Brewers' magical year, which got erased from the record books like the '94 Expos, was just the cost of doing business, collateral damage in the heartless world of Sega game swaps. Were you raised by wolves? Please – and I say this sincerely – be better. R.I.P John Jaha and co.

My lasting childhood memory of Fernando Valenzuela isn't in a Dodger uniform. It's not his brief stop in Philly either. It's Fernando Valenzuela, Oriole. He was on the Baltimore staff in *World Series Baseball* and the only pitcher who had a screwball. I loved him. If I wasn't the Orioles, I played with the Marlins (Charlie Hough) or Pirates (Tim Wakefield). It was a trash move, I admit, like picking E. Honda in *Street Fighter II* and doing the Hundred Hand Slap over and over. So I've heard. I would never stoop to such levels.

Fernandomania ran wild in 1981. The Dodgers called him up in September the year prior and named him the opening day starter the following season. He won his first eight starts, all complete games, and accumulated five shutouts during that span. The historic run turned Fernando into a cultural phenomenon. After a home win over the Expos (9 IP, 2 ER), his ERA *rose* to 0.50. His stardom was unparalleled. He was arguably the most popular MLB player of the last fifty years, a full-on celebrity. Valenzuela would lose his next start, however. The defending champs –

your Philadelphia Phillies – defeated the lefty, 4-0. Schmidt homered. Marty Bystrom threw seven strong. In Game 3 of the World Series that year, he tossed a 149-pitch complete game as LA slipped past the Yanks, 5-4. The Dodgers would go on to win the series in six. Valenzuela, to date, remains the only player to capture both the Rookie of the Year and Cy Young award in the same season.

Fernando was still just 33 when the Phils signed him in June of '94. It was believed by many, though, that he was much, much older than his stated date of birth. In fact, so many people questioned his age that the *Los Angeles Times* once printed a copy of his birth certificate (Jaffe 2021). In the "People Also Ask" section of Google, one of the questions that populates when you search for the lefty is, "How old is Fernando Valenzuela really?" as if Google has the REAL answer in the back.

"Google, how old is Fernando Valenzuela?"

"He's 60, Dave."

"No, no, Google, how old is Fernando Valenzuela *really*?"

whispers

"Between us, Dave? No bullshit? He's 72."

He is wearing No. 33. We are asked to believe that matches his age. Barring his submission to carbon dating, you have to take his word for it (Lyon 1994).

(The '93-'94 Sixers rostered Manute Bol, whose age too was heavily scrutinized. 'Nute was listed at 31 years old that season). Valenzuela last played with the Dodgers in 1990. He moved to the Angels, then to the Mexican League, to Baltimore and then back. The Phils, ravaged by injuries in their rotation, plucked him from the Jalisco Cowboys, and wouldn't you know, I had a cousin who spent some time in Jalisco in '94. What are the chances, right? When the news broke, he sent me a postcard with a quick scouting report detailing what the Fightins were getting.

Hola, Dave!

I'm sure you heard about El Toro donning the red pinstripes. I got Cowboys season tix. Believe me, the kid still has it. Wily, pitches backwards. You're getting a good one.

You like this Bill Romanowski trade for the Birds?

- Cousin Tim

Most believed Valenzuela's big league days were behind him. The Phils were the only organization to contact his agent, Tony DiMarco, after DiMarco sent out feelers to over a dozen teams (Associated Press 1994). Among fans, though, I think there was a healthy curiosity. If nothing else, he was a household name. The Phils wouldn't have another former Cy Young winner take the bump until Cliff Lee's debut in '09 (Zolecki 2009).

"Wait, Chris Brock never won a Cy Young, Dave?"

No.

Fernando was outstanding. Don't let his lone win in a Fightins uniform fool you. Fregosi handed him the pill just four days after signing. He threw 6 innings of 0 ER ball against the Marlins. He made seven starts in total, never giving up more than 3 earned runs. His one win came at the Vet against his former Dodger mates. Valenzuela was pulled in the 9th that game with the Phils up 9-3. Paul Quantrill did his best to cough up the lead, but closer Doug Jones sent the fans home happy.

Valenzuela's final outing in Philadelphia came on the last game before the '94 strike. There was this surreal moment on the telecast when Whitey rattled off his customary happy birthday wishes to some of the Philly faithful.

"Jim and Franklin Bishop will be 99 years old tomorrow. Of course, we won't be on tomorrow." (JDP2 2021).

Damn. That hit me harder than the *Dinosaurs* series finale. The play on the field was an afterthought. (Fernando pitched eight strong but got a no decision. The Phils won, 2-1). With the looming strike, none of it mattered. Valenzuela's stint intersected with a particularly meaningless and dreary time in Phillies history. The '94 team, much like the '94 MLB season, was dead man walking.

For most of the Phillies anyway, the strike was actually a relief. Hopelessly out of the race, playing their worst baseball in two years, Phillies players privately welcome the break in the misery, while publicly lamenting the need for a work stoppage (Fitzpatrick 1994).

Fernando was brought into eat innings while the entire baseball landscape played out the string. But his brief Phillies tenure and subsequent resurgence resurrected his career. He signed with San Diego in '95 and went 21-11 over the next two seasons. Valenzuela is arguably the biggest name that people have *zero* recollection of playing here. It's like you discovered years later that Pelé had a cup of coffee with the Atoms, or Dominique Wilkins played under Johnny Davis. We didn't get El Toro at the height of Fernandomania, but even at 33, or 43, or maybe even 53, Valenzuela was still pretty darn good.

The Man of the People

Name: Sal Fasano

Position: Catcher

Career Slash Line: .221/.295/.392

Phillies Tenure: 2006

"Sal's been dialed in lately."

"Yep, 1-4 last night. Went 1-5 last Sunday. And that Fu Manchu ..."

"She's a beauty, isn't she?"

In response to a Todd Zolecki article that named Chris Coste the biggest cult hero in Phillies history, *The Good Phight* podcast made the case for Sal Fasano (Zolecki 2019). The Good Phight folks are correct here (Stolnis, Roscher, and Klugh 2019). The answer is Sal. Fans were obsessed with the loveable backstop, and truthfully – with respect to Coste and Wilson Valdez – the only other player I'd even consider in Fasano's class was not even a Phillie at all. Well, he was, eventually, but not at the height of the city's infatuation. That would be former Marlins outfielder Logan Morrison who had like a six-month bromance with Phillies Twitter. Outside of Sal spiking the ball down the *third* baseline on an attempted fake throw to *second* (this happened at Joe Robbie Stadium, the House of Horrors), I can't recall anything he did. He played just 50 games for the Fightins. He had an OB% of .284. Yet ask someone which player they'd like to have a bite with, and Fasano tops the list.

Sal was a character actor who drew his fair share of plumber comparisons. Was it tied to a stereotype of the plumbing industry, or because he was an Italian guy who looked like Mario? I personally don't think Sal looked like the overall-wearing,

Tanooki Suit rocking, princess rescuer, per se, but I saw the resemblance with Captain Lou Albano who *played* Mario in the criminally underrated *The Super Mario Bros. Super Show!* Shoutout to the Family Channel. Up next, we have *Shop 'til You Drop*, followed by a six-hour block of *The 700 Club*.

Sal checked all the boxes.

Affable and unpretentious first name? Check.

Nice guy? Check.

A Fu Manchu thicker than the sawgrass in the Everglades? Check.

"When I think of Sal Fasano, however, I think of greatness. Not of Willie Mays or Ted Williams greatness, but of a uniquely excellent human being who, were class and decency the most valued standards of a career, would be the easiest Hall of Fame inductee of all time."

My first interaction with Sal came some eight years ago, when I had been asked by my editors at Sports Illustrated to track down some pudgy, all-or-nothing Triple-A catcher who'd been hit by more than 20 pitches while playing for the Omaha Golden Spikes of the Pacific Coast League. When I dialed Fasano's cell phone, I assumed he'd be either in his apartment or at the ballpark.

"Hey, Jeff, great to hear from you," Sal said after I introduced myself.

"But lemme ask you a favor. Could you call back a little later? I just got hit by another pitch, and I'm in an ambulance heading for the hospital. I think I broke a finger ..." (Pearlman 2017).

We liked having Sal around. Yeah, I'd trust Fasano to replace the PVC piping underneath my hall bathroom sink, but I was more interested in sitting around a campfire with him – cooking up some dogs while he shares his thoughts on pitch counts and the meaning of life. (Once you get past the philosophical discussion, ask him to write up your wedding invitations. No joke, he's a self-taught calligraphist). Sal was our friend. He would do anything for us, and us for him. We look past our friends' imperfections. When Fasano was late on a 91-mph fastball, the collective response was, "Well, Sal's trying his best," not, "I wonder what Paul

Bako is up to."

Sal Fasano was in the bullpen, catching starter Jon Lieber's warm-up for Game 2 of Sunday's doubleheader when he saw the sign. A group of fans, calling themselves "Sal's Pals" were cheering for the backup catcher in the bleachers.

One week into his Phillies career, Fasano already has a fan club.

"I've never had anything like that happen before," Fasano said. "It kind of lifts your spirits and makes you feel good."

Asked what might prompt "Sal's Pals" to embrace a veteran backup, Fasano guessed it's his appearance.

"It's not every day you get (to root for) a guy with a big afro and a Fu Manchu," he said. (Lauber 2006).

Fasano has a point. Garry Maddox hadn't been on the team in twenty years (check out his 1980 Topps card). Sal's Pals were the real deal, and second in my official ranking of Phillies fan groups. (The Wolf Pack tops the list). The fan club was loyal and loud and donned fake moustaches. Given Fasano's personality, "Pals" fit. It was seamless. It wasn't forced – looking at you Padilla's Flotilla. And yeah, 'Padilla' didn't give you much to work with from a rhyme scheme standpoint, but Sal's Pals could've phoned it in and called themselves, Sal's Cows. Fasano famously sent twenty pizzas up to his Pals in the right field upper deck, which had me wondering if I hitched my wagon to the wrong backup catcher. All Mark Parent gave me was angst and some ill-timed double plays.

Normally, these reserve backstops spell the starter on day games. Mariner teammates jokingly called John Marzano, "Johnny NFL," because he "only played Sundays." (Stefano 2021). 90% of the Phillies games I've attended were on Sunday afternoons. Looking back, I don't know if I ever saw Daulton or Lieberthal actually play, but I could reenact Gary Bennett's walk from the on-deck circle to home plate step by step. Due to a strained left hip for the 34-year-old Mike Lieberthal – '06 was his last year in a Phils uniform – Fasano soaked up a lot of innings (Parent 2006). He wasn't some special attraction who was dusted off once a week like Pat

Neshak (I kid, I kid). Big Sal was a fixture. Now the incumbent starter, the team promoted Chris Coste to serve as Fasano's backup. In early July, though, Sal left a game with swelling in his knee (Salisbury 2006). The timing of his injury coincided with Lieby's return, and while Fasano was loved, he wasn't loved for his bat. The team designated him for assignment and stuck with Coste, who had an impressive .881 OPS that season.

The Fightins worked out a trade with New York. The Phils in return received minor leaguer Hector Made, who never advanced past Double-A ball. The Yankees enforced their silly clean-shaven rule, making Fasano trim twenty inches off his luscious locks – one inch for every pizza he sent up to Sal's Pals (King III 2006). His Fu Manchu was also gone, replaced with a moustache so generic that if you glued it above Tom Selleck's lips no one would blink twice. It was a cookie-cutter Sal. It wasn't our Sal. His Pals followed his journey to the Bronx out of loyalty for their blue-collar hero. Philadelphians are good like that. But a Sal Fasano who visits Fantastic Sam's twice a month isn't a Sal Fasano I choose to remember. The burly receiver and the fans built something special. Then New York got their grubby hands on him. They didn't know what do with a Sal Fasano, but we shouldn't be surprised. First, the Yanks clipped Sal's hair. Then they clipped his wings.

The Entitled

Name: Sean Rodriguez

Position: 2B/OF/1B

Career Slash Line: .226/.301/.379

Phillies Tenure: 2019

No one retweets the retraction. A controversial statement or sound clip, that's what goes viral. The clarification, though? Nah, no one cares. That's futile. The damage is already done.

@Wojespn

Sixers sending Hornacek to Utah for K Malone

7:42 PM · Feb 24, 1992

981,523 Retweets 2,635,924 Likes

@Wojespn

Sorry, that's J Malone

7:47 PM · Feb 24, 1992

2 Retweets 8 Likes

It's nothing new, and it transcends sports. It's the same thing in politics, Hollywood, etc. You don't get a do-over. You can apologize. You can have a PR firm or an agent craft a statement, but that doesn't make the front page. Who actually remembers Jimmy the Greek's apology?

Sean Rodriguez called Phillies fans "entitled." Hold on, I'll be right back. Just one sec.

...

...

…

…

…

…

…

Sorry, I'm back. Had to grab my Tom Brady jersey from the dryer.

"Let's go to Jerry in the Northeast."

"Ike, can you believe this guy? Entitled? We're entitled? Philly fans are entitled? I've been a season ticket holder since '73.

"Right. You're loyal. You're a diehard …"

"My dad used to take me to old Connie Mack Stadium. I'd cut this Rodriguez today. I wouldn't even let him on the team bus. The nerve of – "

"Jerry? Jerry? You still there? We may have lost Jerry. Let's go to Wayne in Mount Holly."

Has Sean checked in on the Phils since 2011? What do we have to be entitled about? Do I believe the world owes me something because I watched Tony Gwynn Jr get 105 at-bats in '14? Yeah, I do actually. I am owed something. We're all owed something. Sean has a point. I think I'm entitled to one measly second wild card before my 70th birthday. The problem with accusations from hometown athletes is that the city is put back on the defensive. All past transgressions now resurface. Criticism of Philadelphians is never in a vacuum. Getting labeled as 'entitled' is the gateway drug. It snowballs – pun intended. First, it's Rodriguez' comments. By the early afternoon, I have some out-of-towner texting me about the Santa Claus incident.

"Dude, your city booed Santa."

"IT WAS FIFTY YEARS AGO. SANTA WAS DRUNK."

The entire story came out of left field. We were minding our own business, trying to merge on to the Vine Street Expressway while our favorite baseball team was waist-deep in their annual late summer swoon. Standard fare really. Rodriguez uttered those fateful words – on August 26, 2019 to be exact – *after* a win, AFTER he hit a walk-off home run in the 11th to beat the Pirates. He sabotaged his own moment. It was like if Brandon Graham put on a Tony Romo jersey during the Lombardi Trophy ceremony.

During his postgame comments, Rodriguez called out some Phillies fans for their behavior towards players.

"Think about it. Who is looking bad and feeling entitled when you hear stuff like that?" Rodriguez said about the criticism. "I'm not the one booing. I'm not the one screaming. I'm not the one saying pretty disgusting things at times. That seems pretty entitled. You're just making yourself look pretty bad as an individual, as a person, as a fan. ... There's still a lot of good fans, though, and those are the ones I hear."

Rodriguez said fans really show their true colors "through the thick and thin."

"So when you act a certain way toward somebody because you don't feel like they're doing what they need to do, just look at life in general. I mean, we want to win. There's nobody in here that doesn't want to win. You got to just basically sit there and say, 'Look, let me see if I can help him get out of what he's in. Let me see if I can be encouraging enough to basically help an individual.' That's the harder thing to do, the easier thing is just to scream 'boo.' 'Let me think of something to say that actually might be encouraging.' You know, it takes effort," Rodriguez said. (CBS/Associated Press 2019).

Sean made some valid points. Sure, a little more positivity wouldn't hurt, but 99.99% stopped reading after being called 'entitled.' The headlines from his post-game comments weren't, "Rodriguez: We want to win." It was, "This guy who has played 55 games with the team called Phillies fans 'entitled.'" The insult triggered a two-fold reaction:

1) How dare you.
2) Wait, who called us 'entitled?'

Predictably, we took the criticism well. Angelo Cataldi told him to "shut up and play." Others wanted him cut. Another local media personality called him a "pathetic dude." (McQuade 2019).

"Do you have any red tape, Casey? I'm changing the number of my Rodriguez jersey to #63 for Joely."

The fallout was immediate.

Rodriguez has been booed loudly since making those comments after his walk-off home run. He was booed when he was announced Tuesday night and before each of his plate appearances. The crowd cheered when he was hit by a pitch Tuesday (NBC Sports 2019).

Well, fans are consistent if nothing else. If you throw us red meat, we're gonna stuff our faces. After being booed once more the following night, he clarified his comments.

"I wasn't trying to insult anybody with what I said," Rodriguez told reporters. "I'm very similar to the Philly fan base. I'm a very passionate person. I'm a passionate player. I show up every day and I don't leave anything in the tank.

"Could I probably have used different words? Yeah, absolutely. I could've said 'love over hate.' I do agree that the fans obviously pay to come watch a game and they feel entitled to want to say something." (NBC Sports 2019).

I do appreciate that Sean elected the 'passionate' route instead of the tired, "I'm sorry if anyone was offended" *mea culpa*. The story quickly blew over. We've all misspoke from time to time. Besides, fans had already turned their attention towards the Birds home opener (They beat Washington 34-27). The outrage towards Rodriguez was real – people were angry – but the anger was more a byproduct of another lost season. You can't lose on the field and ALSO tell us how to act. We have our limits. Jimmy Rollins called fans 'front runners' in August of '08, but then captured a World Series a few months later. After the parade, he could've called us whatever he wanted.

"J-Roll thinks your low self-worth is why you sabotage every relationship you've ever been in. Also, your haircut is stupid."

“I mean, the 2007 NL MVP makes some fair points.”

Winning cures all. Philly has a bad reputation, but I think deep down we’re a tolerant bunch. Right? Right? We can handle a little constructive criticism. The substance, though, of Sean Rodriguez’ message would’ve carried more weight if it didn’t come from Sean Rodriguez. But alas.

2019 was his lone season in Philly.

The 8-Year Absence

Name: Andy Ashby

Position: Pitcher

Career Record: 98-110; 4.12 ERA (4.26 FIP)

Phillies Tenure: 1991-1992; 2000

That was Tuesday night. Barely 24 hours later, in what surely ranks as the signature move of his two-year tenure, general manager Ed Wade announced the breathtaking news that the Phillies had acquired Ashby for two former No. 1 draft picks, right-handers Carlton Loewer and Adam Eaton, plus righthanded reliever Steve Montgomery (Hagen 1999).

I have a laminated index card in my wallet to keep this straight:

Andy Ashby, the pitcher, is NOT related to Alan Ashby, the catcher.

Andy Benes and Alan Benes, however, are both related and pitchers.

The two tenures of Andy Ashby were spread so far apart it's hard to fathom it was the same person. That's why I'm always getting all my Andys and Alans confused. I'd see this workhorse pitching for the Padres and have to remind myself, "Oh, right. That's the old Phillies dude." Eight years after leaving Philadelphia the first time, the Prodigal Son returned. That is a *long* time between stints. Andy was here for the Barcelona Summer Olympics and came back just in time for the Sydney Games. We hadn't seen the guy in ages. Next thing you know, he is spotted at Green Eggs Cafe in a Vin Baker Team USA jersey. If a player is gone for over seven years, they're usually just gone. They don't come back. No one comes back. I know like five players out of a million that returned after a lengthy hiatus. Rick Mahorn, who had a cup of coffee in '99 with the Black Shirts, Larry Andersen, Marlon Byrd,

Dennis Cook, and digging deep into the archives, Jeff Parrett. (If you read this book in twenty years, just preemptively add Jordan Matthews to the list).

Andy Ashby 1.0 made his Phils debut in 1991. In his second career start, he threw an "Immaculate Inning," striking out the side on just nine pitches. Hal Morris, Todd Benzinger, and Jeff Reed bent the knee that inning, but the Phils couldn't crack the José Rijo Code in a 3-1 defeat. (Houston's Pete Harnisch would return the favor two months later. Wes Chamberlain, Dickie Thon, and José DeJesús were Pete's victims). There have been just two Fightins hurlers to accomplish the feat since Ashby – Cole Hamels in 2014 and the irreplaceable Juan Pérez in 2011. Andy struggled in his rookie campaign (1-5 with a 6.00 ERA) but showed enough promise to earn a spot in the rotation entering the '92 season. Ashby pitched admirably. The team won all three of his starts before a broken hand in late April sidelined him until August (Frey 1992). The layoff wasn't kind to him. His numbers jumped, and he finished the year with a 7.54 ERA. The Phils left him unprotected for the upcoming expansion draft ('93 was the first year of existence for the Rockies and Marlins), but any sting of losing the young righty to Colorado was mitigated by the same-day acquisition of Danny Jackson.

Fast-forward to November of '99 and Double A was back and better than ever, busting bats and busting spines. It was a new and improved Andy Ashby. You hadn't seen him since high school, but here he was at the ten-year reunion fresh off a juice cleanse and a makeover from *The Ricki Lake Show*.

"Whoa, is that Andy from Stage Crew? He looks great."

This wasn't your uncle's Andy Ashby. This was a two-time All-Star. This was the guy who pitched the Padres to an NL crown in '98. This was a frontline starter who, paired with Curt Schilling, created one of the most formidable 1-2 punches in the National League. Couple that with Paul Byrd, who won 15 games the season prior, and young upstarts, Robert Person and Randy Wolf, and my only concern was cleaning up the Vet's championship parade before Temple's Homecoming. ESPN.com wasn't nearly as encouraged. They penciled in the Phils for a third-place finish in the NL East and #17 in their preseason power rankings, while adding this:

While Schilling tries to get back before May 1, the Phillies must try to survive without him. It will not be easy, even with the addition of Andy Ashby, who has solid enough credentials to be at least an interim staff ace (Brookover 2000).

"Interim staff ace." It was a good to put it. As far as #2 starters went, Ashby was one of the better ones. It was like having Jim McMahon in '91. He wasn't Randall, but he could captain the ship. I can't say the same for Jeff Kemp, Brad Goebel, or Pat Ryan, though. There was optimism surrounding the staff. They were the only team in the majors with three All-Stars the previous year in their rotation (Byrd was the other).

The Phillies are confident they will be able to stay the course because of the addition of two-time All-Star Andy Ashby.

"He's a bonafide No. 1," Brogna said. "Take it from someone who has hit against him, his stuff is as good as anybody in the league. And don't let that little boy face fool you, Andy is one fierce competitor." (Bostrom 2000).

Little Boy Face started opening night in Arizona. I remember this game, and the controversy that involved the team's best hitter. Not wanting to put Bobby Abreu in an early season funk facing dominant lefty, Randy Johnson, Francona benched the star right fielder for Kevin Sefcik (Conlin 2000). You can see the loser energy from that last sentence radiating off the page. Ashby allowed 6 ER in 6 innings in a 6-4 loss. The major talking point surrounding the team was treading water early as they navigated through a difficult early schedule. Buy some time. Stay afloat in April until Schilling returned. Welp. The best-laid plans. The S.S. Fightins took in water. By May 1st, they were 7-17.

The team never clawed into contention. Ashby couldn't claw his way to a quality start. A June 17th outing against Baltimore was particularly glaring. He gave up 7 ER along with 12 hits in 6 2/3 innings. It was like Francona was waiting for the Padres' Andy Ashby to finally arrive, to turn on the switch, while pitch after pitch found an Oriole bat. Ashby had a 6.27 ERA as the calendar turned to June. The preseason assumption was that the free agent-to-be would re-sign (Andy made his residence in Scranton), but by summer, it was clear he had no intention of sticking around. Ed Wade conceded as much.

"Knowing what I know now, I'm disappointed we traded three young pitchers for a guy who doesn't want to be here," Wade said. "There are no do-overs. And we believed it was the right deal. But knowing what I know now, would I make the same deal? No, I wouldn't trade for a guy I'd end up having to turn around in another trade six months later (Roberts 2000).

A struggling, lame duck pitcher who didn't want to be here made Ashby a prime target for fans. The tumultuous relationship reached a boiling point during a rain delayed start against the Brewers at home.

A few fans directly behind the dugout were standing and screaming. Ashby took a step into the dugout, then leaned back and yelled over top at a guy who appeared to be berating him the most.

The brief exchange was X-rated.

In the bottom of the inning, when public-address announcer Dan Baker introduced Rob Ducey as the two-out pinch-hitter for Ashby, the few remaining fans cheered with gusto.

The reason was not a love affair with Ducey (Silary 2000).

Wade moved Ashby in early July for Bruce Chen and Jimmy Osting. Predictably, he was productive in Atlanta – like this story could end any other way. Phillies fans were Reverse Chris Boniol'd, which is like getting Reverse Wet Willy'd, but instead of getting a mouthful of earwax, Andy shoved eight post-All-Star break wins down our gullets. He pitched four more years in the majors, never returning to Philadelphia for Round 3. It was for the best.

He is currently one of the owners of the AAA Scranton/Wilkes-Barre RailRiders.

The (Un)Common Card

Name: Kenny Lofton

Position: Center Field

Career Slash Line: .299/.372/.423

Phillies Tenure: 2005

I attended a card show at the Wildwood Convention Center not too long ago. It was my first card show since mom took me to the Bucks County Mall in the early 90s and handed me $2.

"Don't buy the first thing you see, Dave. Look around first."

A minute later, I ran back to mom waving a 1990 Pro Set Christian Okoye in the air. What were the chances that this Near Mint beauty of the Nigerian Nightmare was only $2? Pretty high it turned out. The premier card of that generation was the 1989 Upper Deck Ken Griffey Jr. I needed a lot more than two bucks to purchase one of those. If you had an '89 Upper Deck Griffey, you were the 1%. You could try and hide your wealth under a pair of hand-me-down Zubaz, but you weren't fooling anyone.

"Your dad drives a Lexus, Todd. Don't bullshit us."

Kids who collected cards were separated by those who had that rookie, and those who didn't. It's maybe the only card from that era with a sustained value. Cards were overproduced. The market was too saturated. I went to this Wildwood trade show looking for cards of players in this book. Any card that is worth a damn – like pre-1960's stuff for instance – was under a glass case, well protected. The common cards, or the cards I was sifting through, were jammed inside shoeboxes, condition be damned. The seller didn't ask me for a backstory or raise an eyebrow when I asked for the price of seven Don Carmans ($.25 each). Every player in this book was in that shoebox. Every player. Except for one. And the only explanation I can offer was that he was too good. Kenny Lofton was too good for that box, and he was too good for this book.

I don't get to discuss a player's Hall of Fame candidacy too often in my line of work. Would I vouch for Hersey Hawkins, if asked? Obviously. Say the word, Hawk, and I'll write you a glowing letter of recommendation so elegant that even your high school English teacher would approve.

And for the reasons stated above, I feel that Hersey "The Hawk" Hawkins would be a welcomed addition to the NBA Hall of Fame Class of 2023.

Thank you for your time.

The Warmest of Regards,

Dave

In 2013, Kenny finished 20th in the Hall of Fame voting, just behind Bernie Williams, the 447th most well-known Yankee ever. Kenny received a paltry 3.2% of the vote. Craig Biggio, elected in 2015, was the leading vote getter that year (68.2%) and recorded a .281/.363/.433 line across 20 seasons. Lofton hit .299/.373/.423 in 17 campaigns. What are we doing here? Why such the large vote discrepancy? Their numbers are identical. Did having the dirtiest helmet in league history separate Biggio from the pack? If we're electing athletes solely based on unique helmets, then let me know when Birds kicker, Paul McFadden, and his single bar facemask lands in Canton. I'll pitch in for gas if someone can pick me up.

"Listen, Dave, it's the Hall of Fame, not the Hall of Very Good."

Oh, pipe down. I don't care who is or isn't in the Hall of Fame. Elect Jack Morris. Don't elect Jack Morris, whatever. I'm too busy trying to clean up the WWE Hall of Fame (Koko B. Ware, really?). But scribes only giving Lofton 3.2% of the vote is comically inept. Getting yanked from the ballot after one year was insulting. A 6x All-Star, a 4x Golden Glove winner, 622 stolen bases, are you not entertained? Kenny deserved better. The Phils acquired the 38-year-old Lofton from the Yankees in December '04 for Félix Rodríguez. History says it should've been a disaster. 38-year-old ballplayers are either relievers or plodding first basemen, not centerfielders, and not base stealers. But all Kenny Lofton did in his one season here was everything. Ok, to be fair, there was one thing he wouldn't do. (Hold that thought).

The Phillies have been openly searching for an upgrade in center since the middle of last season. They asked about Steve Finley before the trade deadline and inquired again when he became a free agent at the end of the season. They considered Scott Podsednik from the Brewers and Ryan Freel from the Reds, but concluded there wasn't a match.

That led them back to Lofton, another player they had looked at before. He replaces Marlon Byrd who, if not traded, likely will open next season at Triple A Scranton/Wilkes-Barre (Hagen 2004).

Lofton had a low bar to clear. It was like a rookie Donovan McNabb taking over for Doug Pederson. Byrd would eventually carve out a nice career, but not in 2004. In '04, he struggled, still adjusting to the rigors of the big leagues. Marlon recorded just a .608 OPS, which was a stone's throw away from the town of Mini Martville. Lofton hit a massive .335 and had a .392 OB%. Let that sink in for a moment. In his first game in a Fightins uniform, he took a Liván Hernández offering and roped it over the right field wall. Oh, that reminds me. Speaking of walls:

After the opener, he said, "I played in Wrigley Field. If you can handle the sun and wind there, you can play anywhere."

After chasing down long drives and smacking into the wall the next two games, Lofton had a change of heart.

"The wall doesn't give," Lofton said. "That's unusual. It's like running into a brick wall, and that's not something outfielders want to deal with. I'm not going to run into that wall. I'm not stupid. I'm not going to kill myself." (Bostrom 2005).

"Can you believe this guy, Matt? Who does he think he is?"

"What a prima donna."

"No heart. Won't even run into a brick wall for this city."

"He's a bum! Time to give Marlon Byrd another look."

The wall comments rubbed people the wrong way. If you won't run into concrete for this city, what else won't you do? Break up a double play? Bunt a man over? I was less concerned. He was our speedy outfielder, not a sledgehammer. The irony isn't lost on me, though. You know what's coming. A year later, Aaron Rowand did exactly what Kenny Lofton vowed to never do. He crashed into the wall face first to catch a Xavier Nady blast with the bases loaded and broke his nose in the process.

Lofton signed with the Dodgers following the '05 season, closing the chapter on one of the greatest, most unassuming seasons in recent Phillies memory. Up until recently, center field wasn't a huge issue. The team transitioned to Rowand then Victorino. The position was in good hands. Now, you'll occasionally see someone pining for the days of yore, when Kenny patrolled center field.

"What's Kenny Lofton up to?"

"Anyone else remember Lofton playing here?"

It's rare, though. You don't hear his name much. His '05 season has been largely cast aside. If you discuss household name center fielders in the twilight of their career, he's an afterthought compared to Dale Murphy (But still ahead of Andy Van Slyke. Everyone has suppressed the AVS Era). Philadelphia was his 9th of eventual 11 different stops in his big league journey. Maybe that's one explanation for his low Hall of Fame tally. You can't truly appreciate someone who leaves so quickly. Lofton played for nine different franchises in the final five years of his career alone. It was hard to keep tabs on his whereabouts. 30-something Kenny Lofton never stayed in one place long, but wherever he was, he was always on base.

The 'Pen Pal

Name: Pat Neshak

Position: Pitcher

Career Record: 36-25; 2.82 ERA (3.60 FIP)

Phillies Tenure: 2017-2019

Dear Mr. Neshak:

I hope this letter finds you well.

I'm a little rusty at asking for autographs, so please bear with me. My last letter to a pro athlete was an ill-fated attempt to Patrick Ewing in the early 90s that still haunts me today.

I know you're an avid card collector. As someone who knows ball, can we agree that the yellow '91 Fleer set is the worst of all time? I'd take the gargantuan '89 Bowman over it and those monsters didn't even fit into a card sleeve.

Thank you for signing. I felt that one autograph from a Phils All-Star deserves another.

All the best,

Dave

Pat Neshak is a noted card collector and autograph hound. He offers this deal to fans: If you mail him an autographed card, he'll send you back a signed one of himself (McLauchlin 2021). I took him up on it. I'm not an autograph guy, though. I don't have a stockpile of signatures stashed away in a wine cellar.

"Maddie, can you please run down and get the signed '01 Topps Jeff Brantley? It should be right next to the 2016 Louis Latour Gevrey-Chambertin Pinot."

I didn't have anything at my disposal, so I had to purchase a signed card. I don't want to insult the guy, but I also can't be spending 50% of my *Phillies Odyssey* budget on a Steve Carlton auto. Which begs the question: What do you trade the man who has everything? Turns out, a signed 1995 Leaf Heathcliff Slocumb card. I don't regret the trade – you gotta give to get – but once I had the Slocumb autograph, I was kinda bummed to see it go. We didn't even have 24 hours together.

My older sisters played competitive softball. Trading pins was a huge deal at these national tournaments. I'd carry around this pin-covered hotel towel through the sports complex, trading with other kids. Depending on the team, or the pin's design, you'd sometimes have to make a two-for-one swap. I understood. It was a necessary evil, but every PTBNL (pin to be named later) meant something. It was tough to watch the ones you didn't have duplicates of go. So after the Neshak transaction, I did what any sane, rational person would do. I went out and bought a second signed Heathcliff Slocumb card.

A team's ineptitude is measured by one of two levels. If your only All-Star representative is your closer that means you're shitty. If your only All-Star representative is a middle reliever? That means you're really fucking bad. You're one step above sending your team trainer as your lone rep.

"Phils are 28 games under .500, but I'm happy Scott Sheridan is finally being recognized."

"Couldn't have said it better myself, Jim. Sheridan is a pro's pro."

Neshak making the 2017 All-Star Team isn't an indictment on Pat (he was outstanding), but it spoke volumes about the team. Of hitters with more than 300 plate appearances that season, only one had an OPS of over .800 (Aaron Altherr). Nola was good. So was Neris. But outside of that? The cupboard was bare. All-Star rep options were limited. I led a half-assed campaign for Cesar Hernandez, but my heart wasn't really in it. Every team has a passable reliever on standby. Well, except for the 2020 Phils – there's always an exception to the rule. Former Phil Mike Williams made the '03 All-Star Team with Pittsburgh and finished the season 1-7 with a 6.24 ERA. But he had 25 saves, so that was good enough. Having my favorite team only send a reliever to All-Star Weekend was a bummer, but beggars can't be choosers. We had no choice but to rally behind our lone bullpen arm.

I spent the '96 All-Star Game screaming at Bobby Cox to put in Ricky Bottalico. I even petitioned to get him an at-bat. Ricky Bo did take the bump, and for 25 years, I thought he was the winning pitcher in that contest. I *just* learned otherwise, like July of 2021 to be exact. Bottalico did NOT get the win. I had the same reaction when I heard that Coca-Cola used to be made with blow. Ricky pitched the 5th inning in a game the NL led the whole way. Seemed clear cut. Silly me for following the actual rules of baseball. John Smoltz is listed as the NL winner for pitching the first two innings. The guy got the victory even though he was lifted before the opening credits of *Wings*.

It was at this 2017 All-Star Game where the Zack Greinke/Pat Neshak beef originated. The squabble isn't quite Jordan and Isiah Thomas, but there were some fireworks. Neshak approached the starting pitcher and asked if he would sign a few items. Zack agreed. Fast-forward a few weeks later, Neshak, now a member of the Rockies after a mid-season deal involving J.D. Hammer, sent some cards over to the Diamondbacks clubhouse. Greinke had a change of tune. He wouldn't sign. Pat tracked him down during batting practice and asked once more. Zack again says "no," telling the reliever he "wears him out." (ESPN 2017). It's a tough look for all parties. Neshak comes off a bit thirsty. Greinke appears to renege on a verbal promise for one reason or another. That encounter though, never would've seen the light of day, if Neshak, under the handle, "heat17," didn't put Greinke on blast on a SportsCollector.net message board.

"I asked him at the all star game if he would sign for me and he said he would... so a couple weeks ago we played them and I sent over the cards I needed signed... basically 3 league leaders cards with Kershaw and Wainwright already done and 2 from 2015 to complete the set. He said no... I waited around for him during batting practice and went up to him and he totally denied having the conversation at the

all star game... I then asked why this was a problem and he said it's because "I wear him out." Hard to wear someone out when he has never signed for me. This is the only a-hole in major league baseball that has been a turd to me." (ESPN 2017).

User heat17 bringing the, well, the heat. The 'turd' at the end is the chef's kiss, like AI stepping over Tyronn Lue. I figure most pro athletes have a gentlemen's agreement. You see post-game jersey and sneaker swaps, what are a few autographs between combatants, right? I'd have signed it, Pat. I'll sign this book if you asked me. I'll even slip a pack of 1990 Fleer cards inside the cover.

Neshak had a minuscule 1.12 ERA in 40 innings for the Phils that season. 1.12! My goodness, someone hand me a cigarette. The sidearmer made things uneasy for hitters, even at 36 when the Fightins inked him to a deal. After a successful stop in Colorado to finish the year, Pat was back. The ol' sign a guy, trade a guy, sign him again move, ala Aroldis Chapman, or Rick Aguilera if you're a Twins fan over the age of 40. Neshak was also effective in '18 (a terrific 2.59 ERA), but each stint was clouded by the one question that no one could provide a definitive answer to.

Is Pat Neshak available to pitch?

It seems silly on the surface, redundant even. Why wouldn't the pitcher be available to, ya know, pitch? But this was a sub-plot that lingered for years. The issue surfaced from conflicting reports provided by Pat and Gabe Kapler, and before that, Neshak and skip Pete Mackanin. Either the managers didn't know the phone number for the bullpen, or the veteran needed more time to warm-up than my late grandma's Ford Tempo. In a game at Wrigley in May 2019, cameras caught Neshak shaking his head no from the bullpen in the bottom of the 8th. The implication there was that Pat was responding to a question of whether or not he was ready.

"It looked really bad on TV and people were like 'Neshek isn't ready,'" the pitcher said. "If (critics) are going to characterize me as 'I'm not coming into the game,' then know that was my first pitch. No one saw when the phone call (to initially get up) was made.

"(Manager Gabe Kapler) got me up on a 1-0 pitch on (Jason) Heyward. That's when I got the call. I got on the mound and threw two pitches and then he called down. That's what they showed on TV. He said, 'Is he ready?' And I said 'No. I'm not ready yet. I've thrown two pitches.'" (NBC Sports 2019).

The Phils would concede three runs that half inning, but manage to squeak one out in extras. The next night, the venerable Juan Nicasio blew a 9th inning save opportunity. Neshak didn't pitch then either. And that's the thing. The only reason why Neshak's availability was such a sore spot with fans and management is because he was good. Everyone wanted him in there. No one was in line at Dunkin' asking why Mike Morin didn't pitch the 7th the night before. I understand arm fatigue and overexposure, but half my life has been spent watching Hector Neris throw splitters. The guy needs an occasional day off. This usage concern popped up during his first tenure too. From June 22nd, 2017:

Phillies reliever Pat Neshek is having a tremendous, All-Star season, but the restrictions on his usage have become a real concern.

Neshek, who has a 0.63 ERA and 30 scoreless appearances out of 31, induced an inning-ending double play Thursday to get the Phillies to the ninth with a two-run lead. He threw just five pitches in the 5-1 win.

But even if the Phillies didn't tack on two insurance runs in the bottom of the eighth, Neshek was not going back out for a save situation in the ninth, Mackanin said.

"I asked him to go back out," manager Pete Mackanin said. "He said he would rather not; he didn't feel like he had it." (NBC Sports 2017).

Neshak threw just five pitches that game. But when questioned by reporters, the reliever said Mackanin never asked him to go back out (Baer 2019). How do you pick sides here? What's a jury supposed to do with that? Someone is lying to my face; I just don't know who. Neshak threw just 18 innings in 2019. Days after the controversy in Chicago, he was placed on the IL with shoulder soreness. He pitched once more in June before a hamstring injury ended his Phillies tenure. He has been unavailable ever since.

(Depending on who you ask).

The Shaving Cream

Name: Tomás Pérez

Position: Everywhere

Career Slash Line: .240/.290/.342

Phillies Tenure: 2000-2005

"I will bring the pies with me wherever I go," Pérez said, trying to force a smile. "I know that at 32 years old, I can still help another team." (Narducci 2006).

My buddy and I went to Citizens Bank Park for the first time on May 28th, 2004: Phils vs. Atlanta. We loved the news digs. The Bank was beautiful. Like everyone else, I held a special place in my heart for the Vet, but not for aesthetic reasons. The Vet was like a gray hoodie you've owned for a decade and washed once a year. It was a piece of shit, but it was your piece of shit. I once heard the expression that the difference between Las Vegas and Atlantic City is that people go to Vegas expecting to win, and I think there's something to that. I had watched the Phillies so often just waiting for the other shoe to drop – the backbreaking bases clearing double or the costly error or the pop-up with two runners in scoring position.

Maybe the Phils and I needed a proverbial change of scenery, like *Sister, Sister* moving from ABC to The WB. I had this renewed awakening walking into the Bank. Maybe the Phils could change. Maybe I could change. Maybe I could be this kinder, gentler Phillies fan, spreading love and positivity. Maybe I could even treat the opponents with some respect –

Wait, who is that in right? I know that face. I've seen that person before. Is that, is that J.D. Drew?

BOOOOOOOOOOOOOOOOOO!

BOOOOOOOOOOOOOOOOOO!

"Quick, pull the batteries from this here Game Boy."

Ok, so change doesn't happen overnight. While Drew was a *very* deserving target, my buddy and I hurled some serious heat at someone much less deserving. This isn't even therapeutic to discuss. I feel terrible about it, but we really gave it to little-used Tomás Pérez. Let me clearly state: It had nothing to do with Tomás Pérez, the player. I liked Tomás! He just wasn't Jim Thome. Thome, banged up with an injured finger, got a rest day with lefty Mike Hampton on the bump. Like Mike Hampton? 4'7" Mike Hampton? (He's actually 5'10", whatever). You don't leave *Hamilton* saying, "Yeah, Lin-Manuel Miranda needed an off day. I get it. His understudy needed the reps." We asked for Thome and they gave us Tomás.

Trailing 2-1 in the bottom of the 8th, Pérez came up with Utley on first. We did everything short of Morse code to get Charlie's attention.

"Put in Thome! Pinch-hit Thome!"

We had zero pull. Pérez stayed in and promptly ripped a double down the right field line to knot things up at 2. In the bottom of the 10th, Tomás stepped up to the plate once more.

"Gotta be Thome here," my friend shouted. "What is Charlie waiting for? Charlie! I know you can hear meeeee!"

We had short memories. Pérez' double two innings prior may as well have been off a Doyle Alexander fastball from 1986.

"We got a power bat on the bench," I hollered. "He's rotting there, Charlie! Grab a bat, Jim!"

Tomás hit a walk-off homer.

The team also had to pay Perez back for all of the shaving cream pies he's delivered to the stars of the games the past few seasons.

Those pies are becoming more famous than anything Mrs. Smith cooks up.

Perez got lathered pretty good, too.

"I'll take it," he said. "I have to enjoy it because it does not happen many times

to me." (Bostrom 2004).

Ah, the shaving cream pies. Like Gallagher taking a sledgehammer to a watermelon, Tomás was a prop comic. He didn't do observational humor. Nobody was safe. Any walk-off hero got a face full of Barbasol. Tomás had a shtick. It made him standout. A Popeye impression got Joey Gladstone on *Star Search.* It doesn't take much. The shaving cream was Tomás' accessory and if Mystery from VH1's *The Pick-up Artist* taught me anything, it's the importance of accessorizing. And negging. Can't forget the negging.

The Fightins signed Pérez on December 15th, 1999. The Sixers clipped the Raptors that night, 93-91, thanks to 37 from Iverson. Bruce Bowen chipped in 2, for those wondering. It was a good night all the way around. Tomás' versatility was his greatest attribute. He hit from both sides of the plate and played everywhere. There has always been this fascination with position flexibility. Hell, there's nothing more attractive in fantasy baseball than someone with SS/2B/OF/DH eligibility. As long as Josh Harrison has a pulse, he'll always have a job on my squad. Being good is negotiable. That you can plug the guy anywhere is the appeal.

"Rex Hudler is hitting .122, Allison. He's really scuffling. It may be time to cut ties."

"Yeah, but he can play seven positions. Allows Francona to stock up on bullpen arms. It will pay dividends in the back end."

Pérez' numbers were always secondary. His popularity transcended his talent. Fans loved him – well, my buddy and I notwithstanding. Teammates loved him. Mike Lieberthal said, "He is one of my favorite players I ever played with." (Narducci 2006). He was a team first guy. Catcher and centerfield were the only spots where Tomás didn't play. (An interesting aside: On September 6, 2000, utility infielder Scott Sheldon played all nine positions in a single game for the Rangers. Detroit's Shane Halter and Andrew Romine would later duplicate the feat). Pérez got his chance on the bump in a 17-3 loss to Houston in '02. Hector Mercado allowed 7 earned runs in 2/3 of an inning before Tomás stopped the bleeding. To

Mercado's credit, though, he only issued one free pass. Silver linings?

Perez faced two hitters in his big-league pitching debut without allowing a hit. That qualified as the best performance by a Phillies pitcher last night.

"It's not that easy," reliever Rheal Cormier told Perez as he checked out of the clubhouse. (Brookover 2002).

He became the first position player to pitch for the Phillies since Glenn Wilson in 1987. Pérez had a lengthy six-year run in Philly, but shaving cream sales in the Delaware Valley dipped following the '05 season after the Phils brought in infielders Alex Gonzalez and Abraham Nunez.

"I saw it coming," said Perez, who hit .233 in just 159 at-bats last season. "I knew right away when they signed those guys." (Narducci 2006).

It was time for Tomás to take his act on the road. He played a couple more years in the bigs, rounding out his career in Tampa Bay and Houston.

The Inside Job

Name: Turk Wendell

Position: Pitcher

Career Record: 36-33; 3.93 ERA (4.62 FIP)

Phillies Tenure: 2001-2003

After returning from injury in 2003, Wendell bounced back with a 3.38 ERA in 56 appearances for Philadelphia. He said he was asked by reporters if he was happy about the fans finally being on his side.

"And I said 'Not really, if they're true fans they should boo me now, too. They shouldn't just jump on the bandwagon,'" Wendell said. "If you don't like somebody you don't like somebody. Don't just like em' cause you're doing well and hate em' cause you're doing bad." (Tasch 2020).

Turk Wendell, my nemesis. At least Jeff Conine looked me in the eye before snatching the Wild Card from my clammy hands. Wendell was a saboteur; a plant sent by New York to infiltrate the Phillies bullpen and destroy our proud franchise from the *inside*. I'm no dummy. I've played *Stratego*. I know the value of the Spy. Asking a Mets reliever to help the Fightins bullpen is like naming Ben DiNucci the Birds' Quarterbacks Coach. A Met is a Met is a Met is a Met. Every one of his quirks – the slamming of the rosin bag, the brushing of his teeth between innings, the chewing of black licorice (the grossest candy out there) – annoyed me more and more with each passing pitch. His notorious shark tooth necklace overtook the puka shell necklace as the douchiest accessory of the early 2000s. Wendell's only saving grace was that he wasn't a Cowboys fan.

For him, though, the preferred label is "routine" – something that puts human beings, who are habitual by nature, in a comfort zone. Even when he was in Little League, this was evident. He wore the same Dallas Cowboys shorts under his uniform until "2,000 or so washings kind of wore them out." (Costello 2014).

Ok, I spoke too soon. In late July of '01, the Phils lost three consecutive games via walk-off homer. How do you come back from that? I don't mean the team. I mean us. Do you know how hard it was for ME to dust myself off the mat and tune into Channel 17 the following night? That's fortitude. Watching Wendell and Cormier take the somber steps to the dugout while the Mets (twice) and the Rockies (once) celebrated at home plate is entrenched into my brain. Here's the postmortem for your records.

The Philadelphia Phillies are probably already sorry they traded Wayne Gomes. While Gomes was winning his debut with the San Francisco Giants, the Phillies bullpen had another meltdown – losing for the third straight time on a game-ending homer.

Todd Helton's second solo homer of the game, a one-out shot in the ninth inning, gave Colorado a 7-6 victory over the Phillies on Tuesday night.

"We've got veteran pitchers down there who are not getting it done," Phillies manager Larry Bowa said. "This is not a one-time happening."

Newly acquired Turk Wendell gave up three runs without retiring a better in the eighth to help Colorado rally from four runs down to tie it. Rheal Cormier (5-5) lost it again.

The Mets' Robin Ventura homered off Wendell on Saturday, and Mike Piazza connected against Cormier on Sunday. Cormier has lost his last four outings – three on game-ending homers (Associated Press 2001).

When I was 8, I received a book listing the school mascot for every Division-1 basketball team (Give or take 300 colleges). I memorized it cover to cover. Almost thirty years later, I can still rattle off the nickname of an Illinois directional school without missing a beat. Like how the Western Illinois Leathernecks are fixtures of my childhood, I can close my eyes and see Turk Wendell serving up that meatball to Robin Ventura.

Turk pitched only 15 2/3 innings for the Fightins after coming over at the trade deadline. Still, it was plenty of time to inflict maximum damage. He went 0-2. He had a 7.47 ERA. He gave up four homers, all seemingly of the back-breaking variety. I would've been more tolerant and accepting of his idiosyncrasies if he retired a few more hitters, or, at the very least, provided concrete evidence that showed he wasn't still in the Mets back pocket. But I can only the play the hand I was dealt. Wendell pitched in the majors for 11 seasons. His oddball mannerisms followed him to four different NL cities, but the stench of the Mets only traveled with him to Philadelphia.

The Phils acquired Turk and former Fightin, Dennis Cook, on July 27th for the well-traveled Bruce Chen and Adam Walker***. One day later, Wendell gave up the walk-off to Ventura.

***There were no winners from this trade. Chen was ineffective in New York. Perhaps so disenfranchised with the outcome – I like to believe this is the reason anyway – neither team completed a trade with each other for another 17 years (Boye 2018). The Asdrúbal Cabrera deal ultimately ended the Chen/Wendell/Cook Hangover.

It was later discovered that the righty was pitching hurt. Years of overuse with the Mets (he threw 285+ innings the previous 3 ½ seasons) led to elbow issues that weren't properly diagnosed until after his arrival (Tasch 2020). On the *New York Post's Amazin' But True* Podcast, Turk didn't shy away from his struggles here and the shitty response it solicited from some despondent fans.

Well I mean, I'm not going to sugar coat that either. When I came over to the Phillies, I mean, I sucked," Wendell said. "I was getting paid a lot of money so I'm trying to push myself to honor the amount of money that I was making. You know, my elbow was sore and I'm not really gonna say anything and that's just probably my stupid competitiveness, too. I try to tell kids today play the game smarter, not harder. But I want to live up to the contract that I'm being paid. So I'm not pitching well and

I'm getting fan mail that says they wish I'd die, that if they saw me, they'd kill me, they wish I was in the Twin Towers when they went down. All this kind of crazy stuff...and you know getting all kinds of different death threats, thinking what the heck? I'm just here to play ball." (Tasch 2020).

Trying to rid himself of the bad juju after coming over, the superstitious Wendell changed numbers in August. Originally #99, in exclusive company with Mitch Williams and So Taguchi, the reliever gave Tomás Pérez a Rolex watch in exchange for his #13 (Brookover 2001). Rolexes are seemingly the going rate for a number switch, but I'm not a watch guy. My wrists need to breathe. If anyone from my 1995 travel hoops teams wants my #42 (in honor of Jerry Stackhouse), you'd better sweeten the deal. A few Pogs, at least one Slammer, maybe a Stephen Starr gift card.

In 2004, Larry Bowa faced criticism for the perceived overtaxing of his bullpen. Bo, as Bo was known to do, fired back.

Bowa's claim that "two or three of [the Phillies beat writers] are doing everything in your power but sticking a bleeping knife in my back" seems a bit overdone, especially in the light that two veteran relievers last season faded after particularly tough stretches (Hayes 2004).

The elbow injury forced Turk to miss the entire '02 season. He bounced back in '03, not allowing a run in his first 12 appearances. The team wanted to monitor his workload given the injury history. That was the original plan anyway, but Bowa would call on Turk for a stretch of three consecutive games in mid-August. Afterwards, Wendell raised concerns about a tired arm. Before the three-game stretch, his ERA was 1.93. Afterwards? 9.24 (Hayes 2004).

That was his final season in a Phils uniform. Wendell was a showman, whether that was his authentic personality, or just a calculated act for attention is in the eye of the observer. Personally, I just wanted him to get people out. Turk Wendell was a lot of things, but to me, he was just a Met. I had a hard time seeing anything else.

The Relief Pitcher

Name: Wilson Valdez

Position: SS/2B/3B

Career Slash Line: .236/.281/.313

Phillies Tenure: 2010-2011

But Valdez wasn't out there to lose; he was going to use every pitch in his limited arsenal to try and stop this game from having a 20th inning. He would never pitch again, nor had he ever pitched before. But when all you get is limited action, the last thing you can do is limit yourself (Klugh 2019).

The Wilson Valdez Game. As far as memorable regular season contests from the Dynasty Years go (Yes, I'm calling one world championship and 5 NL East Titles a dynasty), not sure there is a better candidate for #2 outside The Wilson Valdez Game. (I rank Roy Halladay's perfect game #1). Maybe Ryan Howard almost stuffing Scott Barry into a locker? The Phils/Reds game on May 25th, 2011 went 19 innings. Neither team scored for *days*. It lasted over 6 hours, which was like watching the '98 Birds play a double header (Not so fun fact: That Eagles team threw just 7 TD passes the entire season). You know where you were on that night. This game isn't some hidden gem. People don't see a clip of this and go, "Oh, right! Valdez pitched a game for us. I completely forgot."

Everyone knows The Wilson Valdez Game. It has no other known aliases. As pitcher after pitcher after pitcher mowed down opposing hitters, delirium took over.

11:47 P.M.

"What are opponents hitting against Danyz Báez in his seventh time through a lineup?"

12:23 A.M.

"Where can I find a comprehensive list of Larry Andersen's 'Shallow Thoughts'?"

12:51 A.M.

"Has a mop-up guy ever won a Cy Young?"

1:05 A.M.

#9: If a guy is a good fastball hitter, should I throw him a bad fastball? (Shenk 2015).

"Hmm. Never thought of it like that, LA."

If there's any plotline forgotten from this game, it's that the much-maligned Danyz Báez threw five shutout innings. It was like getting into your car with the gas tank on "E," yet still making it to SugarHouse without dipping into your Wheel of Fortune slots funds. We were on borrowed time; someone was looking out for the Fightins on this night. I can't speak to Peter Bourjos' whereabouts, but there definitely were some Angels in the Outfield. Forget Valdez – that was the real miracle. The bridge to Wilson, getting the ball to him, took a Herculean effort. Manuel couldn't ask Danys to go six (!), so out of options, the loveable skip gave the pill to his infielder. By the 18th, 19th inning, it's less baseball, more a war of attrition. The *next* day's game takes focus. Who, if anybody, will be available? What if tomorrow's starter struggles? Does the team need to make roster moves to bring in some fresh arms? Games over 15 innings are like 2 A.M. text messages to your ex. It seems harmless at the time, but you'll be dealing with the fallout for the next week.

I had two thoughts going through my head when the telecast came back for the top of the 19th.

"Hey, a position player is pitching!"

"God, work is gonna be ass tomorrow."

Wilson's first hitter was Joey Votto. The reigning NL MVP worked a 3-1 count, wanting to see Valdez' full complement of pitches, before flying out to deep center. The righty reliever then hit known villain Scott Rolen with a 75-mph breaking ball, reminding the Reds that the inside of the plate belonged to him. He then induced a flyout from Jay Bruce. When Cincinnati's Carlos Fisher's pop-up hung in the air, Tom McCarthy correctly predicted the crowd's reaction.

"Pop-up ... right side ... this place is gonna go nuts. Polanco under it. Puts it away. How about Wilson Valdez!" (MLBGlobal11 2011).

Rollins would score on a Raúl Ibañez sac fly in the bottom half for the victory. Valdez became just the second player in MLB history to start a game in the field and record the win. The other was a guy named George Herman Ruth.

(Ruth started the October 1st, 1921 game in left. He then pitched 4 innings of relief, notching the win over Connie Mack's Philadelphia A's, 7-6).

Aside from his late inning heroics on the bump, Valdez was also a back-to-back recipient of the prestigious Mike Lieberthal Double Play Award, given annually to the Phillie who grounded into the most tailor-made 6-4-3 twin killings. Past winners include:

1996: Mike Lieberthal

1997: Mike Lieberthal

1998: Mike Lieberthal

1999: Mike Lieberthal

2000: Mike Lieberthal

2001: Johnny Estrada

2002: Mike Lieberthal

2003: Mike Lieberthal

2004: Mike Lieberthal

2005: David Bell

Valdez was economical. The average MLB game in 2011 was 2 hours and 53 minutes. The average length of a game that Valdez started – even accounting for that May 25th night? 1 hour and 43 minutes. I know. I couldn't believe it myself when I heard. Every Valdez at-bat with a runner on was like giving Tom Glavine a 15-foot strike zone. Games flew by. I didn't miss the opening scene of *Law & Order: SVU* for two years. Runners that reached base ahead of Wilson were erased just as fast. He didn't walk and he didn't hit the ball in the air. It was like Bob Barker ushered Valdez to a Plinko board, but the only landing spots were groundballs to second or short. I became so frustrated with Valdez' rally killers that I started #DoublePlaysForCharity. I wanted to channel my frustration for good, so I gave money to St. Jude's every time Wilson rolled one over. By the third week, I had to put donations on my credit card.

The Phils traded the bullpen arm to Cincinnati in January 2012 for Jeremy Horst. The Reds figured, if you can't hit him, acquire him. I'm glad Valdez got out when he did. A lengthier tenure and more at-bats in Philly would've chipped away at the goodwill he had with fans. Wilson did something extraordinary and that remains his legacy. We went to sleep for a few hours knowing we may never witness anything like that again. We hit snooze on our alarms, or got a second coffee in the morning, or maybe just skipped class or called out of work all together. Work *was* ass for me that next day, and you're damn right it was worth it.

The Switch Hitter

Name: Jeff Juden

Position: Pitcher

Career Record: 27-32; 4.81 ERA (4.83 FIP)

Phillies Tenure: 1994-1995

Where to begin? There is so much meat on the Jeff Juden bone that I briefly considered scrapping the other 49 chapters and writing, to the best of my knowledge, the first ever Jeff Juden biography. The working title was, *Jeff Juden: I Did It My Way*, and I was already in talks with Penguin Publishing about a modest advance and a tentative release date of Spring 2023. There's a lot going on with Juden. Just when I thought I had an outline complete; I'd read about the trade to Cleveland (more on that later), the beef with Chuckie Carr (more on that later), or his band's album (MORE ON THAT LATER). Not to mention the stuff with Jim Fregosi – yes, more on that later. OR the GRAND SLAM.

More to come on that, too.

Juden has lived a full life. He was traded four separate times and pitched for eight teams in eight seasons. He was 6'7", 265 lb. and rocked more gold jewelry than Kama after melting the Undertaker's urn. You weren't sure if he was the Phils 5th starter or some dude sent by your bookie to break your thumbs because you're short $300. The back of his 1994 Pinnacle card labels him as a, "Hard-nosed and an intimidating presence." Show me the lie. He looked like every high school bully in an 80s movie, but the only reason he wasn't in Cobra Kai is because 6'7" 265 lb. dudes don't fuck around with karate.

The Cleveland Trade

Jeff had a reputation. You don't get passed around like Olive Garden breadsticks without one. But a mid-90s fastball translates and he was always considered this worthwhile gamble.

"If Juden figures it out, Mike ..."

"Uh huh. The kid's stuff is dynamite."

Each of these eight teams hoped they had the secret sauce; that they knew the combination to unlock Big Jeff's potential. Cleveland got their chance at the '97 trade deadline, but the move – Montreal's Jeff Juden for reliever Steve Kline – got a lukewarm response from Cleveland's *own* front office almost instantly. It's like they made a move just to make a move, and then we're like, "Oh shit. I guess we got Jeff Juden now." 15 years ago, BK and I traded our kickers in fantasy football (I think Jeff Wilkins was involved), and I couldn't tell you why. It was the same thing. The day of the trade, Cleveland GM Mike Hart called the hurler "just a guy." Then a few hours later, he acquired him (Pluto and Hamilton 2014).

Hart tells this story that happened the day after the deal.

"John, why did you ever send me Juden?" asked Hargrove.

"Well," admitted Hart. "I really don't know."

Juden was 0-1 with a 5.46 ERA in eight games for the Tribe. He was known mostly for answering reporters' questions with grunts and taking a guitar with him everywhere (Pluto and Hamilton 2014).

Inconsistency be damned, Juden had an unabashed confidence. Before Game 7 of the World Series against Florida, Jeff walked up to Mike Hargrove and said, "If you want to win this thing, put me out there." (Anderson 2010).

"He laughed at me. I was dead serious. I hadn't lost against the Marlins, up to that point. I think I was a career 5-0." (Anderson 2010).

This was straight out of *Little Big League* when Joey would tell Twins manager, Billy Heywood, "You should start Webman. He always beats the Rangers."

Chuckie Carr

Now, Carr, too, was a character. You may best remember Chuckie from Sega's *Tony La Russa Baseball* and *World Series Baseball*. If you laid a bunt down the third baseline, the CPU had to just eat it. Virtual Chuckie was maybe the fastest player since Tecmo Bo Jackson. Carr once was given the 'take' sign from the third base coach while ahead in the count, 2-0. He swung anyway and popped out. When confronted by Brewers manager, Phil Garner, Carr responded, "That ain't Chuckie's game. Chuckie hacks on 2-0." (Nelson 2017).

Juden hit Carr with a pitch while Chuckie was with Houston. The outfielder shouted at him while walking down the first baseline. When asked about the incident, Juden responded concisely, "Chuckie Carr is an idiot." (Harvey 1998). Jeff was traded to Cleveland five days later.

A year earlier, Jeff and his Expos teammates were involved in another scuffle with Houston. 'Stros pitcher Danny Darwin beaned Henry Rodriguez, which ignited the melee. The brawl was simmering down until you see five Houston players attempting to restrain Juden, who is *dying* to mix it up. The diminutive John Cangelosi then crept up behind Jeff, while he's preoccupied with half the Houston pitching staff, and hit the righty with a modified German Suplex. Which was bullshit. Juden's back was turned. That cheap stunt enraged the big hoss. Jeff and Cangelosi then exchanged a few haymakers, and lemme tell you, the 150 lb. infielder could scrap. A lot of punches landed, which is a baseball brawl rarity. Bert Sugar and I scored the round 10-9 in favor of Cangelosi (MLB 2015).

Time in Philadelphia

The Phils acquired Juden, Doug Jones, and Doug's luscious moustache in December of '93 for Mitch Williams. (It should be noted that Jones was very, very good in his lone season here. He had a 2.17 ERA and made the All-Star Team). Jeff, however, only made 15 starts in Philly across two seasons. He missed one spring training outing due to an infected tattoo on his calf (Hagen 1994). Wildwood is the Calf Tattoo Capital of the world so I can guess where Juden made his summer residence. A sluggish start in Philly led to his demotion to Scranton/Wilkes-Barre.

Soon after, elbow surgery put him on the shelf until the summer of '95. Juden notched just three wins for the Phils, but one of those victories created a lasting memory.

On Friday, August 25th, 1995, the Phils hosted the Dodgers on national TV. NBC's *Baseball Night in America* was the backdrop, with Greg Gumble and Joe Morgan on the call. That alone was an anomaly. Outside of ESPN's *Sunday Night Baseball*, major league games weren't often presented on this national, primetime stage. It felt different. It felt bigger. I hate when the Birds play on primetime, because if/when they lay an egg, I have to hear the talking heads ramble on about the Eagles' countless shortcomings. As if I'm not already acutely aware that we can't keep a wide receiver in front of us or convert a 3rd and 1 with any sense of regularity. But *Baseball Night in America* with my Fightins squaring off against Hideo Nomo? I was pumped. I was into it. I had my pretzel and chip sandwiches ready to go.

Nomo was not the hero on this night. The Phils chased the superstar after just three innings. They pounded the Dodgers for 17 runs. Gregg Jefferies hit for the cycle, Charlie Hayes added 4 RBIs, and Jeff Juden capped off the night with one of the most historic Fightins feats outside of Roy Halladay's NLDS no-hitter.

He won someone $10,000 in the *Daily News* Home Run Payoff.

I don't want to say the *Daily News* Home Run Payoff is a racket. I don't have the exact numbers in front of me. This is purely conjecture mind you. I don't have all the data, but – BUT – it sure seems like every Home Run Payoff inning took place in the bottom of the 3rd when traditionally the back part of the lineup was due up.

"Desi Relaford up next, and he's batting for Robin S. of Mayfair."

Of course he is. I'm in no position to speak for Robin S. of Mayfair, but I'm guessing she doesn't like her chances. 98.73% of the *Daily News* Home Run Payoff contestants are represented by light-hitting middle infielders or pitchers. Those are facts. My mom has been selected three separate times across twelve years, and David Newhan represented her each time. How is that possible? I've been picked once, and Tom Prince bunted on my behalf. Swing away, Tom. College tuition is very expensive. But on this night, there was a magic in the air. On this night, the Phils were playing on *Baseball Night in America*, the granddaddy of them all. On this night, Jeff Juden got a 3-2 fastball over the middle of the plate and he didn't miss. The big man went oppo, belting a grand slam in the 4th (not great for my 3rd inning Home Run Payoff thesis) and we had ourselves a $10,000 jackpot winner.

"We were actually sitting watching the game that night, because it was a big hype, with Nomo coming in. We were all sitting here watching the game and the kids were really into it. And I had actually stepped away from the TV and they knew what inning to put the radio on. They were the ones that had informed me that my name was called."

"I kept asking the kids, 'Who's batting? Who's batting?'" she had said the *evening of Juden's slam, "and they were telling me, 'Jeff Juden, Jeff Juden.' I wasn't even sure who Jeff Juden was."* (Berkery 1995).

Due to budget concerns, the Home Run Payoff was discontinued after the 1988 season, but was reintroduced in '94, following the popularity of the previous year's NL Champions (Vetrone Jr. 2003). Just in time, too, because Juden called his shot.

"(Hideo) Nomo was pitching against us and all the talk before the game was about Nomo," Juden said. "He was on the big screen and they were making a big deal of him and I said I was going to hit a home run. I called the shot. (Third base coach) Larry Bowa called me out, saying I was a pitcher and I can't be calling home runs. I really think he was pissed, but then he did ask me if I wanted a high five or a low five when I rounded third base. I told him it better be a low five because there's no way you're gonna reach me for a high five." (Thomas 2019).

Juden lost his next three starts, though, and you could sense Fregosi was tiring of the big righty. He would be pulled from the rotation in September. After a sluggish outing against the Astros, the skip took a veiled shot in the postgame presser.

"We started very quickly, and we couldn't get anything going after that," Fregosi said. "Drabek is a professional pitcher who didn't have his best stuff." There seemed to be an unmentioned comparison.

"[Juden] does some things that hurt him," Fregosi said. (Hagen 1995).

Fregosi then took, um, a more direct approach when Juden asked why he was pulled from the rotation (Knuckleballer Dennis Springer started three games in his place).

"Because you're the most unprofessional player I've ever seen, you big, fat, lazy piece of (garbage)." (Olney 1995).

Well then. I'm not convinced Fregosi used 'garbage' there either. A month later, the Phils traded Juden and minor leaguer Tommy Eason to San Francisco for Mike Benjamin.

Nuke 14

The band. Jeff Juden is front man for Nuke 14, which is now my third favorite band that contains numbers behind blink-182 and 112. Come on, like your shoulders don't start moving when you hear "Peaches and Cream?" I don't know what I thought former Phillies did after retirement. Shane Victorino golfs. Kruk's on TV. I guess they all have to pass the time somehow, but I wasn't expecting to discover Jeff Juden's rock band and their inspirational lyrics in 2021. What's next? Is Gary Bennett a highly regarded figure in the art community? Is Terry Adams performing stand-up at the Laugh Factory? I listened to Nuke 14's album, *Anything You Wanna Be*, in its entirety. It's an acquired taste – not necessarily my cup of tea – but I've unironically seen Puddle of Mudd live so I don't have the most refined musical palate.

In my first draft of this Juden novella, I finished with Nuke 14. A random Phillie as front man of a band perfectly captures the spirit of the *Odyssey* series (franchise?). I was done. I had hit on all the major plot points: Fregosi, the tattoo, the altercations. I was good. I felt comfortable with where I ended on Juden's saga. Until I read this "Where Are They Now" feature in his local newspaper, *The Herald News.*

Interestingly, Juden, after doing some serious digging himself, could turn out to be the lone switch-hitting pitcher in major league history to have four RBIs in two different games, hitting from each side of the plate.

"For some reason, I'm not recognized as a switch hitter," said Juden, who has been contacting various MLB teams and stat services to set the record straight. "I just want to get the stats right." (Thomas 2019).

Well I'll be damned. Maybe I had a higher calling. Maybe the purpose of *A Phillies Odyssey* isn't to JUST shine the spotlight on the forgotten. Maybe its purpose is to right some wrongs. Jeff Juden didn't realize it yet, but he needed me. I'm a troubleshooter. I solve problems, and all I had was time and 24 different tabs about the big fella up on my Chromebook.

He ripped a grand slam from the right side off LA's John Cummings. Three years later, on May 2nd, 1998, he had a four-ribbie game *batting left-handed*. I found the visual evidence. Jeff ripped a three-run double off Cincinnati's David Weathers, and then followed that up with an RBI groundout (Garrigan 2019). He is the first pitcher to record separate 4 RBI games from each side of the plate since the dead ball era. Wandy Rodriguez, Carlos Zambrano, eat your heart out. I then contacted friend of the program, Baseball-Reference, and explained Juden's plight. I provided visual proof, along with a business card and my resumé listing my esteemed credentials. I'm the self-appointed public defender for all random Philly athletes after all. I work on unopened Starting Lineup action figures and Pat Neshak autographs.

"Think we can sort this out?"

B-R was receptive. The situation looks promising, but there is a lot of bureaucratic red tape to cut through. I trust that all parties will come together and do the right thing. But in the meantime, we wait. The wheels of justice turn slowly after all.

The Utility Man

Name: Eric Bruntlett

Position: SS/2B/OF

Career Slash Line: .231/.303/.330

Phillies Tenure: 2008-2009

Ten, 20, 30 years from now, when Philadelphians look back on the 2008 World Series, this is what they're going to remember: "Eva," and Moyer's performance, and Chooch's rocket, and back-to-back bombs from Utley and Howard.

And they will remember Bruntlett, the runner in scoring position, sliding safely home with the clock approaching 2 o'clock on Sunday morning (Sheridan 2008).

Beep, beep, beep. World F'n Champion coming through. Make way, make way. Eric Bruntlett, better late than never. I didn't think you were gonna show. I gave up hope. I thought I'd have to stall some more, deliver a 1,500-word filibuster about Taylor Featherston. But you get a pass, Eric. Rules are rules. You brought us a parade. You and your friends gave us one of the greatest moments of our lives. You hit a gorgeous .217/.297/.297 in 2008. Look at that line – she's a beauty. If a camera adds ten pounds, then a championship adds 100 points. Come to think of it. We sure this .217 batting average is correct, Baseball-Reference? Did you forget to carry the one?

I don't have one bad memory of Eric Bruntlett, our bearded little rabbit's foot. Did he ever pop out with the bases loaded and less than two outs? That's not rhetorical. I'm asking you. I don't know. All Bruntlett did was win. A throw-in with the Brad Lidge trade, Bruntlett was the World F'n Champions' Swiss Army Knife, carving up the competition through steady glove work and pinch running.

Some Shit for Brains Mets Fan: "We can't let Chris Coste get on."

Some Other Shit for Brains Mets Fan: "Definitely not. Just saw Bruntlett doing some calisthenics in the dugout. He'll slice us up on the basepaths."

Bruntlett and his facial hair were ahead of their time. Today, there would be countless sites peddling a "Fear the Beard" Bruntlett tee. Some merchandise just sells itself. And before you say, "Oh, come on, Dave, who's buying a t-shirt of a utility player?", ask yourself what the plan is for that Carson Wentz jersey stuffed in the back of your closet. Which piece of clothing has the longer shelf life? Ryan Fitzpatrick has been in the NFL for 43 seasons solely because of his beard. You think anyone would care about his noodle arm if he had a five o'clock shadow? (I know, I know. Fitz kills the Birds. Let's move on).

Monumental things happened when Bruntlett was around. He was like Forrest Gump in that regards – or Scott Bakula in *Quantum Leap* if that helps you. He homered off David Price in Game 2 of the '08 Series. In Game 3, Eric led off the bottom of the 9th of a 4-4 game. The consummate team player, he wore a J.P. Howell fastball like Rudi Stein, getting on base by any means necessary. A wild pitch chased him to second and an errant throw down by Rays' catcher Dioner Navarro advanced Eric to third. A trickler down the third baseline off the bat of Chooch would plate the infielder for the walk-off. In the series clinching victory a few nights later, Bruntlett replaced Burrell on the basepaths after Pat's 7th inning double. He would score the game-winner on a Pedro Feliz single. Eric wasn't necessarily fast – this wasn't an Endy Chávez type deal – but he knew how to score. Bruntlett was like fellow Stanford alum Tommy Vardell in that regards.

August 23rd is Eric Bruntlett Day. Do you celebrate? Back in '09, Brad Lidge was on the bump in Queens trying to preserve a 9-7 victory. The Mets had runners on first and second with nobody out when Jeff Francoeur lined out to EB at second. Bruntlett then touched the bag and tagged out Daniel Murphy for the unassisted triple play. Or, as Moses Malone notated in his official scorebook, "Fo', Fo', Fo'." To date, it remains the last unassisted triple play in MLB history. (Mickey Morandini also accomplished the feat in 1992). The Phils released Bruntlett after the World Series loss to the Yanks. He spent some time in AAA the next season with Washington and New York, but it was a far cry from a sold-out Citizens Bank. The '09 World Series was his last appearance in a major league uniform.

I was disappointed to learn he's not in the Stanford Cardinal Hall of Fame (Go Stanford 2021). The committee found room for John Elway, Ed Sprague, Bob Boone, Jeffery Hammonds, and Mike Mussina, but I guess elite defense from the middle infield and a .316 batting average junior year is commonplace? Who knew? Guess I'll go tell Luke Appling to get off his high horse. I reached out to the official Stanford Baseball Twitter account to see how I can right this wrong – who can I call – but there must be an issue with the Silicon Valley Wi-Fi or something. I never heard back. Guess we need to produce multiple Bruntlett t-shirts now. A "Fear the Beard" and a "Bruntlett 4 HoF" tee (he wore #4, you see) to complete the set. Eric Bruntlett deserves it. He did his best work in October. He helped get us a parade. It's the least we can do.

The Inspiration

Name: Ben Rivera

Position: Pitcher

Career Record: 23-17; 4.52 ERA (4.40 FIP)

Phillies Tenure: 1992-1994

The name of my original blog was called, Where Is Ben Rivera. For the uninitiated, Ben Rivera was the 5th starter for the '93 Phillies World Series team. He won 13 games that season at the tender age of 25, pitched a handful of times the following year, and then completely vanished. Never pitched in the majors again. And what I found so fascinating was that no one ever questioned Rivera's whereabouts. He was seemingly erased from Philadelphia's consciousness. I'm walking down Market Street holding a sign saying, "Where Is Ben Rivera?" and I can't even get a honk or a wave or even a head nod. – A Sixers Odyssey: Exploring the Forgotten Players of 76ers Yesteryear.

I suppose it was inevitable. All roads eventually lead to Ben Rivera. In a perfect world, in a perfect scenario, I, founder of Where Is Ben Rivera Inc., would scour the globe until everyone's favorite 5th starter was unearthed. Philly's Favorite Ben has returned, I would shout from the mountain tops. Or Twitter. Probably Twitter.

"I found Ben! This is not a drill!" I'd tweet. We would do the full court blitz with the press – print, TV, podcasts, you name it. Ben and I'd make the rounds together. The reunion would lead to spin-offs. My original blog would be the *Baywatch* to www.BenRiveraNeverLeft.com's *Baywatch Nights*. I'd be David Hasselhoff. Actually, Ben would be Hasselhoff. He's the star here. Only one small problem, though. Ben Rivera wasn't that difficult to find. He isn't some recluse. I wasn't tasked with hunting down J.D. Salinger. Ben has just been living his life. He is a youth pitching coach for Vaughn Sports Academy in Florida, and by Vaughn Sports Academy, I mean former Red Sox slugger, Mo Vaughn. Yeah, that's right. The entire staff is filled with former ballplayers. I signed up for a pitching clinic from Ben, another with Juan Rincon, and actually have to cut this chapter short because I got a 3 o'clock piano lesson with Esteban Yan. I'm shipping my family off to Disney and taking the rental over to Boca Raton.

"Don't wait up for me. Me, Rincon and the boys are grabbing a bite after their shift."

I'm happy to hear Rivera is doing well. I didn't want to Google Ben and find him down on his luck, or see a mugshot, or any negative story or press. I've already cut Curt Schilling out of my life. Some others from that team are on thin ice. I've never met Ben. I haven't been able to get a hold of him (but not for a lack of trying). I considered booking a one hour pitching lesson – for the content – but a 37-year-old man with a fastball that only touches 52 flying down to the Vaughn Sports Academy, where, according to their website, "kids of all ages and expertise can come to practice baseball," would register pretty high on the creepiness scale (Vaughn Sports Academy 2021).

"Hoping you can help with my arm slot, Mr. Rivera. My mechanics are a mess."

My original plan was to never cover forgotten players. I just wasn't particularly good at writing about current ones. I had to find my lane. It's not a new concept. Heck, aren't all relievers just converted starters by trade? So thirteen years after the launching of Where Is Ben Rivera, it's finally time to discuss Ben Rivera.

He got his start with Atlanta in 1992, but I don't acknowledge or recognize Ben Rivera, former Brave. According to Dr. Darlene McLaughlin, psychiatrist and clinical assistant professor at Texas A&M, "If the brain registers an overwhelming trauma, then it can essentially block that memory in a process called disassociation – or detachment from reality. The brain will attempt to protect itself." (Science Daily 2016). Makes perfect sense to me. My brain has also suppressed the second Aunt

Viv from *The Fresh Prince of Bel-Air*. Rivera is a Phillie and has only ever been a Phillie. His major league career, if I had the keys to Baseball-Reference, would have a start date of May 28th, 1992, when the Fightins acquired Ben for pitcher Donnie Elliot.

(Rivera is the subject of the second clerical error detailed in this book. Atlanta accidentally left Ben unprotected in the '88 Rule 5 Draft. They also had the #1 pick. Realizing their mistake, they used the first overall selection to reclaim him. So in 1988, for a hot minute, members of the Atlanta organization were literally like, "Wait, where is Ben Rivera?"). (Hagen 1992).

Lee Thomas conceded that Ben was a project, but he was out of minor league options and the Phils had recently jettisoned *R.B.I Baseball* legend, Danny Cox (Hagen 1992). Rivera got a few spot starts in June, and by August, became a fixture in the rotation. He hurled two complete games that month, including a 10-2 victory over his former team. I was there with my pops. It made sense that the games I attended with my dad were on Sunday afternoon, because he fell asleep at 8:00 every night. When I was 6, I BEGGED my parents to take me to see *Dick Tracy* with Warren Beatty, because I loved the cartoon. I thought Flattop and Mumbles were the coolest. They finally relented. I don't remember much about Big Boy Caprice's henchmen, but Madonna sure opened my eyes to a lot of other things that Saturday afternoon. My dad was asleep by the opening credits.

The seeds were planted on August 30th. Rivera outdueled the previously 19-4 Tom Glavine. Todd Pratt, Tom Marsh, and Juan Bell rounded out the lineup, but no matter. Ben had this one under control. My pops even stayed awake.

"That Rivera looked pretty good," he said, walking down the six-mile ramp from the 700 Level. (If you're keeping track, I have an outstanding record against Atlanta. Please refer back to the Tomás Pérez and Kevin Jordan chapters. Push comes to shove; I'll get Freddie Freeman out myself).

There was excitement surrounding the '93 club. The '92 Phils scored a boatload of runs – 686 to be exact, which was second in the National League behind the

Pirates. Problem was they couldn't get anyone out. They allowed the most runs in the NL by a healthy margin. Most season outlooks drew the same conclusion: If the lineup could stay healthy, if their rotation can string together any semblance of consistency…

It was the original, "If Kyle Kendrick can get ahead in the count …" which I mass texted every March for seven consecutive years.

There is no clear-cut favorite in the National League's East Division.

And even though the Phillies finished last in 1992 and have the worst record in the National League over the last five years, they have the best-hitting team in the division. If their pitching holds up, they are a good bet to win their first title since 1983. (Carroll 1993).

That was *Lancaster New Era* sports columnist, Bill Carroll, calling his shot. Rivera put any questions surrounding the final spot in the rotation to rest in spring training. He turned heads – not just Jim Fregosi's, but opposing skips as well.

Jim Leyland was still working on his initial bag of sunflower seeds when Ben Rivera's first pitch, a fastball, produced a sharp crack from the catcher's mitt. Immediately, the Pirates' manager reached for the notepad and pen in his rear pocket.

There's no record of what he inscribed there, but it probably read something like this: Wow!" (Fitzpatrick 1993).

He made 30 starts for the NL East champs. The 5.02 ERA was unsightly, yeah, but the advanced numbers suggested that our guy was a bit unlucky. That Ben Rivera's 13-9 record should've been even better. That Ben should've won 15, maybe 17 games. Where Is Ben Rivera? At the '93 All-Star Game if I had any say.

Fifth starters play this unique role on teams. Good teams have a serviceable one, a guy that can eat innings and keep you in games. But they're a luxury in the playoffs. Postseason rotations are shortened. Bullpens and benches are tightened up. Back-end starters are like the SATs. They'll help you get into college, but you're on your own from there. Ben appeared in only two postseason games, one coming in the World Series. He had a rough Game 3 in relief of Danny Jackson. (Game 3 is not to be confused with Game 4 which was the nightmare 15-14 loss. I fell asleep in the 5th up 12-7. My mom told me the final score the next morning and I ran upstairs and cried).

With Mulholland moving to the Yankees in the offseason, the organization expected Rivera to make another leap in his progression. His '94 numbers ballooned, though. A loss in velocity left the team wondering if his struggles were injury-related or tied to some extra pounds he was carrying.

"Ben Rivera is not an 82-83 miles-per-hour fastball guy," Thomas said. "He is an 88-89 guy. But he's not throwing that way, and there has to be a reason. We're going to do our best to find out what that is. Whether he's out of condition or overweight, we want to find out. We know he is overweight." (Brookover 1994).

The tipping point was a disastrous start against the Marlins, where he gave up 5 earned runs in just 2 innings of work.

"Ben's problem was that he did not throw the ball worth a bleep," Fregosi said bluntly. (Hagen 1994).

The official reason for Rivera's disabled list stint was a strained right shoulder (Carchidi 1994). He would make three more appearances in July before the strike and that was it. That was the last time we heard from Ben Rivera. With question marks surrounding his velocity, the team moved on from the big righty. He was released days before Christmas that same year.

When you don't write about the Utleys or the Schmidts or the Howards, you understand that most of these players' tenures end with a thud. It's a quiet exit or a disappointing stint or a lingering injury that expedites their departure. It's a byproduct of covering the forgotten. There is this fantastic writer, Kyle Whelliston, who used to run the college basketball site, Mid Majority. He didn't cover major conference hoops – wouldn't even acknowledge their existence. He wrote about the little guy, the small schools taking on these big programs with their seemingly unlimited budgets and resources. Despite the first-round upsets in the NCAA

Tournament, or the occasional Cinderella run, he wrote, almost poetically, "It always ends with a loss." (Steinberg 2011). I wish Rico Brogna was a 3x All-Star with the Fightins or Ken Ryan broke the single season save record. But if they did, they wouldn't be in this book. I can't have it both ways. For the bulk of these players, they're forgotten by so many because there isn't any reason to remember.

Ben is the Godfather of all this. In our hunt for Ben Rivera, we re-discovered 76 former Sixers and 49 more Phils. Maybe some former Birds are next. Hopefully I have some more stories in this tired old Chromebook. Time will tell. In the interim, we can rest easy. Ben seems good. Ben Rivera seems happy.

We can call off the search.

Bibliography

"Your View/Rockland Speaks Out." *The Journal News*. July 2, 1989.

1980s Sports Home. "1985 MLB All Star Game High Quality Metrodome Minneapolis Minnesota." *YouTube*. September 11, 2019. Accessed: February 7, 2021. https://www.youtube.com/watch?v=WV6scZo_-D8.

Aliaksandr, A. "Tyler Goeddel's Great Throw." *YouTube*. May 14, 2016. Accessed June 2, 2021. https://www.youtube.com/watch?v=L9ZYDU_6N4A.

Anderson, Shawn. "Talkin' Baseball with Jeff Juden." *SeamHeads*. April 26, 2011. Accessed May 13, 2021. https://seamheads.com/blog/2011/04/26/talkin-baseball-with-jeff-juden/.

Ashburn, Rich. "Believe Me, Jeltz Could Be an Above-Average Hitter." *Philadelphia Daily News*. November 10, 1988.

Ashburn, Rich. "It Wasn't Perfect, but It Was Carman's Best." *Philadelphia Daily News*. August 21, 1986.

Associated Press. "Atlanta Signs No. 1 Pick." *The Item*. June 20, 1989.

Associated Press. "Braves Fall from Grace." *The Tribune*. May 13, 1996.

Associated Press. "Conine Sparks Florida Comeback." *ESPN*. September 23, 2003. Accessed April 2, 2021. https://www.espn.com/mlb/recap/_/gameId/230923128.

Associated Press. "David Wright's RBI Single in 14th Leads Mets Over Phillies." *ESPN*. May 31, 2014. Accessed July 9, 2021. https://www.espn.com/mlb/recap/_/gameId/340531122.

Associated Press. "Error, Argument Prompt Williams to Bench Bell." *Hartford Courant*. July 28, 1988.

Associated Press. "Jordan's Grand Slam Caps Phils' Rally." *Citizen's Voice*. April 21,

2001.

Associated Press. "McMillon Makes Grand Phils Debut." *Intelligencer Journal*. August 19, 1997.

Associated Press. "Minor League Player Gets Nearly $1 Million in Lawsuit." *MassLive*. March 24, 2019. Accessed April 9 2021. https://www.masslive.com/redsox/2014/07/minor_league_player_gets_nearl.html.

Associated Press. "Phillies Deal Milbourne to Yanks; Call Up Jeltz." *Sunday News*. July 17, 1983.

Associated Press. "Pinch Homer Rescues Phillies." *The Daily News*. June 16, 1995.

Associated Press. "Police: Phillies' Michaels Didn't Get Special Treatment." *Citizens' Voice*. July 6, 2005.

Associated Press. "Poor Pitching Gives Phillies Another Loss." *Deseret News*. August 1, 2001.

Associated Press. "Valenzuela Attempts Comeback with Phils." *The Daily Item*. June 28, 1994.

Baer, Bill. "There Was Another Miscommunication Between the Phillies and Pat Neshak." *Yahoo Sports*. May 21, 2019. Accessed July 28, 2021. https://sports.yahoo.com/another-miscommunication-between-phillies-pat-024505315.html.

Baker, Geoff. "Vision Program Has Mariners' Russell Branyan Seeing Improvement." *Seattle Times*. May 12, 2009. Accessed August 5, 2021. https://www.seattletimes.com/sports/mariners/vision-program-has-mariners-russell-branyan-seeing-improvement/.

Balukjian, Brad. *The Wax Pack*. Lincoln, NE. University of Nebraska Press, 2020.

Bamberger, Michael. "Dodgers Top Phillies, 2-1, After Brawl." *The Philadelphia Inquirer*. August 21, 1990.

Bamberger, Michael. "Williams, Cubs Hold On for 2-1 Win." *The Philadelphia Inquirer*. April 11, 1990.

Barnwell, Bill. "The Year the NFL Went Insane and Gave a Kicker the MVP Award." *Grantland*. June 30, 2015. Accessed February 9, 2021. https://grantland.com/the-triangle/the-year-the-nfl-went-insane-and-gave-a-kicker-the-mvp-award/.

Baseball Happenings. "How Don Carman Remained Batterymates with Darren Daulton Through His Final Hours." *Baseball Happenings*. April 21, 2020. July 22, 2021. https://www.baseballhappenings.net/2020/04/how-don-carman-remained-batterymates.html.

Baseball Roski. "Barry Bonds Crushes a Home Run off Matt Beech, Phillies." *YouTube*. March 2, 2021. Accessed April 10, 2021. https://www.youtube.com/watch?v=-Hq3AAzTzco.

Baseball-Almanac. "1996 Baseball Draft." *Baseball-Almanac*. 2021. Accessed May 13, 2021. https://www.baseball-almanac.com/draft/baseball-draft.php?yr=1996.

Baseball-Almanac. "Official No Hitters." *Baseball-Almanac*. 2021. Accessed April 10, 2021. https://www.baseball-almanac.com/pitching/official-no-hitters.shtml.

Baseball-Cube. "1988 Philadelphia Phillies - [Baseball America] - Prospect Ranks." *The Baseball-Cube*. 2021. Accessed September 13, 2021. http://www.thebaseballcube.com/prospects/years/byTeam.asp?Y=1988&T=22&Src=ba.

Baseball-Cube. "1996 Philadelphia Phillies - [Baseball America] - Prospect Ranks." *The Baseball-Cube*. 2021. Accessed April 11, 2021. http://www.thebaseballcube.com/prospects/years/byTeam.asp?Y=1996&T=22&Src=ba.

BaseballDaysofYore. "Phillies Huge Comeback vs. Dodgers – 1990." YouTube. 2011. Accessed August 12, 2021. https://www.youtube.com/watch?v=-JHPGipLPrE.

Berkery, Joe. "Juden a Lucrative Bat for Family." *Philadelphia Daily News*. August

26, 1995.

Bernstein, Ralph. "For Once, Schmidt Will Blow His Cool." *The Times Leader*. April 4, 1987.

Bostrom, Don. "'89 Phils Are Dead but Set for '90." *The Morning Call*. October 8, 1989.

Bostrom, Don. "Call to Arms." *The Morning Call*. April 2, 2000.

Bostrom, Don. "Cool, Calm Phillies Rookie Pat Burrell Is a Reluctant Hero." *The Morning Call*. August 13, 2000.

Bostrom, Don. "Michaels Charged with Assaulting Police Officers." *The Morning Call*. July 4, 2005.

Bostrom, Don. "Phillies Fans, Don't Panic; Things Can't Be as Bad As They Seem." *The Morning Call*. April 10, 2005.

Bostrom, Don. "Tomas Says *No Mas* to Braves." *The Morning Call.* May 29, 2004.

Bowen, Les. "Phillies Rally from 10-0 Deficit to Win, 15-11." *Philadelphia Daily News*. June 9, 1989.

Boye, Paul (@paul_boye). *Twitter*. July 20, 2021. https://twitter.com/paul_boye/status/1417671232191975426.

Boye, Paul (@paul_boye). *Twitter*. July 27, 2018. https://twitter.com/paul_boye/status/1022970623608406016.

BravesDugoutPod. (@BravesDugoutPod). *Twitter*. April 18, 2020. https://twitter.com/BravesDugoutPod/status/1251698381375844352?s=20.

Brookover, Bob and Salisbury, Jim. "Phils Deal Giambi for Young Pitcher." *The Philadelphia Inquirer*. December 16, 2002.

Brookover, Bob. "Big Cat Means Big Things for Braves." *ESPN*. March 29, 2000. Accessed August 24, 2021. https://www.espn.com/mlb/poweralley/000329.html.

Brookover, Bob. "Campusano Arrives." *The News Journal*. March 4, 1991.

Brookover, Bob. "Carman Making Another Pitch with Phillies." *Courier-Post*. February 20, 1994.

Brookover, Bob. “Long Day Ends in Loss.” *The Philadelphia Inquirer*. June 1, 2014.

Brookover, Bob. “Omar Daal Spared Date with Infamy as Phils Rout Cubs.” *The Philadelphia Inquirer*. September 27, 2000.

Brookover, Bob. “Phillies’ Joyride Halted by Astros.” *The Philadelphia Inquirer*. May 14, 2002.

Brookover, Bob. “Phils Get a Win as Daal Avoids Historic Loss.” *The Philadelphia Inquirer*. September 22, 2000.

Brookover, Bob. “Phils’ Lee and Giambi Focusing on the Present.” *The Philadelphia Inquirer*. August 7, 2002.

Brookover, Bob. “Rivera to Get Physical, 30 Days in Florida.” *Courier-Post*. May 9, 1994.

Brookover, Bob. “Unhappy Brogna Remains a Phil as Trade Deadline Passes.” *The Philadelphia Inquirer*. August 1, 2000.

Brookover, Bob. “Unheralded Pickups Carry a Load for Phils.” *The Philadelphia Inquirer*. April 1, 2011.

Brookover, Bob. “Will New Number Cure Wendell.” *Lancaster New Era*. August 6, 2001.

Calcaterra, Craig. “An Irish Wake for Manny Ramirez.” *NBC Sports*. April 11, 2011. Accessed April 29, 2021. https://mlb.nbcsports.com/2011/04/11/an-irish-wake-for-manny-ramirez/.

Cameron, Dave. “The 25 Best – and Five Worst – Free Agent Values.” *FanGraphs*. November 2, 2012. Accessed February 26, 2021. https://blogs.fangraphs.com/the-25-best-and-five-worst-free-agent-values/.

Cameron, Dave. “The Real Big Trade.” *FanGraphs.* December 15, 2009. Accessed June 17, 2021. https://blogs.fangraphs.com/the-real-big-trade/.

Carchidi, Sam. “Beech Whips Maddux in Debut.” *The Philadelphia Inquirer*. August 9, 1996.

Carchidi, Sam. “Greene Gets a Phony Phone Call of Congratulations.” *The Philadelphia Inquirer*. May 24, 1991.

Carchidi, Sam. "Infielder Iguchi Joins Phils." *The Philadelphia Inquirer*. July 28, 2007.

Carchidi, Sam. "Phils Deal in Bid to Bolster Bullpen." *The Philadelphia Inquirer*. July 28, 2001.

Carchidi, Sam. "Phils Foil No-Hit Bid, But Pirates Win." *The Philadelphia Inquirer*. August 4, 1990.

Carchidi, Sam. "Schilling Works Without Pain, May See Action in Two Weeks." *The Philadelphia Inquirer*. June 7, 1994.

Carroll, Bill. "Phils Good Bet to Win NL East." *Lancaster New Era*. March 31, 1993.

Carter, Scott. "A Failure to Communicate." *The Tampa Tribune*. September 16, 2005.

CBS. "White Sox Bench Coach Mark Parent Ejected Before Game Starts." *CBS Chicago*. August 26, 2013. Accessed June 8, 2021. https://chicago.cbslocal.com/2013/08/26/video-white-sox-bench-coach-mark-parent-ejected-before-game-starts/.

CBS/Associated Press. "Sean Rodriguez Calls Phillies Fans 'Entitled' for Booing Players After Hitting Walk-off home Run Against Pirates." *CBS*. August 27, 2019. Accessed August 26, 2021. https://philadelphia.cbslocal.com/2019/08/27/philadelphia-phillies-sean-rodriguez-fans-entitled-booing-players-walk-off-home-run/.

Cohn, Bob. "25 Years Ago, ex-Pirates Pitcher Jim Rooker Made Good by Trekking from Philly to Pittsburgh." *Tribune Live*. October 3, 2021. Accessed July 12, 2021. https://archive.triblive.com/sports/pirates/25-years-ago-ex-pirates-pitcher-jim-rooker-made-good-by-trekking-from-philly-to-pittsburgh/.

Collins, Donnie. "Barons Say Hello, Goodbye to Calero." *The Times-Tribune*. March 24, 2002.

Conlin, Bill. "'Big C' Looking Good in Cleanup Spot." *Philadelphia Daily News*. May 4, 1990.

Conlin, Bill. "Abreu Takes the Easy Way Out." *Philadelphia Daily News*. April 5,

2000.

Conlin, Bill. "Pennant Cleaver." *Philadelphia Daily News*. March 19, 2007.

Conlin, Bill. "Unlike Phils, Giants Put Chips on Table." *Philadelphia Daily News*. August 1, 2001.

Cooney, Kevin. "Laying Out the Phillies' Blueprint for the Offseason." *The Daily Intelligencer*. October 7, 2007.

Corbett, Jim. "Philadelphia Takes Advantage Over the Somnambulant Mets." *Poughkeepsie Journal*. April 9, 1988.

Costello, Rory. "Turk Wendell." *Society for American Baseball Research*. 2021. Accessed August 30, 2021. https://sabr.org/bioproj/person/turk-wendell/.

Divish, Ryan. "Cliff Lee is a Mariner." *The Olympian*. December 17, 2009.

Donnellon, Sam. "Oh, What a Relief Geary Has Been." *Philadelphia Daily News*. July 14, 2006.

Donnellon, Sam. "Phillies Hit Their Marks." *Philadelphia Daily News*. December 12, 1996.

Egan, Nicole Weisensee. "Cops Probing Michaels' Quick Release." *Philadelphia Daily News*. July 5, 2005.

Eichel, Larry. "Houston Balked at His Role, Bowa Says." *The Philadelphia Inquirer*. September 2, 2003.

En-Academic. "Sil Campusano." *En* Academic. 2021. Accessed March 24, 2021. https://en-academic.com/dic.nsf/enwiki/6583561.

ESPN.com News Services. "Fallout from Saturday's Release Continues." *ESPN*. September 1, 2003. Accessed May 13, 2021. https://www.espn.com/mlb/news/story?id=1607091.

ESPN.com News Services. "Phillies Complete Halladay Deal." *ESPN*. December 16, 2009. Accessed June 16, 2021. https://www.espn.com/mlb/news/story?id=4748216.

ESPN.com. "Pat Neshak Says Greinke Backed Out on Autograph Promise." September 20, 2017. Accessed July 27, 2021.

https://www.espn.com/mlb/story/_/id/20768268/pat-neshek-colorado-rockies-rips-zack-greinke-arizona-diamondbacks-alleged-autograph-snub.

Farnsworth, Dan. "Evaluating the 2016 Prospects: Philadelphia Phillies." *FanGraphs*. March 21, 2016. Accessed June 1, 2021. https://blogs.fangraphs.com/evaluating-the-2016-prospects-philadelphia-phillies/.

Feldman, Loren. "Jim Fregosi Profile: Chewing the Fat." *Philly Mag*. March 1996. Accessed May 17, 2021. https://www.phillymag.com/news/2014/02/14/jim-fregosi-profile-chewing-fat/

Fernandez, Bernard. "So Far, Interleague Play OK with Phils." *Philadelphia Daily News*. June 14, 1997.

Fitzpatrick, Frank. "Phils Fit in a Win Before the Strike." *The Philadelphia Inquirer*. August 12, 1994.

Fitzpatrick, Frank. "Rivers Gets More Pop on His Fastball." *The Philadelphia Inquirer*. March 9, 1993.

Flintoff and Dunn. "Flintoff & Dunn's Tribute to Australia's US Major League Players." *Flintoff & Dunn*. 2021. Accessed May 20, 2021. https://www.pflintoff.com/AUSMajor.htm.

Floyd, Jay. "Prospect Nation 2016: #12 OF Tyler Goeddel." *Phillies Nation*. January 21, 2016. Accessed June 1, 2021. https://www.philliesnation.com/2016/01/prospect-nation-2016-12-of-tyler-goeddel/.

Fredericks, Larry. "Expos Say Greene's Pitches Were Far from the Plate." *The Philadelphia Inquirer*. May 24, 1991.

Frey, Jennifer. "Ashby Joins the DL Crowd." *Philadelphia Daily News*. April 27, 1992.

Fung, Adrian. "April 4, 1988: Angry George Bell Hits Unprecedented Three Home Runs on Opening Day." *Society for American Baseball Research*. 2021. Accessed March 24, 2021. https://sabr.org/gamesproj/game/april-4-1988-

angry-bell-hits-unprecedented-three-home-runs-opening-day/.

Galloway, Matt. "Mike Sweeney, whose 2001 Brawl Lives in Perpetuity, Relates to Fighting Royals." *CJ Online*. April 25, 2015. Accessed July 19, 2021. https://www.cjonline.com/article/20150425/SPORTS/304259830.

Gammons, Peter. "Phillies Could Be Big Spenders." *ESPN*. November 2, 2002. Accessed July 26, 2021. https://web.archive.org/web/20021111061849/http:/espn.go.com/gammons/s/2002/1102/1454708.html.

Garrigan, Mike. "Jeff Juden 3 Run Double in 4 RBI Game." *YouTube*. January 28, 2019. Accessed May 27, 2021. https://www.youtube.com/watch?v=1EhC_PZNTjA.

Go Stanford. "Stanford Athletics Hall of Fame." 2021. Accessed August 27, 2021. https://gostanford.com/honors/stanford-athletics-hall-of-fame.

Gonzalez, John. "Sweeter Than Sweet." *The Philadelphia Inquirer*. August 31, 2010.

Gordon, Bob. *Game of My Life Philadelphia Phillies: Memorable Stories of Phillies Baseball*. Skyhorse Publishing, 2013.

Grathoff, Pete. "Oddly, Mike Sweeney Says He Had a Beer in Hand When He Got Called Up by the Royals." *The Kansas City Star*. July 7, 2020. Accessed July 19, 2021. https://web.archive.org/web/20200707183749/https:/www.kansascity.com/sports/spt-columns-blogs/for-petes-sake/article244051697.html.

Gross, Dan. "Phillie on Celeb-Date Game." *Philadelphia Daily News*. July 21, 2005.

Hagen, Paul. "2 Slams Propel Beech to 2nd Win." *Philadelphia Daily News*. August 19, 1997.

Hagen, Paul. "Agent: It's No Secret Dall Hopes to Pitch Elsewhere." *Philadelphia Daily News*. November 9, 2001.

Hagen, Paul. "Beech Gets Annual Win." *Philadelphia Daily News*. August 13, 1997.

Hagen, Paul. "Catching up with Brogna." *MLB*. October 12, 2016. Accessed

February 8, 2021. https://www.mlb.com/news/phillies-alumni-rico-brogna-c205870220.

Hagen, Paul. "Heroes Big and Small." *Philadelphia Daily News*. May 29, 1996.

Hagen, Paul. "Juden No Relief for Starters." *Philadelphia Daily News*. September 11, 1995.

Hagen, Paul. "Missing 20 Is Plenty for Daal." *Philadelphia Daily News*. September 27, 2000.

Hagen, Paul. "Phillies Bring Ashby Back." *Philadelphia Daily News*. November 11, 1999.

Hagen, Paul. "Phils Deal Mabry for 'Other' Giambi." *Philadelphia Daily News*. May 23, 2002.

Hagen, Paul. "Phils Dialing for Deals." *Philadelphia Daily News*. May 29, 1992.

Hagen, Paul. "Phils Finally Get Their Man." *The Philadelphia Inquirer*. April 8, 1991.

Hagen, Paul. "Phils Get Lofton for Reliever." *Philadelphia Daily News*. December 4, 2004.

Hagen, Paul. "Ryan's In Groove After Shaky Start." *Philadelphia Daily News*. April 25, 1996.

Hagen, Paul. "Schilling Vows His Struggles Won't Continue." *Philadelphia Daily News*. March 23, 1994.

Hagen, Paul. "Shutout Has Fregosi Hinting at Change." *Philadelphia Daily News*. May 6, 1994.

Hagen, Paul. "Up All Night in Philadelphia." *MLB*. July 2, 2013. Accessed March 15, 2021. https://www.mlb.com/news/the-20th-anniversary-of-the-philadelphia-phillies-and-san-diego-padres-game-that-ended-later-than-any-other-game-in-major-league-history/c-52443502.

Hagen, Paul. "Wait Is Over; Slocumb to Red Sox." *Philadelphia Daily News*. January 30, 1996.

Hagen, Paul. "Whiten Steps Right In." *Philadelphia Daily News*. July 26, 1995.

Halvonik, Steve. "Chamberlain All Smiles at Results of Waiver." *Pittsburgh Post-Gazette*. September 4, 1990.

Hammond, Rich. "Phillies Revolt Against Bowa." *Los Angeles Daily News*. September 7, 2003. Accessed May 13, 2021. https://www.seattlepi.com/news/article/Phillies-revolt-against-Bowa-1123639.php.

Harvey, Randy. "He's not a Disney Character, But He Really Is Animated." *Los Angeles Times*. August 11, 1998.

Hayes, Marcus. "Dialing Long Distance." *Philadelphia Daily News*. September 27, 2006.

Hayes, Marcus. "Eaton Left Off Playoff Roster, and He Knew It Was Coming." *Philadelphia Daily News.* October 3, 2007.

Hayes, Marcus. "Make Broom for Phils." *Philadelphia Daily News*. August 31, 2007.

Hayes, Marcus. "Phils Try to Reduce Marlins' Thievery." *Philadelphia Daily News*. April 21, 2004.

Hayes, Marcus. "With Conine, Phils Add Another Sure Vet." *Philadelphia Daily News*. August 28, 2006.

Hayes, Marcus. "Wolf Howls in Laugher." *Philadelphia Daily News*. August 12, 2004.

Henderson, Joe. "This Trade More about Character Than Talent." *The Tampa Tribune*. November 29, 2007.

Hochman, Stan. "Where Dandelions Don't Grow." *Philadelphia Daily News*. July 22, 1987.

Holeva, Larry. "9 Players Still Face Demotion." *The Times-Tribune*. March 26, 1997.

Holeva, Larry. "Phils Sign Melendez to Triple-A Contract." *The Times-Tribune.* April 10, 1995.

Holeva, Larry. "Phils' Longmire Out of Options." *The Times-Tribune*. March 22,

1997.

Housenick, Mandy (@thephilshouse). *Twitter.* May 20, 2011. https://twitter.com/inthephilshouse/status/71757843052756993.

Housenick, Mandy. "Dubee's Laundry List for Aumont to Tackle." *The Morning Call*. July 10, 2013.

Jaffe, Chris. "10th Anniversary: Giambi-Mabry Trade." *The Hardball Times*. May 22, 2012. Accessed July 15, 2021. https://tht.fangraphs.com/tht-live/10th-anniversary-giambi-mabry-trade/.

Jaffe, Jay. "Remembering Fernandomania, 40 Years Later." *FanGraphs*. April 9, 2021. Accessed August 3, 2021. https://blogs.fangraphs.com/remembering-fernandomania-40-years-later/.

JDP2. "1995: Phillies Home Companion Vol. VII: Silver & Bronze." *YouTube*. February 25, 2021. Accessed July 13, 2021. https://www.youtube.com/watch?v=5Y8I6HBBwx4.

Jerardi, Dick. "Phils, Mets Have a Brawl." *Philadelphia Daily News*. September 28, 1989.

Johnson, Marcel. "1993 MLB Pennant Winner – Tony Longmire The Biggest Off-Field Game of His Life." *I Am Necessary*. July 11, 2020. Accessed September 21, 2021. https://anchor.fm/iamnecessary/episodes/1993-MLB-Pennant-Winner--Tony-Longmire-The-biggest-off---field-game-of-his-life-eghq6b.

JSP2. "1994: Mets at Phillies – August 11, 1994 (Game 115 – Last Game Before Strike." *YouTube*. February 23, 2021. Accessed August 2, 2021. https://www.youtube.com/watch?v=L8wM-SYWdMg.

Juliano, Joe. "Phillies Edge Braves and Grab Second Place." *The Philadelphia Inquirer*. August 11, 2007.

Kaegel, Dick. "Sweeney Instigates Brawl and KC Win." *The Kansas City Star*. August 11, 2001.

Kern, Mike. "Manto Strong-Arms Bristol." *Philadelphia Daily News*. April 13, 1982.

Kim, Myung Oak and Gross, Dan. "Phils' Skipper: Michaels 'Not a Troublemaker.'"

Philadelphia Daily News. July 5, 2005.

King III, George A. "Sal Psyched for Pinstripe Chance." *New York Post*. July 27, 2006.

Klapisch, Bob. "Mets Nail Samuel." *Daily News*. June 19, 1989.

Klkatz. "Lenny Dykstra vs. Rick Dempsey." *Penn Live*. March 22, 2007. Accessed August 14, 2021. https://www.pennlive.com/philadelphiasports/2007/03/lenny_dykstra_vs_rick_dempsey.html.

Klugh, Justin. "Limited Action: Wilson Valdez Used One Inning to Become a Legend." *The Good Phight*. May 28, 2019. Accessed September 15, 2021. https://www.thegoodphight.com/2019/5/28/18640851/limited-action-wilson-valdez-used-one-inning-to-become-a-legend.

Klugh, Justin. "Macho Low, Part 7: Jeff Manto Knows How to Spot a Slugger." *The Good Phight*. May 23, 2018. Accessed June 25, 2021. https://www.thegoodphight.com/2018/5/23/17380424/phillies-1993-macho-low-part-7-jeff-manto-and.

Klugh, Justin. "Three Guys Named Kevin to Replace Larry Andersen on Road." *The Good Phight*. January 8, 2018. Accessed May 20, 2021. https://www.thegoodphight.com/2018/1/8/16865640/phillies-larry-andersen-kevin-jordan-stocker-frandsen.

Lalli. "The Long Walk Home." *Philly Sports History*. June 8, 2011. Accessed July 12, 2021. https://web.archive.org/web/20181020132920/http:/phillysportshistory.com/2011/06/08/the-long-walk-home/.

Lancaster New Era. "New Era Sports Poll Letters." *Lancaster New Era*. April 23, 1987.

Lauber, Scott. "Phillies Notebook: Slow Start Doesn't Worry Phils' Bell." *Courier-Post*. April 11, 2006.

Lawrence, Ryan. "Bench Options Should Improve in 2014 Season." *Philadelphia*

Daily News. October 13, 2013.

Lemire, Joe. "Losing 20 Games Isn't for the Faint of Heart, or Game's Worst Pitchers." *SI*. September 5, 2011. Accessed August 9, 2021. https://www.si.com/more-sports/2011/09/05/20-losses.

Ley, Tom. "The Time Paul Silas Let a Clippers Beat Writer Make a Draft a Pick." *Deadspin*. May 7, 2015. Accessed March 8, 2021. https://deadspin.com/the-time-paul-silas-let-a-clippers-beat-writer-make-a-d-1702952979.

Lidz, Franz. "This Job's a Gas." *Sports Illustrated*. May 29, 1989. Accessed February 8, 2021. https://vault.si.com/vault/1989/05/29/this-jobs-a-gas.

Lyon, Bill. "Valenzuela Isn't Delivering Inside Stuff." *The Philadelphia Inquirer*. June 28, 1994.

Maaddi, Rob. "Phillies, Bell Wait for Thome." *York Daily Record*. November 27, 2002.

Macnow, Glen. "Glenn Wilson Fought a Battle Fans Never Knew." *Philly Metro*. March 22, 2017. Accessed February 9, 2021. https://philly.metro.us/glen-macnow-glenn-wilson-fought-a-battle-fans-never-knew/.

Made the Cut. "Randy Wolf Showing Off His Eephus." *YouTube*. October 3, 2020. Accessed June 5, 2021. https://www.youtube.com/watch?v=qDKDahaiNnE.

Marcus, Steve. "Phils Ruin Carter's Birthday with Jeltz Hidden-Ball Trick." *The Central New Jersey Home News*. April 10, 1988.

McCann, Pat. "The Anatomy of David Herndon's Short but Sweet Major League Career." *Panama City News Herald*. May 28, 2016. Accessed August 3, 2021. https://www.newsherald.com/article/20160528/SPORTS/160528995.

McLauchlin, Jim. "Pitcher Pat Neshak Is an Autograph Collector, Too. And He's Got a Deal for You." *Beckett*. 2021. Accessed July 27, 2021. https://www.beckett.com/news/pitcher-pat-neshek-is-an-autograph-collector-too-and-hes-got-a-deal-for-you/.

McQuade, Dan. "Phillies Fans Are Currently Feuding with the Guy Who Hit a Walkoff Home Run Last Night." *Deadspin*. August 27, 2109. Accessed August

26, 2021. https://deadspin.com/phillies-fans-are-currently-feuding-with-the-guy-who-hi-1837623420.

Miller, Randy. "Bank on It." *The Daily Intelligencer*. October 11, 2007.

Miller, Sam. "Pebble Hunting: The Meaning of Russell Branyan." *Baseball Prospectus*. March 23, 2012. Accessed August 4, 2021. https://www.baseballprospectus.com/news/article/16276/pebble-hunting-the-meaning-of-russell-branyan/.

MLB. "Bell Hits for the Cycle Against the Expos in 2004." *YouTube*. February 9, 2018. Accessed July 25, 2021. https://www.youtube.com/watch?v=fsdMjD0eR10.

MLB. "Benches Clear After Rodriguez Hit by Pitch." *YouTube*. February 11, 2015. Accessed May 25, 2021. https://www.youtube.com/watch?v=rX52mpX7ZrU.

MLB. "COL@PHI: Wolf Reflects on His Time with the Phillies." *YouTube*. August 13, 2016. Accessed June 5, 2021. https://www.youtube.com/watch?v=SMVKmk_B2Q8.

MLB. "Phils, Mets Skirmish at Home Finale." *YouTube*. April 30, 2013. Accessed June 15, 2021. https://www.youtube.com/watch?v=B1PNt5iktGE.

MLB. "Splash Hits." *MLB*. 2021. Accessed June 3, 2021. https://www.mlb.com/giants/ballpark/splash-hits.

MLB. NYM@PHL: Jeltz' Hidden Ball Trick on Carter. *YouTube*. June 1, 2018. Accessed July 11, 2021. https://www.youtube.com/watch?v=k33VCYzuWKk.

MLBGlobal11. "2011/05/25 Valdez Wins It in Relief." *YouTube*. May 25, 2011. Accessed September 15, 2021. https://www.youtube.com/watch?v=MCpc8m32p0s.

Mrb 1946. "Wanted to Share a Story about Greg Maddux." *Reddit*. 2014. Accessed July 23, 2021. https://www.reddit.com/r/Braves/comments/2pi5re/wanted_to_share_a_story_about_greg_maddux/.

Murphy, Gregg. "Glove Stories with Murph: Randy Wolf and Charlie Manuel."

Glove Stories with Murph. May 26, 2021. Accessed June 6, 2021. https://glovestories.com/shows/.

Nagatsuka, Kaz. "Marines' Iguchi Knows Key to Playoff Success." *Japan Times*. November 1, 2010. Accessed April 10, 2021. https://www.japantimes.co.jp/sports/2010/11/01/baseball/japanese-baseball/marines-iguchi-knows-key-to-playoff-success/.

Narducci, Marc. "Phillies Say Goodbye to the Pie Guy." *The Philadelphia Inquirer*. April 3, 2006.

NBC Sports. "Conflicting Messages Real Concern Over Usage." *NBC Sports*. June 22, 2017. Accessed July 28, 2021. https://www.nbcsports.com/philadelphia/philadelphia-phillies/conflicting-messages-real-concern-over-usage-restrictions-pat-neshek.

NBC Sports. "Phillies Reliever Pat Neshak Makes Clear He Was Willing to Pitch Monday Night." *NBC Sports*. May 21, 2019. Accessed July 28, 2021. https://www.nbcsports.com/philadelphia/phillies/phillies-reliever-pat-neshek-makes-clear-he-was-willing-to-pitch-monday-night.

NBC Sports. "Sean Rodriguez Says Sorry to Phillies Fans." *NBC Sports*. August 28, 2019. Accessed August 26, 2021. https://www.nbcsports.com/philadelphia/phillies/sean-rodriguez-says-sorry-to-phillies-fans-admits-he-used-wrong-word.

Nelson, Amy K. "Wolf Still Has Loyal Fans in Philly." *ESPN*. October 18, 2009. Accessed June 5, 2021. https://www.espn.com/mlb/playoffs/2009/news/story?id=4576060.

Nelson, James. "Outfielder Chuckie Carr Cemented His Legacy." *Milwaukee Journal Sentinel*. May 16, 2017.

Neyer, Rob. "Mariners Pulling Off a Heist." *ESPN*. December 15, 2009. Accessed June 17, 2021. https://www.espn.com/blog/sweetspot/post/_/id/1778/mariners-pulling-off-a-heist.

Nightengale, Bob. "D-Rays' Kids Set for Major Promotion." *USA Today*. July 28, 2006.

Olney, Buster (@Buster_ESPN). *Twitter*. December 15, 2009. https://twitter.com/Buster_ESPN/status/6698753735?s=20.

Olney, Buster. "Cheap Seats." *The Spokesman-Review*. October 15, 1995.

Olney, Buster. "Manto's U-Turn." *The Baltimore Sun*. June 16, 1995.

Oppedisano, Dana. "Carman Answering Mail – 15 Years Later." *Naples Daily News*. December 5, 2006. Accessed July 20, 2021. http://archive.naplesnews.com/sports/other/carman-answering-mail--15-years-later-ep-405313257-345765042.html/.

Owl Sports. "Jeff Manto." *Owl Sports*. 2021. Accessed June 25, 2021. https://owlsports.com/honors/hall-of-fame?hof=287.

Parent, Rob. "Hip Injury May Put Lieberthal on DL." *The Philadelphia Inquirer*. June 10, 2006.

Parent, Rob. "Phillies Wild Card Race: Jeff Conine Hops to It." *The Philadelphia Inquirer*. August 29, 2006.

Pascarelli, Peter. "Dykstra Fills Inspiration Void." *The Philadelphia Inquirer*. June 19, 1989.

Paul, Keith. "Jeremy Giambi Cited for Pot at McCarran." *Las Vegas Sun*. December 12, 2001. Accessed July 15, 2021. https://lasvegassun.com/news/2001/dec/12/jeremy-giambi-cited-for-pot-at-mccarran/.

Pearlman, Jeff. "The Greatest Guy in the Majors." *ESPN*. April 6, 2007. Accessed August 7, 2021. https://www.espn.com/espn/page2/story?page=pearlman/070406&sportCat=mlb.

Pfeiffer, Eric. "Biotechnology All Stars." *Forbes*. May 31, 1999. Accessed June 1, 2021. https://web.archive.org/web/20120206061144/http://members.forbes.com/

asap/1999/0531/090a_2.html.

Pluto, Terry and Hamilton, Tom. *Glory Days in Tribe Town: The Cleveland Indians and Jacobs Field 1994-1997*. Gray & Company, 2014.

Riccaboni, Ian and Corino, Steve. "Phillies Nation Podcast Episode 9: The Phillies Are Awesome (LIVE)." *Phillies Nation Podcast*. May 14, 2016. Accessed September 10, 2021. https://www.philliesnation.com/2016/05/phillies-nation-podcast-episode-9-the-phillies-are-awesome-live/.

Roberts, Kevin. "Ashby's Change-of-Heart Killing the Phillies' Future Plans." *Courier-Post*. July 2, 2000.

Roberts, Kevin. "Bad Back Will Give Bell Extra All-Star Break." *Courier-Post*. July 12, 2003.

Roberts, Kevin. "Bowa Believes Fans Will Warm to David Bell." *Courier-Post*. June 19, 2003.

Roberts, Kevin. "Houston: Phils Have a Problem." *Courier-Post*. September 1, 2003.

Roberts, Kevin. "Phillies' Otero Returns After an Ugly Hand Injury." *Courier-Post*. May 16, 1997.

Roberts, Kevin. "Phillies' Portugal Pledges a Return from Elbow Injury." *Courier-Post*. May 5, 1997.

Roberts, Kevin. "Scouting Report: Chad Ogea." *Courier-Post*. August 29, 1999.

Salisbury, Jim. "Done Deal: Michaels to Indians." *The Philadelphia Inquirer*. January 28, 2006.

Salisbury, Jim. "Extra Bases." *The Philadelphia Inquirer*. July 3, 2006.

Salisbury, Jim. "In Scranton, Bottalico Accentuates the Positives." *The Philadelphia Inquirer*. June 17, 1998.

Salisbury, Jim. "Lieberthal Homer Beat Slugging Cards." *The Philadelphia Inquirer*. August 19, 1999.

Salisbury, Jim. "Phillies Give Tyler Houston the Boot." *The Philadelphia Inquirer*. August 31, 2003.

Salisbury, Jim. "Phillies Providing a Chemistry Lesson." *The Philadelphia Inquirer*. July 9, 1998.

Salisbury, Jim. "Phils Acquire Another Starter, Dealing Spradlin." *The Philadelphia Inquirer*. November 14, 1998.

Salisbury, Jim. "Phils Hope to Unearth an Offense in Denver." *The Philadelphia Inquirer*. July 31, 2001.

Salisbury, Jim. "Reds' 9 Homers Leaves Phils Leaving Unarmed." *The Philadelphia Inquirer*. September 5, 1999.

Santoliquito, Joseph. "Another Phillies Fan Claims He Was Ejected by Gabe Kapler, But the Team Says it May Have Been a Player." *PhillyVoice*. August 14, 2019. Accessed July 12, 2021. https://www.phillyvoice.com/phillies-fan-ejected-gabe-kapler-oracle-park-san-francisco-giants-sean-rodriguez/.

Schwarz, Glenn. "It's Perfectly Clear: Giants Aren't Hitting." *San Francisco Examiner*. August 21, 1986.

Science Daily. "Can You Unconsciously Forget an Experience." *Science Daily*. December 9, 2016. Accessed April 7, 2021. https://www.sciencedaily.com/releases/2016/12/161209081154.htm.

Shenk, Larry (@ShenkLarry). *Twitter*. September 13, 2020. https://twitter.com/ShenkLarry/status/1305230520037634056.

Shenk, Larry. "LA's Shallow Thoughts." *Phillies Insider*. January 29, 2015. Accessed September 15, 2021. https://philliesinsider.mlblogs.com/las-shallow-thoughts-c0fb897329cd.

Sheridan, Phil. "Ace Falters, Pushing Phils to the Brink." *The Philadelphia Inquirer*. September 24, 2003.

Sheridan, Phil. "Bowa Goes Ballistic After Sweep." *The Philadelphia Inquirer*. August 29, 2003.

Sheridan, Phil. "Eaton Could Be Costing the Phils the Pennant." *The Philadelphia Inquirer*. August 12, 2007.

Sheridan, Phil. "For Ryan, Whiffs of Mountain Air." *The Philadelphia Inquirer*. April

26, 1996.

Sheridan, Phil. "Grace: 'Stabbing' Arm Pain in 5th Inning, MRI Test Today." *The Philadelphia Inquirer*. June 3, 1996.

Sheridan, Phil. "Late and Great." *The Philadelphia Inquirer*. October 31, 2008.

Sheridan, Phil. "Phils Like Look of Grace Under Pressure." *The Philadelphia Inquirer*. March 10, 1996.

Sheridan, Phil. "Whiten and Leiper Did Not Produce." *The Times-Tribune*. June 18, 1996

Silary, Ted. "Andy Makes an Ash of Himself." *Philadelphia Daily News*. June 29, 2000.

Silary, Ted. "Carman's Relief Stints Are Short but Sweet." *Philadelphia Daily News*. June 10, 1985.

Silary, Ted. "It's Better Late Than Never." *Philadelphia Daily News*. July 25, 1998.

Skelton, David. "Chad Ogea." *Society for American Baseball Research*. 2021. Accessed April 28, 2021. https://sabr.org/bioproj/person/chad-ogea/#_edn15.

Sokoloski, Paul. "Outfielder Secures Win for Barons." *The Times Leader*. April 6, 1997.

Sports Reference LLC. "American Family Park." *Baseball-Reference.com – Baseball Statistics and History*. 2021. Accessed August 4, 2021. https://www.baseball-reference.com/bullpen/American_Family_Park.

Sports Reference LLC. "Glenn Wilson." *Baseball-Reference.com – Baseball Statistics and History*. 2021. Accessed February 7, 2021. https://www.baseball-reference.com/players/w/wilsogl01.shtml.

Sports Reference LLC. "Matt Beech vs. Batters." *StatHead Baseball.* 2021. Accessed April 10, 2021. https://stathead.com/baseball/batter_vs_pitcher.cgi?pitcher=beechma01&utm_medium=br&utm_source=player-finder-links&utm_campaign=baseball.

Sports Reference LLC. "Pythagorean Theorem of Baseball." *Baseball-*

Reference.com – Baseball Statistics and History. 2021. Accessed April 23, 2021. https://www.baseball-reference.com/bullpen/Pythagorean_Theorem_of_Baseball.

Springer, Jon. "Roger McDowell." *Society for American Baseball Research*. 2021. Accessed May 15, 2021. https://sabr.org/bioproj/person/roger-mcdowell/.

Stark, Jayson. "Expos Batter Phillies." *The Philadelphia Inquirer*. June 13, 1987.

Stark, Jayson. "Schmidt Stays Cool as 2,000th Hit Nears." *The Philadelphia Inquirer*. June 14, 1987.

Stark, Jayson. "Slocumb to Bosox? Thomas Mum." *The Philadelphia Inquirer*. January 19, 1996.

Stefano, John. "John Marzano." *Society for American Baseball Research*. 2021. Accessed September 8, 2021. https://sabr.org/bioproj/person/john-marzano/.

Steinberg, Dan. "It Always Ends with a Loss." *Washington Post*. May 5, 2011.

Stolnis, John and Klugh, Justin and Roscher, Liz. "Episode 336 of Hittin' Season." *The Good Phight Podcast*. November 18, 2019. https://dcs.megaphone.fm/VMP7774587208.mp3?key=a97c635a69bdc23dc5610b4525033771.

Stolnis, John. "Remembering the Michael Martinez Era." *That Balls Outta Here*. October 4, 2013. Accessed June 17, 2021. https://thatballsouttahere.com/2013/10/04/remembering-michael-martinez-era/.

Tasch, Justin. "Ex-Mets Pitcher Wendell Got Death Threats with Phillies." *New York Post*. July 14, 2020.

The Philadelphia Inquirer. "Bristol Rolls by Jenkintown." *The Philadelphia Inquirer*. January 20, 1982.

Thomas, Mike. "Whatever Happened To: Jeff Juden, Eight-Year MLB Veteran Out of Salem High School." *Herald News*. January 16, 2009

TimothyHellmann. "Mike Sweeney Video." *YouTube*. September 2, 2008.

Accessed July 20, 2021. https://www.youtube.com/watch?v=Eih4rqhy1p4.

Topkin, Marc. "Mecir's Injury 'Freak Accident.'" *Tampa Bay Times*. May 15, 1999.

Unterberger, Andrew. "Today in Philly Sports History: Don Carman Publishes List of Clichés." *NBC Sports*. June 18, 2009. Accessed July 22, 2021. https://www.nbcsports.com/philadelphia/today-philly-sports-history-don-carman-publishes-list-cliches-1990.

Vaughn Sports Academy. "Meet the Coaches." 2021. Accessed April 5, 2021. https://vaughnsportsacademy.com/

Verducci, Tom. "Larry Bowa Sees Red." *SI Vault*. September 15, 2003. Accessed May 12, 2021. https://vault.si.com/vault/2003/09/15/larry-bowa-sees-red-theres-playoff-fever-in-philadelphia-where-the-combustible-manager-has-his-disgruntled-phils-headed-for-a-wildcard-berthor-a-colossal-flameout.

Vetrone Jr., Bob. "Sticks and Milestones." *Philadelphia Daily News.* March 28, 2003.

Weisman, Jon. "An Epic ~~Dodgers Collapse~~ Phillies Comeback, 30 Years Ago Today." *Dodgers Thoughts*. August 21, 2020. August 14, 2021. https://www.dodgerthoughts.com/2020/08/21/an-epic-dodgers-collapse-phillies-comeback-30-years-ago-today/.

Wikipedia. "Don Carman." *Wikipedia*. 2021. Accessed July 20, 2021. https://en.wikipedia.org/wiki/Don_Carman.

Wikipedia. "Mike Grace (pitcher)." *Wikipedia*. 2021. Accessed March 23, 2021. https://en.wikipedia.org/wiki/Mike_Grace_(pitcher).

Wikipedia. "Omar Daal." *Wikipedia*. 2021. Accessed August 9, 2021. https://en.wikipedia.org/wiki/Omar_Daal.

Wikipedia. "Tadahito Iguchi." *Wikipedia*. 2021. Accessed April 10, 2021. https://en.wikipedia.org/wiki/Tadahito_Iguchi.

Wilson, Glenn and Halk, Darrell. *Headed Home: An MLB All-Star's Search for Truth*. Brenham, TX. Lucid Books, 2012.

Wuench, Tony (@twuench). *Twitter*. March 16, 2021.

https://twitter.com/twuench/status/1371865497147424768?lang=en.

Zolecki, Todd (@ToddZolecki). *Twitter*. July 31, 2009. https://twitter.com/ToddZolecki/status/3063666961.

Zolecki, Todd. "Bell Finally Tolls in Phillies' Victory." *Lancaster New Era*. May 16, 2003.

Zolecki, Todd. "Geary Sent Down; Davis Get Call." *The Philadelphia Inquirer*. September 1, 2007.

Zolecki, Todd. "The 33-Year-Old-Rook: Coste Remains a Cult Hero." *MLB*. November 14, 2019. Accessed August 7, 2021. https://www.mlb.com/news/chris-coste-phillies-cult-hero.

Zolecki, Todd. "Wolf May Sign with Dodgers." *The Philadelphia Inquirer*. November 27, 2006.

Zoo With Roy. "Mike Sweeney Cares (Care Bears Theme)." *YouTube*. October 6, 2013. Accessed July 20, 2021. https://www.youtube.com/watch?v=bzEI845UFoA.

Made in the USA
Middletown, DE
21 December 2022

20097991R00158